"*Thomas Merton's Holistic Spirituality* is one of the best books about Merton ever written. Patrick O'Connell's achievement is to have created a masterpiece through nine chapters that are a magisterial integration of themes at the heart of Merton's theology and lived experience. With his extraordinary grasp of the meanings inherent in the entire corpus of Merton's legacy, O'Connell argues for the monk's 'catholicity' in finding unities that transcend all dualisms. His book invites readers to appreciate, appropriate, and apply the values of Merton's integrating vision, which posits that the history of religious traditions is perennially dynamic and remains vital for our times."

— Jonathan Montaldo, co-editor with Patrick Hart of *The Intimate Merton: His Life from His Journals*

"Writing from a position of authority, after devoting a lifetime to the careful study of Thomas Merton's work, Patrick O'Connell imparts to the fortunate reader a compassionate and comprehensive, wise, and winsome account of Merton's complex and yet elegantly simple spirituality. This is a rare book, ideal for both the expert and the novice—a study that is steeped in scholarship and arcane knowledge of theological and spiritual thought yet is also accessible to the common reader who may be encountering Merton for the first time. O'Connell's book is as compelling as his subject, Merton himself, unfolding like a well-told tale that kept this reader engrossed from start to finish."

— Angela Alaimo O'Donnell, author of *Flannery O'Connor: Fiction Fired by Faith* and *Radical Ambivalence: Race in Flannery O'Connor*

"One of the best short introductions to the spirituality of Thomas Merton that I have ever read: wise, grounded, thoughtful, incisive and, best of all, well written."

— James Martin, SJ, author of *Jesus: A Pilgrimage* and *In All Seasons, For All Reasons*

"In a time of cultural, political, and even religious polarization and fragmentation, spiritual seekers need resources that are grounding and integrating. Patrick O'Connell's latest book on the holistic spirituality of Thomas Merton arrives at just the right time! O'Connell, widely recognized as the unofficial 'Dean of Merton studies,' brings his encyclopedic knowledge of Merton's life and work to many of the spiritual questions of our time in a thorough yet accessible manner. Readers familiar with Merton already will appreciate the way this book synthesizes many of the monk's disparate interests and insights, while those new to him will find no better introduction to Merton's spirituality than this book!"

— Daniel P. Horan, professor of philosophy, religious studies, and theology, Saint Mary's College, Notre Dame, Indiana

"Steeped in fifty-plus years of reading, writing, and reflecting on Thomas Merton, Patrick O'Connell is well-equipped to provide an incisive and comprehensive analysis of Merton's spirituality and evolving thought. The author's ability to juggle pertinent sections of multiple Merton passages demonstrates not only his academic acumen but also his prayerful interaction with the texts. The paschal mystery, central to Merton's incarnational, sacramental view of the Christian life, is here illuminated through a prism of lenses with depth and clarity. If you have room on your bookshelf for only one more interpretation of Merton's work, this book is the one to read and savor."

— Monica Weis, SSJ, emerita professor of English, Nazareth University, author of *The Environmental Vision of Thomas Merton* and *Thomas Merton and the Celts*

"Only a truly comprehensive scholar could render such a comprehensive synthesis of the kaleidoscopic genius of Thomas Merton. That seasoned scholar is none other than Patrick O'Connell, the 'summa cum laude' of Merton studies, whose latest contribution elucidates the unified wisdom of a modern spiritual master."

— Kathleen Noone Deignan, CND, professor emerita of religious studies, Iona University, New York

Thomas Merton's Holistic Spirituality

Patrick F. O'Connell

Foreword by
Bonnie B. Thurston

LITURGICAL PRESS
Collegeville, Minnesota

litpress.org

Cover: Photograph of Thomas Merton. Used with permission of the Merton Legacy Trust and the Thomas Merton Center, Bellarmine University.

© 2026 by Patrick F. O'Connell
Published by Liturgical Press, Collegeville, Minnesota. All rights reserved. No part of this book may be used or reproduced in any manner whatsoever, except brief quotations in reviews, without written permission of Liturgical Press, Saint John's Abbey, PO Box 7500, Collegeville, MN 56321-7500. Printed in the United States of America.

Library of Congress Cataloging-in-Publication Data

Names: O'Connell, Patrick F. author
Title: Thomas Merton's holistic spirituality / Patrick F. O'Connell ; foreword by Bonnie Thurston.
Description: Collegeville, Minnesota : Liturgical Press, 2026. | Includes bibliographical references and index. | Summary: "Drawing on both well-known and relatively little-studied sources, renowned Merton scholar Patrick F. O'Connell examines key themes and motifs that exemplify Merton's commitment to what he called "final integration," an inner unity grounded in the experience of divine love that extends to embrace the entire human community and all creation"—Provided by publisher.
Identifiers: LCCN 2025039834 (print) | LCCN 2025039835 (ebook) | ISBN 9798400802683 trade paperback | ISBN 9798400802690 epub
Subjects: LCSH: Merton, Thomas, 1915–1968 | Spirituality—Catholic Church
Classification: LCC BX4705.M542 O26 2026 (print) | LCC BX4705.M542 (ebook)
LC record available at https://lccn.loc.gov/2025039834
LC ebook record available at https://lccn.loc.gov/2025039835

Contents

Foreword by Bonnie B. Thurston   vii

Preface   xi

1 Tradition and Innovation   1

2 Traditional Roots, Innovative Shoots:
Merton's Ecological Conscience   23

3 The Paschal Heart of Merton's Spirituality   41

4 Wisdom and Prophecy:
The Two Poles of Merton's Spirituality   65

5 Awakening in Eden: Merton and the Recovery of Paradise   89

6 Merton's Vision of the Kingdom   111

7 "What I Wear Is Pants":
"Lay" Spirituality and Monastic Reform   131

8 From Communication to Communion:
Merton on Language and Silence   157

9 Final Integration:
Culture, Multiculturalism, Transcultural Consciousness   183

Bibliography   207

Acknowledgments   217

Index   219

Foreword

Recently many good (and some not-so-good) books on Thomas Merton have been published. Most are either "Merton and" or "Merton on" studies; that is, they explore Merton and someone else's thought, his influence on someone else or theirs on him, or they concentrate on particular interests in or aspects of Merton's thought. Few have been comprehensive. This study most certainly is. Whether Merton is writing about social justice or monastic renewal, cultural critique or interreligious dialogue, poetry or any of the other myriad things he addressed, his thought originates from his life of prayer, his spirituality. Using "holistic spirituality" as the touchstone, Patrick O'Connell has written one of the most helpful analyses of Merton's thought that I have read. This Foreword may seem hyperbolic because I personally found the book so helpful and "spot on." O'Connell provides a much needed assessment of the Merton corpus from the standpoint of his spirituality. But fasten your intellectual seat belts. If you think you know Merton, there is turbulence ahead. But I think you will find, as I did, that the "shaking up" is well worth the discomfort.

O'Connell (to paraphrase Merton in *Conjectures of a Guilty Bystander*[1]) clarifies something of the tradition that lived in Merton and in which he lived, what O'Connell describes as "a perennial wisdom to a world that has largely lost touch with its roots" (13) to say the least—his analysis is remarkably inclusive. In addition to the fact that the author cites many less well-known or infrequently read Merton works, itself helpful, the book exhibits three primary strengths. The first is its author. Only a Merton polymath, one who may have

---

[1] Thomas Merton, *Conjectures of a Guilty Bystander* (Garden City, NY: Doubleday, 1966) 176.

written, edited, and critiqued more than any other contemporary Merton scholar, could have produced this analysis. O'Connell's synthesis probes the taproot of Merton's thought (see chapter 3) and argues convincingly that, from beginning to end, Merton's holistic spirituality is paschal and contemplative. Only one who not only knows Merton's work at its deepest level, but has also personally appropriated its paschal implications, could have produced this synthesis.

Second, O'Connell, the consummate scholar, is also a literary stylist. His writing is lucid, easily accessible to the general reader. The book is beautifully written. The clarity of the periodic sentences and the precision of the adjectives and adverbs warm this (former) English teacher's heart. O'Connell renders Merton's sometimes intricate and dense texts more accessible. He not only knows and understands the Merton corpus thoroughly, but can communicate it to those others of us who are less knowledgeable than he.

Third, the book as a whole, chapter by chapter, is carefully organized. That so much material can be so accurately summarized and communicated reflects a very well-organized mind. O'Connell begins with Tradition and Innovation in Merton's writing (chapters 1 and 2), and the essentially Paschal Heart of Merton's spirituality (chapter 3), then moves on to Merton's essential concerns: Wisdom and Prophecy (chapter 4), Recovery of Paradise (chapter 5), Merton's Vision of the Kingdom (chapter 6), and Lay Spirituality and Monastic Reform (chapter 7). "From Communication to Communion" (chapter 8) provides the background material for "Final Integration," which is not only a matter of multiculturalism, but also of transcultural consciousness (chapter 9). O'Connell's analysis highlights Merton's awareness that deeper understanding is found in paradox. Structurally, chapters are written to highlight opposites that intersect and coalesce: matter/spirit; self/other; human/divine; theocentric/Christocentric; paschal/personal transformation; grace/nature; kingdom/church.

This is not a quick read, but a book for pondering and prayer. Because the book's erudition is presented in clear, understandable prose, it is wonderfully enlightening (perhaps especially to us who think we know Merton well). Beyond its scholarship and clarity, I recommend this as a book for our times. Chapters 6, 8, and 9 are particularly relevant and practical. Merton's analyses of the turmoil of the 1960s presaged the struggles and horrors of our time and still offer sane alternatives and practical solutions. With Merton, O'Connell's book calls us to "an experiential participation in the paschal mystery" (20). Of Merton O'Connell writes, "Secure in his own cultural identity, he was not threatened by different ideas or customs, and so was able to respond to them creatively rather than to react defensively" (189). Merton's spirituality arose from his True Self (see *New Seeds of Contemplation*[2]), passed through his paschal heart, and so was not only holistic, but inclusive.

The various themes of Merton's holistic spirituality converge in a final, supreme one: compassion, the compassion found in and emanating from his paschal heart. Merton, and O'Connell's book, challenge us to discover and develop it in ourselves. Merton writes, "paradise is all around us. . . . It is wide open. . . . but we do not know it" (90). Merton's spirituality, masterfully analyzed and summarized in O'Connell's astute and accessible book, challenges us to "know it," and live the truth that "the kingdom . . . has come near" (Matt 4:17; 10:7). Even in these dark days, the kingdom is not elsewhere, but here, always present and evident when our hearts open and become more paschal. Pat O'Connell's synthesis of Merton's spirituality offers us a hope-filled book when hope is in short supply. I am grateful. I think you will be as well.

Bonnie Thurston

---

[2] Thomas Merton, *New Seeds of Contemplation* (New York: New Directions, 1961) *passim*.

Preface

Early in *Conjectures of a Guilty Bystander*, Thomas Merton's 1966 compilation of revised, augmented, and rearranged selections from his journals of the previous decade, he includes one of his best-known statements:

> If I can unite *in myself* the thought and the devotion of Eastern and Western Christendom, the Greek and the Latin Fathers, the Russians with the Spanish mystics, I can prepare in myself the reunion of divided Christians. From that secret and unspoken unity in myself can eventually come a visible and manifest unity of all Christians. . . . We must contain all divided worlds in ourselves and transcend them in Christ.[1]

Here he articulates one key aspect of his spirituality, his commitment to integrating seemingly disparate concerns and interests, the historical with the contemporary, the spiritual with the secular, contemplative prayer with prophetic critique, monastic stability with lifelong pilgrimage, which will characterize that entire volume and indeed Merton's oeuvre as a whole. Merton exemplifies here what theologian Richard McBrien described as the "both/and rather than an either/or approach to Christian faith and practice"[2] that distinguishes

---

[1] Thomas Merton, *Conjectures of a Guilty Bystander* (Garden City, NY: Doubleday, 1966) 12; this is an expansion of the original journal entry for April 28, 1957, which was focused exclusively on the Greek and Latin Fathers, the Eastern and Western Church (see Thomas Merton, *A Search for Solitude: Pursuing the Monk's True Life. Journals, vol. 3: 1952–1960*, ed. Lawrence S. Cunningham [San Francisco: HarperCollins, 1996] 87).

[2] Richard P. McBrien, *Catholicism*, revised and updated ed. (San Francisco: HarperCollins, 1994) 17; on the previous page, McBrien had developed more extensively what he then summarized here: "Catholicism is characterized . . .

Catholicism at its best, an embrace of the entire range of human experience through which the divine presence is manifested in "epiphanies" great and small, a quest for wholeness—a true "catholicity."

Coming across this passage, and this book, in the immediate aftermath of the Second Vatican Council,[3] during my senior year in college, at a time when I was seeking spiritual and intellectual integration and direction for the future, this first significant contact with Merton's writing was a revelation that would initiate an ongoing fascination with the man and his message not yet exhausted, even after more than five decades of delving into his astonishingly prolific and wide-ranging body of work.[4]

Without any intentional planning or even conscious awareness on my part, when I began to speak and write about Merton some years later, I frequently found myself drawn to topics and themes focused on various aspects of this unifying, synthesizing dynamic, intrinsic to virtually all that he had written. Given the present period of social, cultural, political, and even religious disinformation and disintegration, it seemed an opportune moment to bring together updated versions of some of these studies of constitutive components of what I have come to see as Merton's holistic[5] spiritual vision, as a signifi-

---

by a both/and rather than an either/or approach. It is not nature *or* grace, but graced nature; not reason *or* faith, but reason illumined by faith; not law *or* Gospel, but law inspired by the Gospel; not Scripture *or* tradition, but normative tradition within Scripture; not faith *or* works, but faith issuing in works and works as expressions of faith; not authority *or* freedom, but authority in the service of freedom; not unity *or* diversity, but unity in diversity. In a word, Catholicism is *catholic*" (16).

[3] For an extensive overview of Merton's response to Vatican II both during and after the council, see William H. Shannon, "Vatican Council, The Second" in William H. Shannon, Christine M. Bochen, and Patrick F. O'Connell, *The Thomas Merton Encyclopedia* (Maryknoll, NY: Orbis, 2002) 503–7.

[4] I had the opportunity to write in more detail about my ongoing engagement with Merton's work in "A Long Shelf Life: Growing Up and Growing Old(er) with Thomas Merton," included in the wonderful collection of reminiscences and reflections by more than 100 Merton friends, scholars, and readers assembled for the one hundredth anniversary of his birth: Gray Henry and Jonathan Montaldo, eds., *We Are Already One: Thomas Merton's Message of Hope, Reflections to Honor His Centenary (1915–2015)* (Louisville, KY: Fons Vitae, 2014) 235–40.

[5] Related etymologically, of course, to "catholic": concerning the whole.

cant alternative to that sense of fragmentation and alienation that pervades so much of contemporary life.

This book is intended to be accessible, like Merton himself, to a broad spectrum of readers, Catholic and non-Catholic, ecumenical, interreligious, devout or skeptical, spiritual without being religious, religious with or without being spiritual, academics, and those of any and all walks of life with a modicum of curiosity and a sufficient degree of receptivity, a willingness to consider in some detail Merton's commitment, never fully realized yet never relinquished, to what he called "final integration."[6] Speaking of accessibility, readers who (unlike the present author) may not be fans of footnotes should feel free to skip them, as they are not essential to the thread of structural and thematic development found in the text proper, consisting as they do—already evident in this preface itself—principally of references to sources, citations of additional passages bearing on material found in particular quotations, and frequent extended considerations of largely, though not exclusively, scholarly interest. As they have not been banished to the relative inaccessibility of the back of the book, they can be either looked over or overlooked—according to the preference of the individual reader.

I am grateful for the opportunities I have had to share these presentations with various audiences and to receive their feedback at conferences of the International Thomas Merton Society and ITMS chapter meetings in Cleveland, Chicago, New York City, and Rochester, NY; at Merton conferences in Atchison, KS, Erie, PA, Olean, NY, Toronto, ON, and Worcester, MA; at meetings of the College Theology Society, the Conference on Christianity & Literature, and the Pennsylvania Communications Association; particularly at a week-long conference series sponsored by the Milltown Institute of Theology, Dublin, Ireland, and shortly afterward at a one-day retreat in Victoria, BC, sponsored by the Thomas Merton Society of Canada, which provided the first opportunities to link some of these pieces together. Appreciation is also due—particularly for granting reprinting permissions, where needed—to the journals in which earlier versions of

---

[6] See "Final Integration: Toward a 'Monastic Therapy'" in Thomas Merton, *Contemplation in a World of Action* (Garden City, NY: Doubleday, 1971) 205–17 and chapter 9 below.

these studies first appeared, including *The American Benedictine Review* (ch. 4), *Cistercian Studies Quarterly* (ch. 3), *Cithara* (ch. 9), *Grail: An Ecumenical Quarterly* (ch. 9), *The Journal of Communication and Religion* (ch. 8), *Logos: A Journal of Catholic Thought and Culture* (ch. 5), *The Merton Annual* (ch. 7), *The Merton Seasonal* (ch. 9), *Milltown Studies* (ch. 6), and *Spiritual Life* (chs. 1 and 2). Sincere thanks are also due to all those at Liturgical Press who have brought this volume to publication with grace and efficiency, especially Hans Christoffersen, editorial director; Angela Steffens, production manager; Stephanie Lancour, production editor; Clare Koll, production coordinator; Tara Durheim, marketing director; and Michelle Verkuilen, marketing coordinator.

I am grateful for the wonderful gift of community provided over the nearly four decades of its existence by the International Thomas Merton Society, marked by wisdom, challenge, humor, and abiding friendships, and especially for the gracious and generous Foreword to the present volume provided by one of its finest representatives, theologian, poet, scripture interpreter, and Merton scholar *par excellence*, Rev. Bonnie Thurston. I have been deeply blessed as well by the love and joy of my own family, in which, as my son Michael has recently written, Thomas Merton has sometimes seemed to be "a bit like an extra family member—perhaps a great uncle."[7] Uncle or not,[8] Thomas Merton is someone whom it is relatively easy, and absolutely worthwhile, to encounter and engage with on multiple levels, both diverse and ultimately unified, for reasons that I hope the following pages will help to make clear.

December 10, 2025

---

[7] Michael J. O'Connell, "The Consolations of Thomas Merton: On Re-reading a Spiritual Classic in a Particularly Fraught Time," nothinggold.substack.com (February 1, 2025).

[8] Unbeknownst, I suspect, to Michael, "Uncle Louie" was a favorite nickname for Merton among his novices at the Abbey of Gethsemani; he was also familiarly called "Uncle Tom" by the numerous children of his Louisville friends Tommie and Frank O'Callaghan (see Robert E. Daggy, "A Note on Thomas Merton's 'Old Uncle Tom,'" *Kentucky Poetry Review* 28.1 [Spring 1992] 93–94).

1

Tradition and Innovation

More than five decades after his death at the age of 53, what is it about Thomas Merton that continues to fascinate and attract?[1] As respected and influential (and in some circles controversial) as he was during the twenty years between the publication of his bestselling autobiography, *The Seven Storey Mountain*,[2] and his death at a monastic conference in Thailand on December 10, 1968, interest in Merton over the past half-century has remained remarkably constant, as witnessed most conspicuously by his inclusion as one of four great Americans, "a source of spiritual inspiration and a guide for many people . . . a man of dialogue, a promoter of peace between peoples and religions," in the address of Pope Francis to a joint session of the US Congress on September 24, 2015.[3] There is, of course, no simple

---

[1] See, for example, Gray Henry and Jonathan Montaldo, eds., *We Are Already One: Thomas Merton's Message of Hope, Reflections to Honor His Centenary (1915–2015)* (Louisville, KY: Fons Vitae, 2014), a compilation of over one hundred reflections on Merton by personal friends, fellow monastics, scholars, and readers representing a broad spectrum of locations, ages, and interests. See also Jon M. Sweeney, ed., *What I Am Living For: Lessons from the Life and Writings of Thomas Merton* (Notre Dame, IN: Ave Maria Press, 2018), and Jon M. Sweeney, ed., *Awake and Alive: Thomas Merton According to His Novices* (Maryknoll, NY: Orbis, 2022).

[2] Thomas Merton, *The Seven Storey Mountain* (New York: Harcourt, Brace, 1948).

[3] Pope Francis, "Address of the Holy Father to a Joint Session of the United States Congress – September 24, 2015," *The Merton Annual* 28 (2015) 16–23. For commentary, see Julie Leininger Pycior, *Dorothy Day, Thomas Merton, and the Greatest Commandment: Radical Love in Times of Crisis* (New York: Paulist Press, 2020); Daniel Cosacchi, *Great American Prophets: Pope Francis's Models of Christian Life* (New York: Paulist Press, 2022) 71–88.

explanation for this sustained attention. A number of factors need to be taken into account.

One reason is undoubtedly his personality. Merton seems in many ways to be a coincidence of opposites: down to earth and approachable, yet enigmatic, difficult to figure out; drawn to solitude yet genuinely gregarious; a mystic with his feet firmly planted on the ground; thoroughly American yet cosmopolitan; a committed Christian who was quite comfortable with Buddhists and atheists and other "exotic" types. His life story was idiosyncratic, yet representative[4]—even his unique upbringing, wandering around Europe with his artist father, and his almost equally rare decision, a few short years after his conversion to Catholicism, to settle down within a monastery, then spending the second half of his life exploring and articulating the full significance of this vocational choice, paradoxically became in some sense a paradigm for contemporary alienation and the search for roots. Merton was, in Anthony Padovano's apt phrase, "symbol of a century."[5]

But this is only a partial explanation—it is not just Merton the person but Merton the writer who draws our interest. We cannot help but be impressed by the sheer variety of forms he used: he was autobiographer, spiritual writer, essayist, poet, social commentator, literary critic, even novelist in his pre-monastic days, as well as prodigious letter writer and journal keeper, as the five volumes of collected letters[6]

---

[4] The standard biographies are: Michael Mott, *The Seven Mountains of Thomas Merton* (Boston: Houghton Mifflin, 1984); William H. Shannon, *Silent Lamp: The Thomas Merton Story* (New York: Crossroad, 1992); Jim Forest, *Living with Wisdom: A Life of Thomas Merton*, rev. ed. (Maryknoll, NY: Orbis, 2008).

[5] Anthony T. Padovano, *The Human Journey: Thomas Merton, Symbol of a Century* (Garden City, NY: Doubleday, 1982); reissued as *The Spiritual Journey of Thomas Merton* (Cincinnati, OH: Franciscan Media, 2014).

[6] Thomas Merton, *The Hidden Ground of Love: Letters on Religious Experience and Social Concerns*, ed. William H. Shannon (New York: Farrar, Straus, Giroux, 1985); Thomas Merton, *The Road to Joy: Letters to New and Old Friends*, ed. Robert E. Daggy (New York: Farrar, Straus, Giroux, 1989); Thomas Merton, *The School of Charity: Letters on Religious Renewal and Spiritual Direction*, ed. Brother Patrick Hart (New York: Farrar, Straus, Giroux, 1990); Thomas Merton, *The Courage for Truth: Letters to Writers*, ed. Christine M. Bochen (New York: Farrar, Straus, Giroux, 1993); Thomas Merton, *Witness to Freedom: Letters in Times of Crisis*, ed. William H. Shannon (New York: Farrar, Straus, Giroux, 1994).

and seven volumes of complete journals[7] issued in the closing years of the twentieth century bear witness. More than one hundred books by Merton have been published in the past eighty years, almost half of them since his death.[8] His style makes him almost compulsively readable for many people, whatever the topic or genre. He is typically informal without being disorganized, self-revelatory without being self-centered, accessible without being condescending, and often profound without becoming obscure. He has an uncanny ability to penetrate to the heart of an issue, to separate the wheat from the chaff. He can be exasperatingly inconsistent, but is seldom conventional, commonplace, or repetitious. The reader feels that Merton is interested not only in his subject but in his audience, not merely in conveying information but in developing a kind of community of shared insight. One of his greatest skills as a writer is to be suggestive rather than definitive, to point beyond himself, to relinquish the last word. He invites his audience to make direct contact with authors he discusses,

---

[7] Thomas Merton, *Run to the Mountain: The Story of a Vocation. Journals, vol. 1: 1939–1941*, ed. Patrick Hart, OCSO (San Francisco: HarperCollins, 1995); Thomas Merton, *Entering the Silence: Becoming a Monk and Writer. Journals, vol. 2: 1941–1952*, ed. Jonathan Montaldo (San Francisco: HarperCollins, 1996); Thomas Merton, *A Search for Solitude: Pursuing the Monk's True Life. Journals, vol. 3: 1952–1960*, ed. Lawrence S. Cunningham (San Francisco: HarperCollins, 1996) (subsequent references will be cited as *"SS"* parenthetically in the text); Thomas Merton, *Turning Toward the World: The Pivotal Years. Journals, vol. 4: 1960–1963*, ed. Victor A. Kramer (San Francisco: HarperCollins, 1996) (subsequent references will be cited as *"TTW"* parenthetically in the text); Thomas Merton, *Dancing in the Water of Life: Seeking Peace in the Hermitage. Journals, vol. 5: 1963–1965*, ed. Robert E. Daggy (San Francisco: HarperCollins, 1997) (subsequent references will be cited as *"DWL"* parenthetically in the text); Thomas Merton, *Learning to Love: Exploring Solitude and Freedom. Journals, vol. 6: 1966–1967*, ed. Christine M. Bochen (San Francisco: HarperCollins, 1997); Thomas Merton, *The Other Side of the Mountain: The End of the Journey. Journals, vol. 7: 1967–1968*, ed. Patrick Hart (San Francisco: HarperCollins, 1998).

[8] The definitive bibliography of Merton's writings up to the time of publication is Patricia A. Burton with Albert Romkema, *More Than Silence: A Bibliography of Thomas Merton* (Lanham, MD: Scarecrow Press, 2008). A comprehensive discussion of all Merton's books and pamphlets published up to the beginning of the twenty-first century, along with significant events, figures, and themes in Merton's life and writings, is provided in William H. Shannon, Christine M. Bochen, and Patrick F. O'Connell, *The Thomas Merton Encyclopedia* (Maryknoll, NY: Orbis, 2002) (subsequent references will be cited as *"Encyclopedia"* parenthetically in the text).

whether William Faulkner in the twentieth century or John of the Cross in the sixteenth; he challenges readers to think, and act, for themselves on issues of social justice or nuclear war; not just to read about prayer, but to pray.

But even this does not fully explain the peculiar resurgence of interest in Merton today. Is it perhaps that he was ahead of his time? There is a quality about much of Merton's thought that can, I think, legitimately be termed prophetic, not in the sense of foretelling the future, but of discerning and articulating the will of God in ways that both address and transcend particular issues and circumstances of the present. As he explains at a meeting of Cistercian novice masters in June 1968, a few months before his death, "the biblical notion of prophecy . . . is not a matter of picking derby winners but of being attuned to what is happening, being able to read the signs of the times and see how they are manifesting God's will for the whole world as well as for ourselves."[9] Merton would certainly never claim to have all the right answers but hoped to be able to raise some of the right questions[10] and so to provide resources for discerning fruitful approaches to issues relevant but not exclusive to the tumultuous 1960s and still far from fully resolved decades later. In the age of Black Lives Matter, his reflections on racism and structural sin[11] have attracted renewed attention.[12] His warnings about the potential dangers of an

---

[9] Thomas Merton, "The Present 'Crisis' in Monasticism," *The Merton Annual* 37 (2024) 16. For further discussion of this theme, see chapter 4 below.

[10] See Merton's comment in *Conjectures of a Guilty Bystander* (Garden City, NY: Doubleday, 1966): "It seems to me that one of the reasons why my writing appeals to many people is precisely that I am not so sure of myself and do not claim to have all the answers. In fact, I often wonder quite openly about these 'answers,' and about the habit of always having them ready. The best I can do is to look for some of the questions" (38) (subsequent references will be cited as "*CGB*" parenthetically in the text). See also the similar comments in "A Letter on the Contemplative Life" in Thomas Merton, *The Monastic Journey*, ed. Brother Patrick Hart (Kansas City: Sheed, Andrews and McMeel, 1977) 171.

[11] For an overview, see Patrick F. O'Connell, "Civil Rights Movement" (*Encyclopedia* 60–62) and "Racism" (*Encyclopedia* 377–79).

[12] See in particular "Merton the Opponent of Racism," chapter 6 in Gregory K. Hillis, *Man of Dialogue: Thomas Merton's Catholic Vision* (Collegeville, MN: Liturgical Press, 2021) 169–201 (subsequent references will be cited as "Hillis" parenthetically in the text); "The Spirituality of Racial Justice," Part IV of Daniel P. Horan, *Engaging Thomas Merton: Spirituality, Justice, and Racism* (Maryknoll,

overreliance on technology have taken on an even more urgent significance in light of subsequent developments[13] (what would he have made of the implications of the now ubiquitous phrase *"artificial intelligence"*?). Well before the full recognition of the potentially catastrophic effects of anthropogenic climate change, he had begun to emphasize the crucial necessity of developing an "ecological conscience"[14] to resist environmental exploitation and degradation.[15] His recognition of "the stranger" as a source of "newly living truth, not just a projection of a dead conventional idea of our own,"[16] one "who most differs from ourselves" and yet on a more profound level "is no other than ourselves—which is the same as saying that we find

---

NY: Orbis, 2023) 149–203; "Reaching across the Racial Divide," Part II of Gordon Oyer, *Signs of Hope: Thomas Merton's Letters on Peace, Race, and Ecology* (Maryknoll, NY: Orbis, 2021) 115–201 (subsequent references will be cited as "Oyer" parenthetically in the text); Edward J. Vinski, *Thomas Merton: The Monk of Civil Rights* (Newcastle upon Tyne: Cambridge Scholars Publishing, 2023). An ongoing bibliography of primary and secondary sources on "Merton and Racism" is available on the Thomas Merton Center website at https://merton.org/Research/Bibliographies/Merton-Racism.pdf.

[13] For an overview, see William H. Shannon, "Technology" (*Encyclopedia* 466–70); see also Jeffrey M. Shaw, *Illusions of Freedom: Thomas Merton and Jacques Ellul on Technology and the Human Condition* (Eugene, OR: Pickwick, 2014); Phillip M. Thompson, *Returning to Reality: Thomas Merton's Wisdom for a Technological World* (Eugene, OR: Cascade, 2012); and the essays published in *The Merton Annual* 24 (2011), including proceedings of a September 2011 conference entitled "Contemplation in a Technological Era: Thomas Merton's Insight for the Twenty-First Century."

[14] See "The Wild Places" in Thomas Merton, *Selected Essays*, ed. Patrick F. O'Connell (Maryknoll, NY: Orbis, 2013) 450–51.

[15] For an overview, see Patrick F. O'Connell, "Ecology" (*Encyclopedia* 125–27); see also Monica Weis, *The Environmental Vision of Thomas Merton* (Lexington: University Press of Kentucky, 2011); "When the Forest Is My Bride," Introduction to Thomas Merton, *When the Trees Say Nothing: Writings on Nature*, ed. Kathleen Deignan (Notre Dame, IN: Sorin Books, 2003) 21–41; "An Ecological Consciousness," Oyer, chapter 10 (228–48). For further discussion of this theme, see chapter 2 below.

[16] Thomas Merton, *The Collected Poems of Thomas Merton* (New York: New Directions, 1977) 385; he goes on to add: "The desecration, de-sacralization of the modern world is manifest above all by the fact that the stranger is of no account. As soon as he is 'displaced' he is completely unacceptable. He fits into no familiar category, he is unexplained and therefore a threat to complacency. Everything not easy to account for must be wiped out, and mystery must be wiped out with it" (385).

Christ in him . . . Christ our fellow-pilgrim and our brother,"[17] whose "place is with those others for whom there is no room,"[18] provides a powerful challenge to the reductive, demeaning caricatures of the contemporary migrant "crisis." His insistence on the need for dialogue, highlighted by Pope Francis and epitomized for Merton in the figure of the pontiff's namesake, whose encounter with the sultan "as a messenger not of violence, not of arrogant power, but of humility, simplicity, and love" (*MZM* 112) exemplifies both authentic interreligious dialogue[19] and the exercise of genuine peacemaking[20] that characterizes the children of God in the Sermon on the Mount. Above all is his central recognition that contemplation and action, prayer and protest, are not opposed or even separate, but mutually necessary and mutually enriching dimensions of the Christian life. The wisdom of this holistic synthesis and the need to put it into practice are no less evident and no less urgent today than in Merton's own lifetime.

Merton and the Spiritual Tradition

Merton's reference to the witness of St. Francis is a reminder, though, that his continuing impact is not simply a function of his intriguing personality, his literary skills, and his prophetic vision. Another major factor that must be taken into account is that Merton was able to be fully engaged in the present and open to the future without disregarding or denigrating the past. He is a bearer of that

---

[17] Thomas Merton, *Mystics and Zen Masters* (New York: Farrar, Straus and Giroux, 1967) 112 (subsequent references will be cited as "*MZM*" parenthetically in the text).

[18] Thomas Merton, *Raids on the Unspeakable* (New York: New Directions, 1966) 72.

[19] For an overview, see William H. Shannon, "Ecumenism" (*Encyclopedia* 127–28); and Patrick F. O'Connell, "Interreligious Dialogue" (*Encyclopedia* 220–22); see also William Apel, *Signs of Peace: The Interfaith Letters of Thomas Merton* (Maryknoll, NY: Orbis, 2006); "Merton the Pilgrim to the East," Hillis, chapter 9 (239–80).

[20] For an overview, see Patrick F. O'Connell, "Nonviolence" (*Encyclopedia* 330–33); and "Peace" (*Encyclopedia* 354–55); see also John Dear, *Thomas Merton, Peacemaker: Meditations on Merton, Peacemaking, and the Spiritual Life* (Maryknoll, NY: Orbis, 2015); Jim Forest, *The Root of War Is Fear: Thomas Merton's Advice to Peacemakers* (Maryknoll, NY: Orbis, 2016); "Advancing a Catholic Gospel of Peace," Oyer, Part I (21–113).

communal memory without which we are estranged from one another and alienated from ourselves. One of Merton's greatest gifts to the contemporary church and the wider society is his ability to do justice simultaneously to the realities of continuity and change; he finds the tension between past and present to be not a problem but an opportunity, not destructive but creative. The period since the Second Vatican Council, which coincides with Merton's posthumous presence, has seen, on one hand, an exaltation of the present at the expense of the past, a passion for relevance, for innovation divorced from tradition, and on the other a glorification of the past at the expense of the present, a sterile nostalgia, tradition as hostility to innovation. For Merton, these two attitudes are equally signs of a community in danger of losing its sense of historical identity:

> If society loses its "memory," if it forgets its language of traditional symbol, then the individuals who make it up become neurotic, because their own memories are corrupted by uninterpreted, unused meanings. Then traditions themselves become mere dead conventions—worse than that, obsessions—collective neuroses. To replace one set of conventions with another, however new, does nothing to revive a truly living sense of meaning and of life. This is our present condition. (*CGB* 145)

Merton's entire life and work can be viewed as presenting a third alternative: a re-visioning of the Christian tradition[21] to reveal its continuing vitality. This requires a process of discernment, of mutual clarification, in which the wisdom of the past probes the unexamined presuppositions and challenges the standards and values of a particular era, while the central issues and questions of that era help to distinguish the authentic message of the gospel from the time-bound forms in which it had previously been expressed. It is this creative interchange between past and present that was at the heart of the program of *aggiornamento* of Pope John XXIII, whose vision Merton strongly endorses. He describes himself as being

> neither conservative nor an extreme progressive. I would like to think I am what Pope John was—a progressive with a deep respect and love for tradition—in other words a progressive who

---

[21] For an overview, see William H. Shannon, "Tradition" (*Encyclopedia* 492–93).

> wants to preserve a very clear and marked *continuity* with the past and not make silly and idealistic compromises with the present—yet be *completely open* to the modern world while retaining the clearly defined, traditionally Catholic position. (*CGB* 285–86)

This is not, in other words, a kind of compromise position halfway between old and new. For Merton, faithfulness to tradition demands innovation, not in the sense of novelty but of renewal, of listening and responding to the Word of God in the present, as addressed to the needs and hopes, the fears and opportunities, of one's own time and place. Merton writes, "Tradition is not passive submission to the obsessions of former generations but a living assent to a current of uninterrupted vitality. . . . Fidelity to tradition does not mean the renunciation of all initiative, but a new initiative that is faithful to a certain spirit of freedom and of vision which demands to be incarnated in a new and unique situation."[22]

This incarnational perspective is perhaps the principal key to the unity of Merton's thought and teaching. As the Word of God was enfleshed in the person of Jesus, so disciples of Jesus in each generation are called to incarnate the divine message, to make it audible and visible in their own lives. Salvation, conversion, vocation are not concepts or experiences that present themselves in some timeless supernatural sphere, but must be recognized and responded to in the context of actual events of the times in which one lives. In one of his most trenchant comments, Merton writes, "The great historical event, the coming of the Kingdom, is made clear and is 'realized' in proportion as Christians themselves live the life of the Kingdom in their own space and time."[23] The church, the community of disciples, is called to be a kind of sign or sacrament of God's reign, revealing the concrete meaning and implications of salvation, of life in the Spirit

---

[22] Thomas Merton, *Contemplation in a World of Action* (Garden City, NY: Doubleday, 1971) 22 (subsequent references will be cited as "*CWA*" parenthetically in the text).

[23] Thomas Merton, *Faith and Violence: Christian Teaching and Christian Practice* (Notre Dame, IN: University of Notre Dame Press, 1968) 16 (subsequent references will be cited as "*FV*" parenthetically in the text). For further exploration of this theme, see chapter 6 below.

of the risen Jesus, for the contemporary world. Thus the task, the vocation, of the church remains constant, even as the circumstances alter. We must learn from our predecessors, but are unable simply to imitate them. Here is the essence of Merton's creative response to tradition, in which continuity with the past is joined with responsiveness to the present, and the same mind can be just as deeply engaged by the reflections on love of the twelfth-century Cistercian Fathers as by the moral implications of the Vietnam War. By immersing himself in the scriptures and in the teachings of the great contemplative men and women throughout history, Merton is able to bring this stream of wisdom to bear on questions and issues never faced by previous ages.

Appreciating the Tradition

In analyzing Merton's response to the past, it is perhaps helpful to speak of three dimensions or stages, which can be termed appreciation, appropriation, and application. Appreciation describes Merton's ability to enter into the world of the great teachers of the Christian past in order to discover why and how they lived and wrote as they did. His approach is not one of scholarly detachment but rather a not-uncritical empathy that is able to appreciate, in the root sense of to evaluate properly, in historical context, the vision and values of forefathers and foremothers in the faith.

For example, in discussing the rise of monasticism in the fourth century, Merton considers it as a response to the loss of fervor and the inevitable compromises that followed the legalization of Christianity and the entrance of Christians into the power structure of Roman society. He writes:

> They did not reject society with proud contempt, as if they were superior to other men. On the contrary, one of the reasons they fled from the world of men was that in the world men were divided into those who were successful and imposed their will on others, and those who had to give in and be imposed upon. The Desert Fathers declined to be ruled by men, but had no desire to rule over others themselves. . . . The society they sought was one where all men were truly equal, where the only authority

under God was the charismatic authority of wisdom, experience, and love.[24]

Here he emphasizes that to learn from the desert solitaries, as he clearly intends that we should, we must recognize where they are coming from, what they are responding to: theirs too was an incarnational, sacramental spirituality, providing a sign of the kingdom for their own time. This does not mean that the sign is no longer valid, but that there is a danger of misreading it unless we are aware of the circumstances in which it was given. Properly understood, then, the early hermits are not misfits or misanthropes but signs of contradiction and of hope to an authoritarian political structure and an often lukewarm church—not totally unfamiliar institutions even in more modern periods.

Appropriating the Tradition

The second dimension, or stage, is appropriation, making the tradition one's own by allowing it to come alive in one's own experience. This is incarnation on a personal, existential level. Merton was interested in the spiritual teachings of the past not as an historian but as a practitioner, as one who sought the face of God and desired to learn from those who had preceded him on the pilgrimage to the mountain of God, whether it be called Zion or Sinai, described as an ascent of Mount Carmel or of Mount Purgatory, the "seven storey mountain" of Dante's *Divine Comedy*. Internalizing these classic teachings is not an end in itself; they are catalysts, with the potential to mediate the encounter their words inadequately describe. This emphasis on experience rather than abstract theory is itself something Merton learned from the tradition, particularly from his own Cistercian Fathers. Merton's friend Dom Jean Leclercq, the editor of St. Bernard, writes, "Monastic theology appeals to the concrete intuition more than to the discursive and logical analysis of the Scholastics; it is the

---

[24] Thomas Merton, *The Wisdom of the Desert: Sayings from the Desert Fathers of the Fourth Century* (New York: New Directions, 1960) 5 (subsequent references will be cited as "*WD*" parenthetically in the text).

description of an experience of God."[25] We see Merton resonating with this approach, for example, in his love for the English mystic Julian of Norwich. "I pray much to have a wise heart, and perhaps the rediscovery of Lady Julian of Norwich will help me. . . . She first experienced, then thought, and the thoughtful deepening of experience worked back into her life, deeper and deeper, until her whole life as a recluse at Norwich was simply a matter of getting completely saturated in the light she had received" (*CGB* 191–92).[26] By participating in this process of reflection, the reader of Julian is invited to appropriate the experience, to meet not just Julian but Julian's God. This, we sense, is Merton's interest in making the tradition his own.

It is not by chance that so many of Merton's own books are autobiographical, and these generally considered to be among his best. What is handed on in tradition is most fundamentally life: the life of faith, life in the Spirit, which is received not simply by agreeing with ideas and propositions but by living this life as faithfully as possible. While Merton preserves the mystery of his own most intimate relationship with God, all his writings are a record, directly or indirectly, of his own struggles to allow the Word of God to become enfleshed in him. It is here that he finds the coincidence of his own dual vocation of monk and author, as in this reflection included in *Conjectures of a Guilty Bystander*:

> Evening, rain, silence, joy. I believe that, where the Lord sees the small point of poverty, extenuation, helplessness which is the heart of a monk after very long and very dry celebrations in choir, when He sees the point of indigence to which one is reduced, He Himself cannot refuse to enter this anguish, to take flesh in it so to speak, making it instantly a small seed of infinite joy and

---

[25] Jean Leclercq, OSB, "Saint Bernard and the Monastic Theology of the Twelfth Century" in *Saint Bernard, Theologian*, 2 vols. (Berryville, VA: Our Lady of the Holy Cross Abbey, 1961) 1.7.

[26] See also the original version of this passage in his journal entry for December 27, 1961 (*SS* 189), as well as his discussion of Julian in his essay "The English Mystics" (*MZM* 128–53), in which he calls her "the greatest of English mystics" and "one of the greatest English theologians, in the ancient sense of the word," uniting experience and reflection, "a theology of the all-embracing totality and fullness of the divine love" (140–41).

> peace and solitude in the world. There is for me no sense, no truth in anything that elaborately contrives to hide this precious poverty, this seed of tears which is also the seed of true joy. . . . I may speak to others only in so far as I address myself to this same small spark of truth and sorrow in them, to help resolve their doubts, to assuage their anguish, to lighten their grief by helping them to be strong in this same small spark of exhaustion in which the Lord becomes their wisdom and their life forever. What else do the Psalms talk about but this? (*CGB* 247–48)[27]

Here we see the continuity between the experience of the psalmist, the experience of Merton, and that of his readers, a consciousness of the process by which the life of faith is transmitted.

Applying the Tradition

This brings us, of course, to the third aspect of Merton's approach to tradition: application. Merton is concerned to show how the experience of God in earlier days continues to speak to the needs and hopes of the present. Having made the imaginative leap to meet the masters of the past on their own terms, and then having brought them into the present in his own consciousness and experience, he assesses their ongoing significance for the church as a whole and for its individual members. Thus, for example, he concludes his discussion of the Desert Fathers by saying:

> We cannot do exactly what they did. But we must be as thorough and as ruthless in our determination to break all spiritual chains, and cast off the domination of alien compulsions, to find our true selves, to discover and develop our inalienable spiritual liberty and use it to build, on earth, the Kingdom. . . . We need to learn from these men of the fourth century how to ignore prejudice, defy compulsion and strike out fearlessly into the unknown. (*WD* 24)

As so often in Merton, we discover that differences in time and custom are superficial compared with the common quest that makes us

---

[27] See also the original version of this passage in the journal entry for December 25, 1962 (*TTW* 280).

members of the same body. Above all else, this focus on unity is characteristic of Merton's encounter with tradition. In a famous passage (quoted previously in the preface), he writes:

> If I can unite *in myself* the thought and the devotion of Eastern and Western Christendom, the Greek and the Latin Fathers, the Russians with the Spanish mystics, I can prepare in myself the reunion of divided Christians. From that secret and unspoken unity in myself can eventually come a visible and manifest unity of all Christians. . . . We must contain all divided worlds in ourselves and transcend them in Christ. (*CGB* 12)[28]

Here we see that our three dimensions are in practice inseparable, part of a seamless process. Appreciation is found in his respect for each manifestation of the Christian message, his refusal to reject or even to subordinate one or another; by appropriating each of these forms of thought and devotion, Merton discovers their unity in diversity; the goal of visible unity shows that the application has relevance not only to individual lives but to the entire church. Here is the essence of Merton's holistic approach to Christian life.

Retrieval and Re-Presentation

Merton is certainly aware of the importance of these efforts to "clarify something of the tradition that lives in me, and in which I live" (*CGB* 176),[29] but also of the difficulty of communicating a perennial wisdom to a world that has largely lost touch with its roots, cultural as well as spiritual. Commenting on the doctrine of the divine image as found in Adam, in Christ, and in ourselves, and on the Pauline and patristic teaching that Christian conversion involves the passage from identification with Adam to identification with Christ, Merton comments, "We are not used to the perspectives which enabled the Fathers and the New Testament writers to see the mysterious com-penetration of all these realities in the one great reality of

---

[28] See also the original version of this passage in the journal entry for April 28, 1957 (*SS* 87).

[29] See also the original version of this passage in the journal entry for August 22, 1961 (*TTW* 155).

the Person of Christ."[30] In some sense all Merton's work, explicitly or implicitly, is an effort to express these seminal notions in an idiom that can be readily grasped by a twentieth- (or twenty-first-) century audience: the drama of sin and redemption, of alienation and communion, first described centuries or even millennia ago, is still going on, is in fact one in which we ourselves are intimately involved.

This retrieval and re-presentation of the central message of Christianity is evident throughout Merton's work, nowhere more so than in connection with two themes—world and self—where traditional and contemporary attitudes seem to be completely at odds. By briefly considering these two central concepts in Merton's spirituality, we will be able to appreciate how thoroughly his spiritual teaching is both grounded in tradition and engaged in contemporary issues, so that this appreciation will perhaps encourage us in the process of appropriating and applying it ourselves.

The World in Merton's Spirituality

In traditional Christian teaching as commonly understood, "the world" was something to be avoided, part of the unholy trinity, along with the flesh and the devil. To "leave the world," as one would by entering a monastery, was to escape from a host of snares, threats, and temptations. Such an outlook tended to draw a sharp distinction between the natural and the supernatural, the material and the spiritual. It also had the effect of relegating laypeople to a necessarily second-class spirituality, if not worse, since they were unavoidably in contact with the world on a regular basis. In more recent times, a reaction to this negative depiction of the world has developed, taking the form of a strong affirmation of this-worldly existence, a celebration of the secular, the physical, the mundane, the world of the senses.

Merton's response to these divergent attitudes is quite indicative of his entire spiritual teaching. Its starting point can be found in the title of the fourth chapter of *New Seeds of Contemplation*, "Everything That Is, Is Holy." In this chapter, he writes: "In His love we possess all things and enjoy fruition of them, finding Him in them all. And

---

[30] Thomas Merton, *The New Man* (New York: Farrar, Straus & Cudahy, 1961) 134.

thus as we go about the world, everything we meet and everything we see and hear and touch, far from defiling, purifies us and plants in us something more of contemplation and of heaven."[31] Here we encounter that profoundly sacramental vision so characteristic of Merton: creation is a sign of the Creator, an epiphany of the transcendent: earthly things are windows through which we catch a glimpse of God. Moreover, Merton repeatedly points out that this is the genuine teaching of Christian tradition, which has consistently opposed any Manichaean rejection of material reality. He traces this "natural contemplation, which beholds the divine in and through nature,"[32] back to the Greek Fathers of the fourth century, and elsewhere he speaks of the great contemplative theologians and artists of the High Middle Ages, Aquinas, Scotus, Bonaventure, Dante, as having "a basically world-affirming and optimistic view of man, of his world and his work"; for them, "the created world itself is an epiphany of divine wisdom and love" (*CWA* 147). In his rejection of a negative view toward the material world, Merton could certainly be considered an advocate of what has come to be called "creation spirituality."

But this does not mean that Merton simply embraces a glorification of the secular without reservation. He comments, "the stereotype of world rejection is now being firmly replaced by a collection of equally empty stereotypes of world affirmation in which I, for one, have very little confidence" (*CWA* 149). Having shown that the tradition is basically world-affirming, he goes on to examine the more negative elements that are also undeniably to be found in traditional teaching, to see what they could mean, if and how they can be reconciled with a sacramental view of the world, what value they might still be able to convey if properly interpreted.

Merton is no unqualified apologist for the church of the past. He can be, and often is, fiercely critical of the compromises, evasions,

---

[31] Thomas Merton, *New Seeds of Contemplation* (New York: New Directions, 1961) 25 (subsequent references will be cited as "*NSC*" parenthetically in the text); this passage is also found in the original version of the text, Thomas Merton, *Seeds of Contemplation* (New York: New Directions, 1949) 22 (subsequent references will be cited as "*SC*" parenthetically in the text).

[32] Thomas Merton, *The Inner Experience: Notes on Contemplation*, ed. William H. Shannon (San Francisco: HarperCollins, 2003) 68.

even betrayals of the gospel that mark Christian history. He is well aware that hostility to the world has often been a mark of complacent arrogance or of timid insecurity. But he also realizes that this is not always the case. There is a healthy wariness toward the world as well. The problem, he finds, is not in created reality itself but in our attitude toward it, our relationship to it.

> The fulfillment we find in creatures belongs to the reality of the created being, a reality that is from God and belongs to God and reflects God. The anguish we find in them belongs to the disorder of our desire which looks for a greater reality in the object of our desire than is actually there: a greater fulfillment than any created thing is capable of giving. Instead of worshipping God through His creation we are always trying to worship ourselves by means of creatures. (NSC 26)[33]

The danger is basically one of substituting a means for an end, of absolutizing what is relative, which is a good working definition of idolatry. The phrase "the world" as it is frequently used in the tradition is thus a kind of shorthand for a flawed perception of reality, a distorted view which sees the world not as it comes forth from the hand of God but as we try to reorder it to suit ourselves; it is a world of egocentric desires in which we try to force reality, including other persons, to revolve around ourselves; when it refuses to do so, in frustration we maltreat and foul and profane it, transforming it into an image of our interior disorder: this is the world to be fled, a false, unreal mockery of God's creation. Merton writes:

> It is not Christianity, far from it, that separates man from the cosmos, the world of sense and of nature. On the contrary, it is man's own technocratic and self-centered "worldliness" which is in reality a falsification and a perversion of natural perspectives, which separates him from the reality of creation, and enables him to act out his fantasies as a little autonomous god, seeing and judging everything in relation to himself. (CGB 269)

It is not the world itself, then, which must be rejected, but this seductive pseudo-reality of self-sufficiency and godlike control. It

---

[33] A slightly different version of this passage is found in *SC* 23.

entails a change in perspective, above all about oneself. Merton comments, "As far as I can see, what I abandoned when I 'left the world' and came to the monastery was the *understanding of myself* that I had developed in the context of civil society—my identification with what appeared to me to be its aims" (*CGB* 36). But this means that leaving the world does not involve abandoning the world to its fate. It is rather to enter into a new relationship with reality: it is not sufficient to recognize the abyss between the world as sacrament and the world as mirror of sinful, self-deluded humanity. This recognition is also a summons to responsible action, to work toward bringing the second into conformity with the first:

> To choose the world . . . is first of all an acceptance of a task and a vocation in the world, in history and in time, in my time, which is the present. To choose the world is to choose to do the work I am capable of doing, in collaboration with my brother, to make the world better, more free, more just, more livable, more human. And it has now become transparently obvious that mere automatic "rejection of the world" and "contempt for the world" is in fact not a choice but the evasion of choice. The man who pretends that he can turn his back on Auschwitz or Viet Nam and act as if they were not there is simply bluffing. (*CWA* 149)

Here we have a further instance of that incarnational dimension of Merton's thought. The Christian vocation is a call to be a sign and instrument of the kingdom, of God's world as it was meant to be, in the midst of the concrete forces and events that block and contradict this vision. Such a response is possible only because it has already been definitively accomplished in Christ. In what is perhaps his most complete statement about the world, Merton asks:

> Do we really choose between the world and Christ as between two conflicting realities absolutely opposed? Or do we choose Christ by choosing the world as it really is in him, that is to say created and redeemed by him and encountered in the ground of our own personal freedom and of our love? Do we really renounce ourselves and the world in order to find Christ, or do we renounce our alienated and false selves in order to choose our own deepest truth in choosing both the world and Christ at the same time? If the deepest ground of my being is love, then in that very love itself and nowhere else will I find myself, and the

world, and my brother and Christ. It is not a question of either/or but of all-in-one. (*CWA* 155–56)

Here all questions about our attitude toward the world are raised and answered except perhaps one—how do we gain access to such a vision of wholeness? This brings us to the second of our two key concepts: the self.

The Self in Merton's Spirituality

We seem to encounter the same challenge with regard to the self as we did in connection with the world. The traditional terminology about the self often appears to be unrelievedly dour and unattractive. It is filled with negative expressions like self-denial, self-surrender, self-abnegation, mortification, submission, dying to oneself, etc. All this can sound rather masochistic, give evidence of hostility to joy, vitality, life. It seems to suggest hair shirts and regular self-imposed scourging. In reaction, we have a psychology, a theology, of self-acceptance, self-affirmation, self-actualization, celebrating our own uniqueness. From this perspective self-discipline is seen as repressive, and guilt is probably neurotic.

Where does Merton stand on all this? He can be as affirming and as celebratory as the most avid supporter of "feel-good" theology. In his famous "Fourth and Walnut" vision, he talks of being suddenly struck by the hidden beauty of the shoppers in downtown Louisville, and of realizing that "they are all walking around shining like the sun." He says, "if only they could all see themselves as they actually are . . . there would be no more war, no more hatred, no more cruelty, no more greed. . . . I suppose the big problem would be that we would fall down and worship each other" (*CGB* 141–42).[34] But the implication is of course that they don't, can't, see themselves as they really are—that this affirmation is hidden and not easily unveiled.

So the question remains: who or what is being affirmed in so-called self-affirmation? How do we define, or, more importantly, how do we experience, the self? Too often what is affirmed is a mask, a disguise, a self created not in the image of God but in the image of a

---

[34] See also the original version of this passage in the journal entry for March 19, 1958 (*SS* 181–82).

disordered world. Merton's theology of the self[35] is a contemporary elaboration of the gospel paradox that only the one who loses his life will find it, showing the essentially positive significance of all those negative terms in the traditional vocabulary.

The first question, then, is what must be lost. Merton's answer is: that false, superficial identity which each of us creates for ourselves by choosing to be autonomous, self-sufficient. Merton writes, "My false and private self is the one who wants to exist outside the reach of God's will and God's love—outside of reality and outside of life. And such a self cannot help but be an illusion" (*NSC* 34; *SC* 28). Like Adam and Eve in the garden, this self tries to be like God apart from God, denying its genuine likeness freely given to pursue a spurious one that can never be found. It tries to create its identity out of its own works, accomplishments, reputation, possessions—a doomed enterprise because it tries to make something permanent out of what is transitory. Merton comments, "There is no substance under the things with which I am clothed. . . . They are all destined by their very contingency to be destroyed. And when they are gone there will be nothing left of me but my own nakedness and emptiness and hollowness, to tell me that I am my own mistake" (*NSC* 35).[36] This for Merton is the state of sin, not just an act or series of acts but a fundamental attitude or orientation—the choice of illusion over reality, an alienation from the ground of existence and from one's own true identity. Affirmation of this self is simply compounding the illusion.

Thus Merton writes, shortly before his death, that the journey to God "is a path of ascetic self-emptying and 'self-naughting' and not at all a path of self-affirmation, of self-fulfillment or of 'perfect attainment.'"[37] The false self must be recognized, rejected, denied, surrendered, abnegated and the rest, precisely in order that the authentic

---

[35] For an overview, see William H. Shannon, "Self" (*Encyclopedia* 417–20); see also James Finley, *Merton's Palace of Nowhere: A Search for God through Awareness of the True Self* (Notre Dame, IN: Ave Maria Press, 1978), and Anne F. Carr, *A Search for Wisdom and Spirit: Thomas Merton's Theology of the Self* (Notre Dame, IN: University of Notre Dame Press, 1988).

[36] See also the original version of this passage (*SC* 29).

[37] Thomas Merton, *Zen and the Birds of Appetite* (New York: New Directions, 1968) 76 (subsequent references will be cited as "*ZBA*" parenthetically in the text).

self can emerge. This for Merton is the essential meaning of salvation, the central mystery of Christianity:

> We must be saved above all from that abyss of confusion and absurdity which is our own worldly self. The person must be rescued from the individual. The free son of God must be saved from the conformist slave of fantasy, passion and convention. The creative and mysterious inner self must be delivered from the wasteful, hedonistic and destructive ego that seeks only to cover itself with disguises. To be "lost" is to be left to the arbitrariness and pretenses of the contingent ego, the smoke self that must inevitably vanish. To be "saved" is to return to one's inviolate and eternal reality and to live in God. (*NSC* 38)

This is what Paul means when he speaks of being crucified with Christ—redemption is not simply a matter of intellectual adherence to a set of dogmas. It is an experiential participation in the paschal mystery; it is a death to the illusory self in order that the true self, the image of God, may rise through and with and in the resurrected Jesus. Here is the heart of Merton's understanding of self-transformation, and indeed of his entire spirituality.[38] For him, the contemplative experience is fundamentally paschal in character. In one of his last essays, he provides what is perhaps his most compelling description of the central mystery of existence, interestingly enough, in the context of a dialogue with Zen. It is thoroughly traditional, yet, in this setting in particular, quite contemporary. It does justice both to the modern quest for self-realization and to the traditional discipline of self-denial by pointing out that they are, when interpreted properly, not contradictory but correlative, for the self which is to be realized is in fact the real self. He writes:

> It is essential to remember that for a Christian "the word of the Cross" is nothing theoretical, but a stark and existential experience of union with Christ in His death in order to share in His resurrection. To fully "hear" and "receive" the word of the Cross means much more than simple assent to the dogmatic proposition that Christ died for our sins. It means to be "nailed to the Cross with Christ," so that the ego-self is no longer the principle

---

[38] For further discussion, see chapter 3 below.

of our deepest actions, which now proceed from Christ living in us. "I live, now not I, but Christ lives in me." To receive the word of the Cross means the acceptance of a complete self-emptying, a kenosis, in union with the self-emptying of Christ "obedient unto death." It is essential to true Christianity that this experience of the Cross and of self-emptying be central in the life of the Christian so that he may fully receive the Holy Spirit and know (again by experience) all the riches of God in and through Christ. (*ZBA* 55–56)

What, then, is this real self which rises with Christ and is filled with the riches of God? What is ultimately affirmed, Merton tells us, may not resemble very closely the self we're accustomed to, but that is precisely the point. The "yes" we are to speak to ourselves is our "yes" to God, because we are accepting that self which is in God; and it is God's "yes" to us, because it is the self that is in God that is making the affirmation, and it is God's "yes" to all creation, because we are no longer alienated from the unity of all that is. It is the eternal "yes" the Father speaks to the Son, because we are "in Christ." In accents that make the typical jargon of self-actualization sound shallow indeed, but with a tone and content that speak precisely to the needs such talk is intended to meet, Merton points toward the ultimate identity of the true self:

The shallow "I" of individualism can be possessed, developed, cultivated, pandered to, satisfied: it is the center of all our strivings for gain and for satisfaction, whether material or spiritual. But the deep "I" of the spirit, of solitude and love, cannot be "had," possessed, developed, perfected. It can only *be*, and *act* according to the inner laws which are not of man's contriving, but which come from God. They are the Laws of the Spirit, who like the wind blows where He wills. This inner "I," who is always alone, is always universal: for in this inmost "I" my own solitude meets the solitude of every other man and the solitude of God. Hence it is beyond division, beyond limitation, beyond selfish affirmation. It is only this inmost and solitary "I" that truly loves with the love and the spirit of Christ. This "I" is Christ Himself, living in us; and we, in Him, living in the Father.[39]

---

[39] Thomas Merton, *Disputed Questions* (New York: Farrar, Straus & Cudahy, 1960) 207.

In this passage, Merton manages to make the consistent teaching of the Christian contemplative tradition available to a contemporary audience. He is the heir of Bernard and John of the Cross, of Eckhart and Julian of Norwich, indeed of John and Paul, but he speaks our language, the language of an era fascinated yet perplexed by the mystery of our own selves. To a generation entranced by novelty but uncertain about change, he speaks a word of that timeless reality incarnated in time, Augustine's "Beauty ever ancient, ever new." Jean Leclercq says:

> I am not giving in to an ingenuous, admiring expression of friendship when I rank Merton with the Fathers of the Early Church and those of the Middle Ages. Not only, as do all Christians, did he live the same mystery as they did, but he lives it and expresses it in the same way. . . . Just as they drew from the culture of their own times in order to make it a part of their inner experience, so did Merton work in our times toward bringing the good news to the world. (CWA xx)

By being responsive both to the issues and demands of his, and our own, day, and to that cloud of witnesses who have communicated the life of faith from one generation to the next, Merton himself becomes a further link in this chain of *paradosis*, of tradition, the transmission of the living Word through history.

Traditional Roots, Innovative Shoots:
Merton's Ecological Conscience

Recent studies of Thomas Merton's social thought have focused on his growing awareness during the final years of his life of the need for environmental responsibility,[1] particularly after reading Rachel Carson's *Silent Spring*[2] in 1963 and Roderick Nash's *Wilderness and the American Mind*[3] in the last year of his life. In his 1968 review of Nash's book, Merton stressed the importance of the environmental ethic of pioneer ecologist Aldo Leopold as a guiding principle for the present and future. A distorted concept of freedom that in practice has led to ruthless exploitation of the environment by industrial and military institutions had reached the point, Merton believed, of threatening the foundations of life on earth. "Aldo Leopold brought into clear focus one of the most important moral discoveries of our time. This can be called the *ecological conscience*. The ecological conscience is centered in an awareness of *man's true place as a dependent member of the biotic community*."[4] The utilitarian and pragmatic attitude that

---

[1] See Monica Weis, *The Environmental Vision of Thomas Merton* (Lexington: University Press of Kentucky, 2010); see also Kathleen Deignan, CND, "'Love for the Paradise Mystery': Thomas Merton, Contemplative Ecologist," *Cross-Currents* 58.4 (December 2008) 545–69.

[2] Rachel Carson, *Silent Spring* (Boston: Houghton Mifflin, 1962).

[3] Roderick Nash, *Wilderness and the American Mind* (New Haven: Yale University Press, 1967).

[4] Thomas Merton, *Selected Essays*, ed. Patrick F. O'Connell (Maryknoll, NY: Orbis, 2013) 450 (subsequent references will be cited as "*SE*" parenthetically in

sees the natural world principally as a potential source of profit must be countered by an ecological awareness if the process of environmental degradation is to be reversed.

In a February 1968 letter to Barbara Hubbard, Merton stressed the need to "retain a solid ecological consciousness"[5] rather than to become seduced by what he calls a "millennial consciousness" oriented completely toward a vision of a utopian future brought about by technological mastery that tends in actuality to "destroy and repudiate the past . . . by immolating our living earth, by careless and stupid exploitation for short-term commercial, military, or technological ends which will be paid for by irreparable loss in living species and natural resources" (*WF* 74). While the sense of urgency was new, Merton's recognition that a commitment to cherish and protect the environment is an integral dimension of the Christian life was rooted in his deep appreciation of the sacramentality of the natural world, of creation as a sign of the Creator,[6] that was already developing at the time of his conversion in 1938 and continued to deepen as he immersed himself in the resources of the Christian theological and spiritual tradition throughout the course of his monastic life.

The first significant discussion of the natural world in Merton's published work appears in the second chapter of his 1949 book of meditations, *Seeds of Contemplation*, entitled "Things in Their Identity," in which he writes that each created being is a finite manifestation of the infinite Creator. "A tree gives glory to God first of all by being a tree. For in being what God means it to be, it is imitating an idea

---

the text); an abbreviated version of this essay is also found in Thomas Merton, *Preview of the Asian Journey*, ed. Walter H. Capps (New York: Crossroad, 1989) (see 105–106) (subsequent references will be cited as "*PAJ*" parenthetically in the text).

[5] Thomas Merton, *Witness to Freedom: Letters in Times of Crisis*, ed. William H. Shannon (New York: Farrar, Straus, Giroux, 1994) 75 (subsequent references will be cited as "*WF*" parenthetically in the text).

[6] For overviews, see Patrick F. O'Connell, "Creation" and "Nature" in William H. Shannon, Christine M. Bochen and Patrick F. O'Connell, *The Thomas Merton Encyclopedia* (Maryknoll, NY: Orbis, 2002) 91–93, 319–22 (subsequent references will be cited as "*Encyclopedia*" parenthetically in the text).

which is in God and which is not distinct from the essence of God, and therefore a tree imitates God by being a tree. The more it is like itself, the more it is like Him."[7] Merton goes on to emphasize that this does not mean that a particular object is to be understood simply as an imperfect material reproduction of an eternal archetype in the mind of God. It is not by conforming more or less exactly to a generic model that a being realizes its authentic identity, but by embodying its own unique, unrepeatable individuality given by God to it alone. "This particular tree will give glory to God by spreading out its roots in the earth and raising its branches into the air and the light in a way that no other tree before or after it ever did or will do" (SC 24; NSC 29). Precisely because God is infinite, there is an infinite number of ways of reflecting God, so that each created being does so in its own specific manner. Merton continues:

> Therefore each particular being, in its individuality, its concrete nature and entity, with all its own characteristics and its private qualities and its own inviolable identity, gives glory to God by being precisely what He wants it to be here and now, in the circumstances ordained for it by His Love and His infinite Art. The forms and individual characters of living and growing things and of inanimate things and of animals and flowers and all nature, constitute their holiness in the sight of God. Their inscape is their sanctity. (SC 25; see NSC 30)

The reference to "inscape" here makes clear that in this recognition of the holiness of every creature, Merton is drawing on the insights of the Jesuit poet Gerard Manley Hopkins.

Merton made his first acquaintance with the poetry of Hopkins while in prep school at Oakham in England,[8] but it was in the autumn of 1938, as he was being drawn more and more toward the Catholic

---

[7] Thomas Merton, *Seeds of Contemplation* (New York: New Directions, 1949) 24 (subsequent references will be cited as "SC" parenthetically in the text). A revised version of this passage is found in Thomas Merton, *New Seeds of Contemplation* (New York: New Directions, 1961) 29–31 (subsequent references will be cited as "NSC" parenthetically in the text).

[8] Thomas Merton, *The Seven Storey Mountain* (New York: Harcourt, Brace, 1948) 100 (subsequent references will be cited as "SSM" parenthetically in the text).

Church, that he became fascinated with Hopkins' notebooks, as well as deeply impressed with his verse (see *SSM* 211). It was while reading about Hopkins' conversion in G. F. Lahey's biography[9] that Merton felt himself impelled to walk from his apartment near Columbia University to Corpus Christi Church and to tell Fr. George B. Ford, the pastor, that he himself wished to become a Catholic (see *SSM* 215).[10] So impressed was Merton with Hopkins that he had hoped to write his doctoral dissertation on his work (see *SSM* 235).[11]

Inscape was a term invented by Hopkins to describe the inner form of coherence and beauty in particular things. It occurs almost fifty times in Hopkins' journal for the years 1868–1875[12] in a variety of ways, most often "to indicate the essential individuality and particularity or 'selfhood' of a thing working itself out and expressing itself in design and pattern."[13] For example, on June 13, 1871, Hopkins notes, "A beautiful instance of inscape . . . is seen in the behaviour of the flag flower from the shut bud to the full blowing: each term you can distinguish is beautiful in itself and of course if the whole 'behaviour' were gathered up and so stalled it would have a beauty of all the higher degree."[14] Hopkins even discovers inscape "in the random clods and broken heaps of snow made by the cast of a

---

[9] G. F. Lahey, *Gerard Manley Hopkins* (London: Humphrey Milford/Oxford University Press, 1930); for the letter from Hopkins to John Henry Newman that Merton was reading, see 33–35.

[10] Merton also mentions this event in his journal entry for November 27, 1941: see Thomas Merton, *Run to the Mountain: The Story of a Vocation. Journals, vol. 1: 1939–1941*, ed. Patrick Hart, OCSO (San Francisco: HarperCollins, 1995) 455 (subsequent references will be cited as "*RM*" parenthetically in the text).

[11] In his journal entry for June 1, 1939, Merton writes, "The English Dept. won't let me write on G. M. Hopkins for my Ph.D." (*RM* 13).

[12] In a journal entry for October 19, 1939, Merton noted the precision of Hopkins' observation of natural phenomena compared with his own: "The trees, no leaves. I forget what kind of trees they would be, and that should forbid me forever to think this notebook is in the tradition of G. M. Hopkins!" (*RM* 61).

[13] John Pick, *Gerard Manley Hopkins, Priest and Poet* (1942; 2nd ed., New York: Oxford University Press, 1966) 33 (subsequent references will be cited as "Pick" parenthetically in the text). In an unpublished February 12, 1965, letter to Pick, Merton writes, "your book on Hopkins spoke very forcefully to me years ago here" (archives of the Thomas Merton Center, Bellarmine University, Louisville, KY).

[14] Gerard Manley Hopkins, *Poems and Prose*, selected and edited by W. H. Gardner (Baltimore: Penguin, 1953) 124 (subsequent references will be cited as "Hopkins" parenthetically in the text).

broom," commenting: "All the world is full of inscape and chance left free to act falls into an order as well as purpose" (Hopkins 128 [February 24, 1873]).[15] Merton himself will later define inscape as "the inner structure of a living, or organic, or even inorganic created being, the result of its gradual development under the secret action of nature—and the creative hand of God—the trademark of God imprinted in the *individual structure* given to a thing by its history, the mark of God's love and God's wisdom imprinted in the unique identity of a thing."[16]

In *Seeds of Contemplation*, Merton goes on to exemplify just what inscape entails through additional precise descriptions of specific creatures:

> The special clumsy beauty of this particular colt on this April day in this field under these clouds is a holiness consecrated to God by His own Art, and it declares the glory of God. The pale flowers of the dogwood outside this window are saints. The little yellow flowers that nobody notices on the edge of that road are saints looking up into the face of God. This leaf has its own texture and its own pattern of veins and its own holy shape, and the bass and trout hiding in the deep pools of the river are canonized by their beauty and their strength. (*SC* 25; see *NSC* 30)

---

[15] The significance of inscape for Hopkins's verse can be seen in a poem such as the sonnet "As kingfishers catch fire, dragonflies draw flame," perhaps the most clear and intense poetic description of inscape, with its lines: "Each mortal thing does one thing and the same: / Deals out that being indoors each one dwells; / Selves—goes itself; *myself* it speaks and spells, / Crying *What I do is me: for that I came*" (ll. 5–8 [Hopkins 51]). In the collection of religious poetry (never published) that he was assembling in the summer of 1941, Merton included this sonnet among seven Hopkins poems (see Patrick F. O'Connell, "Thomas Merton's Projected Anthology of Religious Poetry," *The Merton Seasonal* 25.3 [Fall 2000] 20–28), and echoed it repeatedly in his own verse: see "The Sowing of Meanings" (ll. 28–30, 36–37) (Thomas Merton, *Figures for an Apocalypse* (New York: New Directions, 1947) 85 (subsequent references will be cited as "*FA*" parenthetically in the text); Thomas Merton, *Collected Poems* (New York: New Directions, 1977) 188–89 (subsequent references will be cited as "*CP*" parenthetically in the text); "Canticle for the Blessed Virgin" (ll. 75–76) (*FA* 46; *CP* 163).

[16] Thomas Merton, *Monastic Observances: Initiation into the Monastic Tradition* 5, ed. Patrick F. O'Connell (Collegeville, MN: Cistercian Publications, 2010) 78. See also Thomas Merton, *The Behavior of Titans* (New York: New Directions, 1961) 92: "It is an intuition of the patterns and harmonies, the 'living character' impressed by life itself, revealing the wisdom of the Living God in the mystery of interplaying movements and changes."

Ultimately, these natural objects serve as models for human beings, likewise called to holiness by freely choosing to be who they truly are, to realize their own authentic identity as images of God. This sensitivity to the beauty of natural objects as signs of the divine presence in creation, an intuition of the "sacred and marvelous" present in the ordinary,[17] continued to mark Merton's response to the world around him throughout the remaining two decades of his life.[18]

The perception of inscape even relates, albeit somewhat indirectly, to Merton's early interest in Franciscan theology and spirituality,[19] which initially drew him toward entering the Order of Friars Minor.[20]

---

[17] Thomas Merton, *Dancing in the Water of Life: Seeking Peace in the Hermitage. Journals, vol. 5: 1963–1965*, ed. Robert E. Daggy (San Francisco: HarperCollins, 1997) 291 (subsequent references will be cited as *"DWL"* parenthetically in the text). See also, for example, the sense of heightened awareness and vivid clarity of detail that radiates through the June 1949 journal description of his first afternoon outside the monastic enclosure after being given permission to spend time alone meditating in the woods (Thomas Merton, *Entering the Silence: Becoming a Monk and Writer. Journals, vol. 2: 1941–1952*, ed. Jonathan Montaldo [San Francisco: HarperCollins, 1996] 329 [subsequent references will be cited as *"ES"* parenthetically in the text]); the climactic section of the celebrated "Fire Watch" passage of July 4, 1952 (Thomas Merton, *The Sign of Jonas* [New York: Harcourt, Brace, 1953] 360; the same passage is also found in *ES* 486); the experience of interrelatedness that characterizes his new life as a hermit in 1965: "I exist under trees. I walk in the woods out of necessity. . . . I know there are trees here. I know there are birds here. I know the birds in fact very well, for there are precise pairs of birds (two each of fifteen or twenty species) living in the immediate area of my cabin. I share this particular place with them: we form an ecological balance" (Thomas Merton, *Day of a Stranger* [Salt Lake City: Gibbs M. Smith, 1981] 33 [subsequent references will be cited as *"DS"* parenthetically in the text]).

[18] For an anthology of passages on the natural world from Merton's journals and other works, see Thomas Merton, *When the Trees Say Nothing: Writings on Nature*, ed. Kathleen Deignan (Notre Dame, IN: Sorin Books, 2003).

[19] See especially Daniel P. Horan, *The Franciscan Heart of Thomas Merton: A New Look at the Spiritual Inspiration of His Life, Thought, and Writing* (Notre Dame, IN: Ave Maria Press, 2014) (subsequent references will be cited as "Horan" parenthetically in the text).

[20] The story of Merton's initial acceptance and eventual rejection by the Franciscans is found in *The Seven Storey Mountain* (261–62, 265–66, 288–92, 294–98); see also Michael Mott, *The Seven Mountains of Thomas Merton* (Boston: Houghton Mifflin, 1984) 123–25, 155–56 (subsequent references will be cited as "Mott" parenthetically in the text).

The very first mention of St. Francis in Merton's journal refers to his sermon to the birds (see *RM* 24), and the Franciscan sense of kinship with all creation is evident in Merton's own early poetry, as, for example, in the lovely early lyric "Evening," in which the young children love "The trees, their innocent sisters" (l. 13),[21] or in the reference to "the hay-colored sun, our marvelous cousin" (l. 9) in "Aubade: Lake Erie" (*TP* [7]; *CP* 35).[22] While teaching at St. Bonaventure College, Merton engaged in a careful study of the *Itinerarium Mentis in Deum*[23] of the great Franciscan theologian after whom the school was named, and copied into his journal the passage from the first chapter, in which Bonaventure presents an overview of the spiritual journey to God that begins with recognizing the "*vestigia Dei*," the traces or "footprints" of God, in the created world (*RM* 270 [12/4/40]). When he was debating with himself about entering the Cistercians, he questioned whether he would be somehow cut off from the natural world: "telling myself some absurd thing about the necessity to love God's creatures—nature etc. The only answer to that is: there is nothing in the Trappist discipline to prevent you loving nature the way I meant it then and do now: loving it in God's creation, and a sign of His goodness and Love" (*RM* 399). Much later, he would recall saying at the time, "I'm a Franciscan; I need nature" at the precise spot that he would pass coming down from the hermitage decades afterward, commenting: "God was telling me something. I have more nature here than I would have had anywhere."[24]

But for close to a decade Merton's strongest Franciscan enthusiasm was for the late thirteenth-century theologian John Duns Scotus, whom he first encountered at Columbia in a course with Daniel Walsh

---

[21] Thomas Merton, *Thirty Poems* (Norfolk, CT: New Directions, 1944) [12] (subsequent references will be cited as "*TP*" parenthetically in the text); *CP* 42.

[22] For a discussion of these poems, see Patrick F. O'Connell, "Sacrament and Sacramentality in Thomas Merton's *Thirty Poems*" in Patrick F. O'Connell, ed., *The Vision of Thomas Merton* (Notre Dame, IN: Ave Maria Press, 2003) 172–76, 176–80.

[23] See the edition and translation by Merton's mentor and friend Philotheus Boehner, OFM: *Itinerarium Mentis in Deum*: Works of Saint Bonaventure II (St. Bonaventure, NY: Franciscan Institute, 1956).

[24] Thomas Merton, *The Springs of Contemplation: A Retreat at the Abbey of Gethsemani*, ed. Jane Marie Richardson (New York: Farrar, Straus, Giroux, 1992) 25–26.

in the fall of 1938 as he was preparing for baptism (see *SSM* 219),[25] and later studied at St. Bonaventure with Fr. Philotheus Boehner (see *SSM* 333, 337). The original version of *The Seven Storey Mountain* had numerous references to Scotus (see Mott 231–32), and he appears frequently in the journal of Merton's early monastic years.[26] In an August 17, 1946, letter to his publisher James Laughlin, Merton confides his desire to write "a book, some 150 pages long, on Scotus," needed because "There is practically nothing about him available, especially in English."[27] Eventually Merton found Scotus too complicated and gave up the idea of a book, noting when he started teaching the scholastics at Gethsemani that "Our life is not designed for theological controversy and Scotus is more than the Cistercian head can bear—at least until somebody distills his essence and gives it to us second-hand" (*ES* 459 [6/13/51]). That somebody was not to be himself, yet Scotus had a formative influence on Merton's spirituality. The key christological idea of Scotus that the incarnation of the Word was not simply a consequence of the fall but the culminating point of creation is evident throughout Merton's work, from his reference in the 1949 poem "Dry Places" to "Christ . . . promised first without scars" (l. 35)[28] to the second paragraph of the final chapter of *New Seeds of Contemplation*, in which he writes: "The Lord made the world and made man in order that He Himself might descend into the world, that He Himself might become Man" (*NSC* 290), a deeply positive perception of the ultimate purpose of creation.

---

[25] On Merton and Scotus, see especially Horan, 97–116. In *Merton and Walsh on the Person* (West Palm Beach, FL: Liturgical Publications, 1987), Robert Imperato discusses the importance of Scotus for Walsh, whose 1933 doctoral dissertation from the University of Toronto was entitled "The Metaphysics of Ideas according to Duns Scotus." George Kilcourse has some insightful pages on Merton and Scotus in *Ace of Freedoms: Thomas Merton's Christ* (Notre Dame, IN: University of Notre Dame Press, 1993) 30–34.

[26] See *ES* 31 [12/10/46], 136–37 [11/20/47], 146 [12/16/47], 158 [1/17/48], 162 [1/28/48], 240 [10/31/48].

[27] Thomas Merton and James Laughlin, *Selected Letters*, ed. David D. Cooper (New York: Norton, 1997) 12.

[28] Thomas Merton, *The Tears of the Blind Lions* (New York: New Directions, 1949) 25–26; *CP* 217; for a discussion, see Patrick F. O'Connell, "Thomas Merton and the 'Edenic Office of the Poet': Three Poems from *The Tears of the Blind Lions*," *The Merton Annual* 32 (2019) 194–200.

As Merton was surely aware, Hopkins's enthusiasm for Scotus was at least equal to his own, and it was due in large part to the Franciscan's concept of *haecceitas*, the unique individual form, or "thisness," present in every created being, in which the Jesuit poet found confirmation and philosophical justification for his own intuition of inscape.[29] In August 1872 Hopkins wrote that "when I took in any inscape of the sky or sea I thought of Scotus" (Hopkins 126) and in his sonnet "Duns Scotus's Oxford" he would call the great Franciscan the one "who of all men most sways my spirits to peace" (l. 11 [Hopkins 40]).[30] While Merton never explicitly refers to the affection and respect of Hopkins for Scotus, the coincidence with his own predilections must have increased his sense of connection with both men, and the affinity of inscape with *haecceitas* no doubt provided added support for his own vivid sense of the sacramental potential of each created being to serve as a unique reflection of its divine source.

For Merton, an appreciative and responsible integration with the natural world is an essential component of any authentic human life, but especially of one that aspires to some sort of contemplative awareness, for the natural world in Merton's view is ultimately a source of revelation (see *DWL* 279), a manifestation of the divine ground of all created reality, which nevertheless infinitely transcends it. In the development of his own monastic life, and particularly in his growing responsibility for instructing young monks that began shortly after his own ordination to the priesthood in 1949 and continued until he

---

[29] For a thorough discussion of the relation of Scotus and Hopkins, see Pick 34–36, 151–53; Pick notes that "we must be careful not to consider the influence of Scotus as too positive an initiating force, for Hopkins had been using the word 'inscape' for almost four years before he took Scotus out of the library. It was not that he found something he had not known. He did not become a disciple of Scotus in the sense that a student adopts the teachings of a master; rather, both of them had the same experience of 'form' as sharply individual and particular" (35). See also William Short, OFM, "Pied Beauty: Gerard Manley Hopkins and the Scotistic View of Nature," *The Cord* 45.3 (1995) 27–36.

[30] Merton himself wrote two poems on Scotus: "Duns Scotus" in *Figures for an Apocalypse* (48–49 [*CP* 164–65]) and "Hymn for the Feast of Duns Scotus" in *Tears of the Blind Lions* (6–7 [*CP* 198–99]).

became a full-time hermit in August 1965,[31] Merton was increasingly influenced by the Greek Fathers of the church, who provided a third important source for his own environmental spirituality, the contemplation of the created cosmos that is the traditional second stage of the spiritual journey for many of the Greek Fathers.

The Ascent to Truth, published four years after *Seeds of Contemplation*, is mainly focused on St. John of the Cross, but the opening chapter, entitled "Vision and Illusion," introduces the Greek patristic concept of "natural contemplation"—*theoria physike* (or *physica* in its Latinized form)—which is described as "a positive recognition of God as He is manifested in the essences (*logoi*) of all things. . . . a kind of intuitive perception of God as He is reflected in His creation."[32] Analogous to the illuminative way, the second of the "three ways" more familiar in the West, *theoria physike* follows the *praktike* of ascetic effort and moral transformation and leads to the *theologia* of unmediated encounter with God, imageless contemplation of the Trinity.[33] In his discussion of *theoria physike* in *The Ascent to Truth* Merton may seem to focus more on illusion than on vision, stressing the "instinctive realization of the vanity and illusion of all things as soon as they are considered apart from their right order and reference to God their Creator" (*AT* 27). He makes clear, however, that a proper appreciation for the created world is possible only insofar as one has become detached from creatures as a source of self-centered gratification, as a means to be manipulated for one's own private ends; this requires "the ascetic gift of a discernment which, in one penetrating glance, apprehends what creatures are, and what they are not" (*AT* 28).

Such a perspective is essential in safeguarding the natural world from exploitation. Throughout his monastic life, Merton remains aware that a contemplative perception of the created universe is by no means automatic; it can be distorted either by despising the material world and embracing "an exaggerated asceticism that tries to

---

[31] For an overview, see Patrick F. O'Connell, "Master of Novices" and "Master of Students" (*Encyclopedia* 288–89, 289–90).

[32] Thomas Merton, *The Ascent to Truth* (New York: Harcourt, Brace, 1951) 27 (subsequent references will be cited as "*AT*" parenthetically in the text).

[33] Bishop Kallistos Ware provides a brief, clear overview of the stages of spiritual growth in the Eastern Church in *The Orthodox Way*, rev. ed. (Crestview, NY: St. Vladimir's Seminary Press, 1995) 105–32.

sever the soul entirely from the rest of creation,"[34] or by demanding more from creation than it can provide by turning it into an end in itself or a means to glorify the self rather than God. As he had written in *Seeds of Contemplation*, "The fulfillment belongs to the reality of the created being, a reality that is from God and belongs to God and reflects God. The anguish belongs to the disorder of our desire which looks for a greater reality in the object of our desire than is actually there: a greater fulfillment than it is capable of giving. Instead of worshipping God through His creation we are always trying to worship ourselves with creatures" (*SC* 23; cf. *NSC* 26).

When Merton considers *theoria physike* in *The Inner Experience*, written largely in 1959, he emphasizes that this "natural contemplation" is not "natural" as distinguished from "supernatural": it is natural with respect to its object rather than its origin, a "contemplation of the divine *in nature*, not contemplation of the divine *by our natural powers*."[35] Again he emphasizes that such an "intuition of divine things in and through the reflection of God in nature" (*IE* 67) is possible only when one has relinquished the desire to possess and control, the craving to find fulfillment in what cannot ultimately satisfy. Detachment frees one from the illusions of a "distorted" view of reality, so that one "sees straight into the nature of things as they are" (*IE* 68). Only in this way is creation properly respected and appreciated, and only in this way can it point beyond itself to its divine source.

In his most extensive discussion of *theoria physike*, the series of conferences on mystical theology he gave to recently ordained monks in the summer of 1961,[36] Merton defines it as "a contemplation according to nature (*physis*) . . . a contemplation of God in and through nature, in and through things He has created, in history. . . . the *gnosis* that apprehends the wisdom and glory of God, especially His

---

[34] Thomas Merton, *Seasons of Celebration* (New York: Farrar, Straus and Giroux, 1965) 136 (subsequent references will be cited as "*SCel*" parenthetically in the text).

[35] Thomas Merton, *The Inner Experience: Notes on Contemplation*, ed. William H. Shannon (San Francisco: HarperCollins, 2003) 68 (subsequent references will be cited as "*IE*" parenthetically in the text).

[36] Thomas Merton, *An Introduction to Christian Mysticism: Initiation into the Monastic Tradition 3*, ed. Patrick F. O'Connell (Kalamazoo, MI: Cistercian Publications, 2008) 121–37; see also xxix–xxxiii (subsequent references will be cited as "*ICM*" parenthetically in the text).

wisdom as *Creator* and *Redeemer*" (*ICM* 122). It is an awareness of the inner coherence, the *logos*, of creatures and of creation as a whole, a recognition and appreciation of the loving presence of the Logos, the creative Word of God, in the creature. In the Greek Fathers, Merton discovers a perception analogous to Hopkins's notion of inscape, but one that is thoroughly integrated into a holistic theology of life with God. Attentiveness to the divine shining through created beings is presented by the Greek patristic tradition as a fundamental dimension of authentic spiritual development. *Theoria physike* is the transition point between active and contemplative lives, arising from a synergy between human effort and divine gift, providing "penetrating intuitions" (*ICM* 122) into the intelligibility of all that God has made. While in his major sources, Evagrius Ponticus and Maximus the Confessor, *theoria physike* culminates in awareness of pure intelligences—the angelic realm—Merton's own focus is above all on the natural world as an epiphany of the divine and on development of the capacity to recognize this manifestation of God in creation as an essential element in spiritual growth. Merton is convinced that the tendency on the part of some spiritual theologians to deemphasize or to skip over completely this encounter with the divine in the created world has been just as harmful to a full and adequate theology of mystical experience as an unwillingness to move beyond the level of images and ideas into the darkness of unknowing. He points out that "both in the West and in the East there developed a tendency to go directly from the ascetic life to contemplation without forms, without passing through *theoria physike*, in the Middle Ages. This is certainly as meaningful a fact as the separation between spirituality and scientific theology, probably much more meaningful. It is here really that the separation has its most disastrous effect" (*ICM* 137). By neglecting the sacramentality of creation, both theologians and practitioners tend to devalue the material world and so to miss its revelatory dimension.

Conversely, an awareness of God's active presence in all that God has made results not simply in insight but in personal transformation:

> Man by *theoria* is able to unite the hidden wisdom of God in things with the hidden light of wisdom in himself. The meeting and marriage of these two brings about a *resplendent clarity* within

man himself, and this clarity is the presence of Divine Wisdom fully recognized and active in him. Thus man becomes a mirror of the divine glory, and is resplendent with divine truth not only in his *mind* but in his *life*. He is filled with the light of wisdom which shines forth in him, and thus God is glorified in him. (*ICM* 125–26)

This contemplative awareness has a dynamic dimension, then, which leads not only to a perception of creation as a revelation of divine power, wisdom, and love, but to a rediscovery of authentic personal identity as reflecting and participating in the divine likeness and of human activity as a way of sharing in the divine creativity.[37] The human person is not merely called to observe the sacramentality of God's works, but "exercises a spiritualizing influence in the world by the work of his hands which is in accord with *the creative wisdom of God* in things and in history" (*ICM* 126). *Theoria physike* is at the heart of a genuine theology of creativity, which is thus an intrinsic element of the mystical journey to union with God. "God Himself hands over to man, when he is thus purified and enlightened, and united with the divine will, a certain creative initiative of his own, in political life, in art, in spiritual life, in worship: man is then endowed with a *causality* of his own" (*ICM* 126). Thus natural contemplation is an aspect of the redemptive work of Christ by which "all creation waits with eager longing for the revealing of the children of God" (Rom 8:19). The restoration of a right relationship with creation as it was meant to be is an anticipation of the ultimate fulfillment of the cosmos in the glorified Christ, the firstborn of the whole creation. As Merton writes in *The New Man*, "This new creation begins with the Resurrection of the Lord and will be perfected at the end of time. . . . The recapitulation of the work of creation sublimated and perfected in Christ is a communion in the divine life, an infusion of the life, and glory and power and truth of God not only into man's spirit but

---

[37] The perspective here is very similar to that found in Merton's essay "Theology of Creativity" (Thomas Merton, *The Literary Essays of Thomas Merton*, ed. Brother Patrick Hart [New York: New Directions, 1981] 355–70 [subsequent references will be cited as "*LE*" parenthetically in the text]), first published as part of a three-part symposium in *The American Benedictine Review* 11 (September–December 1960) 197–213.

also, ultimately, into all the material creation as well."[38] Redeemed humanity is called to participate in this process of extending the effects of Christ's saving work to the rest of creation.

> If man's eye is "lightsome" with the spiritual beauty of grace, wisdom, understanding and divine sonship, then light will pass through him to pervade and transfigure the whole of creation . . . by the creative work of man's own spirit, a work born out of love for God the Creator and for our fellow man. Work that springs from this creative love is patterned on the truth implanted in our very being, by nature, and in our redeemed spirit by the Pneuma who is given us by the Risen Christ. (*SCel* 167–68)

Care for creation is thus a participation in the creative and redemptive work of Christ.

Conversely, the absence of this contemplative perception of the material world, a purely instrumental attitude toward nature, Merton declares, leads in practice to a degradation of creation through an "impersonal, pragmatic, quantitative *exploitation and manipulation* of things . . . a demonic cult of change, and 'exchange'—consumption, production, destruction, for their own sakes" (*ICM* 130). Hence an authentically contemplative response to creation is recognized by Merton as having tremendous practical importance in a world increasingly tempted by a "demonic pseudo-contemplation, {a} mystique of technics and production" (*ICM* 130). The discipline of *theoria physike* includes not only a recognition of the sacred character of the material world but the vocation to respect and nurture that sacredness, to resist any and all efforts to reduce creation to a collection of raw materials to be exploited for purposes of human pride and arrogance.

This early Christian vision of the sacredness of the cosmos is in turn traced by Merton back to the scriptural presentation of wisdom, above all as personified in the eighth chapter of the Book of Proverbs,

---

[38] Thomas Merton, *The New Man* (New York: Farrar, Straus & Cudahy, 1961) 150 (subsequent references will be cited as "*NM*" parenthetically in the text).

where creation is presented as a primordial cosmic revelation, an epiphany of divine Wisdom "playing before God the Creator in His universe. . . . The beauty of all creation is a reflection of Sophia living and hidden in creation" (*WF* 4–5).[39] It is telling that when Merton revises his discussion of "Things in Their Identity" for *New Seeds of Contemplation*, he immediately follows the statement "Their inscape is their sanctity" with an additional sentence: "It is the imprint of His wisdom and His reality in them," and goes on describe the colt's "clumsy beauty" as "consecrated to God by His own creative wisdom" where the earlier version had "by His Art" (*NSC* 30). From this "sophianic" perspective, the cosmos is perceived as a window through which shines the light of the Logos, the Word through which all things came, and come, to be (cf. John 1:2): "God creates things by seeing them in His own Logos" (*NSC* 291).

Thus Merton recognizes an intrinsic relationship between creation as an epiphany of the divine Word and the incarnation as the culmination of this revelatory self-disclosure of God, the perfect manifestation of Creator in creation.

> The whole character of the creation was determined by the fact that God was to become man and dwell in the midst of His own creation. Creation is therefore not a preestablished fact into which the Word will come and fit Himself as best He can at the appointed time. Creation is created and sustained in Him and by Him. And when He enters into it, He will simply make clear the fact that He is already, and has always been, the center and the life and the meaning of a universe that exists only by His will. (*NM* 137)

---

[39] In his prose poem "*Hagia Sophia*," Merton memorably presents the figure of Wisdom as the personification of divine creativity: "Sophia, the feminine child, is playing in the world, obvious and unseen, playing at all times before the Creator. Her delights are to be with the children of men. She is their sister. The core of life that exists in all things is tenderness, mercy, virginity, the Light, the Life considered as passive, as received, as given, as taken, as inexhaustibly renewed by the Gift of God. Sophia is Gift, is Spirit, *Donum Dei*. She is God-given and God Himself as Gift" (*CP* 368). For a comprehensive treatment of Merton's theology of wisdom, particularly in "*Hagia Sophia*," and its relation to the sophiology of the twentieth-century Russian Orthodox theologians, see Christopher Pramuk, *Sophia: The Hidden Christ of Thomas Merton* (Collegeville, MN: Liturgical Press, 2009).

Here again Merton seems clearly to be identifying with the Scotist teaching that the incarnation would have taken place even without the Fall.

Concepts, logical explanations, are not enough to disclose what Merton called this "epiphany of the cosmic mystery" (*LE* 104); such awareness is not available to the detached, "objective" observer but only to one who has what Merton liked to describe as a "sapiential" consciousness, an intuitive, participatory awareness of the "hidden wholeness" (*CP* 363) of all reality, "a kind of knowledge by identification, an intersubjective knowledge, a communion in cosmic awareness and in nature . . . a wisdom based on love" (*LE* 108). For those whose inner eye has been opened, the very existence, order, life, and beauty of the universe, and of each creature within it, reflects and participates in the mystery of the divine Wisdom who made it. As Merton would say from the hermitage: "Up here in the woods is seen the New Testament: that is to say, the wind comes through the trees and you breathe it" (*DS* 41). An appreciation of wisdom is crucial in recognizing the sacramentality of creation and the need for human stewardship of the world as a participation in divine creativity.[40]

It was this sapiential perspective, this perception of the world as sacrament and of human stewardship of creation as a participation in divine creativity, that led Merton to endorse the growing ecological consciousness of the 1960s. He first writes in his journal on December 11, 1962 of his interest in reading Rachel Carson's *Silent Spring*, with its revelations of the effects of indiscriminate pesticide use on bird populations. His response to the objection that one should be concerned about people rather than about nonhuman creatures is that it is not a question of either/or but of both/and: "We are in the world and part of it and we are destroying everything because we are destroying ourselves, spiritually, morally and in every way. It is all part of the same sickness."[41] After reading the book, he wrote an appreciative letter to Carson linking her analysis of contemporary disregard for the environment to other manifestations of the same technological

---

[40] See the further discussion of this theme in chapter 4 below.

[41] Thomas Merton, *Turning Toward the World: The Pivotal Years. Journals, vol. 4: 1960–1963*, ed. Victor A. Kramer (San Francisco: HarperCollins, 1996) 274 (subsequent references will be cited as "*TTW*" parenthetically in the text).

hubris, particularly the threat of atomic destruction. "The awful irresponsibility with which we scorn the smallest values is part of the same portentous irresponsibility with which we dare to use our titanic power in a way that threatens not only civilization but life itself" (*WF* 70). He finds a subconscious hatred of life buried beneath the superficial optimism of an affluent society that utterly fails to satisfy the deepest human desires for interior unity and for a sense of connectedness with all life. The separation from one's own deepest identity results in an alienation from the rest of creation as well. "The whole world itself, to religious thinkers, has always appeared as a transparent manifestation of the love of God, as a 'paradise' of His wisdom, manifested in all His creatures, down to the tiniest, and in the most wonderful interrelationship between them. . . . That is to say, man is at once a part of nature and he transcends it. In maintaining this delicate balance, he must make use of nature wisely" (*WF* 71). But it is this sense of balance that is lost when the unifying vision of wisdom is replaced by the analytic, dominating attitude of scientistic and technical control. The vocation of modern humanity, Merton concludes, is to rejoin technics and wisdom, though he is not optimistic about the willingness to do so. Merton thus sees ecological consciousness as an essential part of an authentic contemporary contemplative awareness, a necessary way of being responsive to the revelation of wisdom in creation. The development of "a tradition that opens out in *full continuity* into a wisdom capable of understanding the mystery of the contemporary world in the light of *theoria*" must include, along with commitment to peace and racial justice, attentiveness to "the great spiritual problem of the profound disturbances of ecology all over the world, the tragic waste and spoilage of natural resources" (*TTW* 330).

Despite the slowness of the Christian community to respond to this critical issue, Merton does see an awareness of the interconnectedness of all creation and a sense of environmental stewardship as an intrinsic element of an authentic Christian and religious consciousness. Even before encountering Leopold's summons to recognize the "true place" of the human being "as a dependent member of the biotic community" (*SE* 450; *PAJ* 106), Merton had written in his journal for Holy Saturday, April 13, 1963, "How absolutely true, and how central a truth, that we are purely and simply *part of nature*, though," he adds, "we are the part which recognizes God" (*TTW* 312). Appreciation of this fact, Merton believes, can have profound consequences for the future of Christianity and the future of the earth. In his response to and articulation of the looming environmental crisis, Merton emerges as a witness that the Christian tradition contains and provides significant resources for a contemporary effort to defend and promote the integrity of creation, which had become a constitutive dimension of his mature holistic spirituality.

3

The Paschal Heart of Merton's Spirituality

Is Thomas Merton's spirituality more accurately described as Christocentric or theocentric? This question first arose some three decades ago in a review of George Kilcourse's ground-breaking study *Ace of Freedoms: Thomas Merton's Christ*,[1] when Christine M. Bochen pointed out that "for Kilcourse, christology is the foundation and interpretive key to Merton's spirituality."[2] While expressing appreciation for the "comprehensive and often compelling case" which the author makes "for reading Merton through the lens of christology" (337), she went on to "question the centrality of christology to Merton's thought and spirituality" (339). She proposed that his approach, while definitely intrinsically Christian, is better described as theocentric than as Christocentric, that it focuses more on God than on the person of Christ. She suggested further that theocentrism facilitates dialogue with non-Christians, and concluded, "The Christian character of Merton's spirituality is not debatable; the degree to which Merton's spirituality is 'Christ-centered' certainly is" (339).

Little attention has been given subsequently to this divergence between two highly respected Merton scholars. Is there further consideration that might contribute to reaching a satisfactory resolution? One might be tempted to try to settle the matter simply by quoting

---

[1] George Kilcourse, *Ace of Freedoms: Thomas Merton's Christ* (Notre Dame, IN: University of Notre Dame Press, 1993).

[2] Christine M. Bochen, "Review Symposium on George Kilcourse's *Ace of Freedoms: Thomas Merton's Christ*: Three Perspectives," *Horizons* 21 (1994) 337 (subsequent references will be cited as "Bochen" parenthetically in the text).

a passage such as the definition Merton provides in the opening chapter of *New Seeds of Contemplation*: "Contemplation is the awareness and realization, even in some sense *experience*, of what each Christian obscurely believes: 'It is no longer I that live but Christ lives in me.'"[3] Surely this is as "Christ-centered" as one could possibly ask for, but it could be argued in response that it is, after all, only a single sentence, and that in fact the following paragraph refers generically to God nine times, and specifically to Christ only in a final characterization of contemplation, as able "to follow the Word 'wherever he may go'" (*NSC* 5). More to the point, this description of contemplation does not exemplify at least one common understanding of Christocentrism, a devotional expression of love for Jesus, the affective *Brautmistik*, "Christ-mysticism," of classical spirituality, which relies heavily on the bridal imagery of union between the Word and the soul, as seen, for example, in Merton's great Cistercian predecessor, St. Bernard.[4] If this is the approach one associates with Christocentrism, it is indeed debatable whether Merton's spirituality fits this label.

Perhaps what needs to be done is to consider the issue from a somewhat different angle. While I believe Bochen has raised important questions, I am not convinced that the alternatives of theocentrism and Christocentrism are necessarily mutually exclusive, nor that these categories are in fact completely accurate or helpful in grasping the essential dynamic of Merton's thought. The verse that Merton quotes from Paul's letter to the Galatians, "It is no longer I that live but Christ lives in me" (Gal 2:20), which is immediately preceded by the statement, "I have been crucified with Christ" (Gal 2:19), suggests that the most adequate way to describe the central focus of Merton's spiritual vision is not as either "theocentric" or "Christocentric" but as "paschal," a term which synthesizes and

---

[3] Thomas Merton, *New Seeds of Contemplation* (New York: New Directions, 1961) 5 (subsequent references will be cited as "*NSC*" parenthetically in the text).

[4] Bernard's use of bridal imagery does not, of course, preclude a strong paschal dimension to his own teaching. See, for example, his sermons of the Song of Songs 21:2, 25:8, and 28:11; Bernard of Clairvaux, *On the Song of Songs* 2, trans. Kilian Walsh, OCSO, *The Works of Bernard of Clairvaux* 3, Cistercian Fathers [CF] 7 (Kalamazoo, MI: Cistercian, 1976) 4, 56, 98; and *On Loving God* 4.11, *Treatises* 2, trans. Robert Walton, OSB, *The Works of Bernard of Clairvaux* 5, CF 13 (Washington, DC: Cistercian, 1974) 103.

transcends the distinctions between these alternatives.⁵ This verse from Galatians reappears in an important passage from *The New Man*, which clarifies and develops the paschal implications of Paul's declaration:

> When we speak of "life in Christ," according to the phrase of St. Paul, "It is no longer I that live, but Christ lives in me" [Galatians 2:20-21], we are speaking not of self-alienation but of our discovery of our true selves in Christ. In this discovery we participate spiritually in the mystery of His resurrection. And this sharing of the death and resurrection of Christ is the very heart of the Christian faith and of Christian mysticism.⁶

For Merton as for Paul, the Christian life is most fundamentally a participation in the crucifixion and resurrection of Jesus, a death to sin and the gift of new life "in Christ." From one perspective it is a theocentric stance, as Jesus' own spirituality is theocentric, focused on God his Father, for to be "in Christ" is to relate to God as Jesus relates to God. From another perspective it can be called Christocentric, not because the focus of attention is on Christ, but because the attentiveness itself is a participation in Christ; Christ is not so much part of the field of vision as the eyes through which one sees, not so much one's partner as one's deepest identity.

For Thomas Merton, it is dying and rising with Christ that leads to discovery of the true self, to realization of authentic community, to contemplative union with God. Moreover, the paschal mystery is

---

⁵ James Finley provides a strongly paschal reading of Merton's spirituality in *Merton's Palace of Nowhere: A Search for God through Awareness of the True Self* (Notre Dame, IN: Ave Maria Press, 1978). Kilcourse includes the paschal aspect of Merton's Christology in his book, especially in his discussion of Christ's *kenosis* (cf. 29, 68, 97, 100–101, 105–6, 203–4, 205, 212, 215), but it is not a central theme of his work.

⁶ Thomas Merton, *The New Man* (New York: Farrar, Straus & Cudahy, 1961) 167 (subsequent references will be cited as "*NM*" parenthetically in the text). Anne E. Carr notes Merton's reliance on this verse from Galatians in *A Search for Wisdom and Spirit: Thomas Merton's Theology of the Self* (Notre Dame, IN: University of Notre Dame Press, 1988) 16, 49; for other passages where Merton quotes the verse, see *NSC* 41; *No Man Is an Island* (New York: Harcourt, Brace, 1955) xv, 98, 185 (subsequent references will be cited as "*NMI*" parenthetically in the text); *Zen and the Birds of Appetite* (New York: New Directions: 1968) 55 (subsequent references will be cited as "*ZBA*" parenthetically in the text).

the common element that links doctrine and experience, liturgy and contemplation, monasticism and other forms of Christian life; it even has a significant contribution to make to dialogue with other religious traditions. To examine some of the passages in which Merton explores these topics in the context of the cross and resurrection is to recognize that what Merton himself calls "the very heart" of faith and of mysticism is indeed "the very heart" of his own spiritual teaching.[7]

The Paschal Mystery and the True Self

Certainly most people familiar with Merton's writings would identify the distinction between false and true selves as a central theme of his spirituality. In her review, Bochen summarizes Merton's view of contemplation as an "awakening to one's true self in God. The true self is the self that knows itself in the ground of its being which is God" (Bochen 339). This focus on the true self grounded in God is certainly characteristic of Merton's thought, but it does not include any explicit consideration of the process by which the true self is discovered. In *The Inner Experience*, Merton describes the "Christian life" in precisely these terms, but with some significant additions: it is "a return to the Father, the Source, the Ground of all existence . . . a return to the infinite abyss of pure reality in which our own reality is grounded, and in which we exist." But this return takes place "through the Son, the Splendor and the Image of the Father, in the Holy Spirit, the Love of the Father and the Son." It is a restoration of "the inner self, purified and renewed," but this restoration "is only possible by detachment and 'death' in the exterior self." This "spiritual self in which [one's] exterior self is destroyed and his inner self rises from death by faith" is not just analogous to Christ's

---

[7] This study will consider the paschal theme in Merton's writings thematically rather than chronologically. While the latter approach has the distinct advantage of tracing the development of Merton's thought in this area, it would be rather unwieldy and repetitious in its moving back and forth among topics. Thematic organization does reveal the pervasiveness of this paschal consciousness throughout Merton's life as it relates to many key aspects of his teaching, but the reader should be aware that Merton's approach to the paschal mystery does not remain static but broadens and deepens in conjunction with his own maturing spiritual vision.

passion but a participation in it, a "communing with God in the death and resurrection of Christ."[8] The full significance of the false self/true self polarity in Merton's thought can be understood only in this paschal context.

Spiritual transformation depends on identification with the crucified and risen Savior, which is possible only because the Savior first identified completely with the rest of humanity. In what might be called the mystery of mutual compassion, God shared fully, in the person of Jesus, in the human condition, endured even the suffering and pain of human death, so that human persons might share fully in the life of God. Merton writes, "the sufferings of all men became His own sufferings; their weakness and defenselessness became His weakness and defenselessness; their insignificance became His. But at the same time His own power, immortality, glory and happiness were given to them and could become theirs" (*NSC* 294).[9] But this new life is available only by passing through death with Christ. Christ's compassion, his "suffering with" humanity, must be reciprocated by humanity's compassion, their "suffering with" Christ. Only in this way will the false self, the self captivated by the illusion of its own autonomy, the self alienated from its divine ground and its own authentic identity and its kinship with the rest of creation, disappear like the insubstantial "smoke self" (*NSC* 38) it is, in order that the true self, created in the divine image, might live. This paschal journey "is the passage through non-being into being, the recovery of existence from non-existence, the resurrection of life out of death" (*NM* 247).[10]

It is the false self that dies with Christ in order that the true self might rise with Christ, a pattern which Merton repeatedly describes throughout the corpus of his writings. In *Life and Holiness*, he writes, "true sanctity means the full expression of the cross in our lives, and this cross means the death of what is familiar and normal to us, the

---

[8] Thomas Merton, *The Inner Experience: Notes on Contemplation*, ed. William H. Shannon (San Francisco: HarperCollins, 2003) 36 (subsequent references will be cited as "*IE*" parenthetically in the text).

[9] See also Thomas Merton, *Seasons of Celebration* (New York: Farrar, Straus and Giroux, 1965) 178 (subsequent references will be cited as "*SCel*" parenthetically in the text).

[10] See also *NM* 16, 154, 191; *NMI* 85–86.

death of our everyday selves, in order that we may live on a new level."[11] A similar passage in *New Seeds of Contemplation* describes the self-surrender in terms of the *kenosis*, the self-emptying of Christ (cf. Phil 2:7), and specifies that the new level of existence is life in union with Christ: "to seek some way of being holy, we must first of all renounce our own way and our own wisdom. We must 'empty ourselves' as He did. We must 'deny ourselves' and in some sense make ourselves 'nothing' in order that we may live not so much in ourselves as in him" (*NSC* 62).[12] *Thoughts in Solitude* emphasizes that the passage from death to life involves a transformed awareness of God's world as it actually is: "The death by which we enter into life is not an escape from reality but a complete gift of ourselves which involves a total commitment to reality. It begins by renouncing the illusory reality which created things acquire when they are seen only in their relation to our own selfish interests."[13] *Contemplative Prayer* points out that this paschal focus is central to the Christian spiritual tradition: commenting on the living flame of love of which John of the Cross speaks, Merton identifies it as "a true awareness that one has died and risen with Christ. It is an experience of mystical renewal, an inner transformation brought about entirely by the power of God's merciful love, implying the 'death' of the self-centered and self-sufficient ego and the appearance of a new and liberated self who lives and acts 'in the Spirit.'"[14]

This "new and liberated self" is actually, of course, the original self, the person God created, rather than the distorted and disguised

---

[11] Thomas Merton, *Life and Holiness* (New York: Herder and Herder, 1963) 60 (subsequent references will be cited as "*LH*" parenthetically in the text); see also Thomas Merton, *Love and Living*, ed. Naomi Burton Stone and Brother Patrick Hart (New York: Farrar, Straus, Giroux, 1979) 231 (subsequent references will be cited as "*L&L*" parenthetically in the text); *NSC* 209–10.

[12] See also *LH* 162.

[13] Thomas Merton, *Thoughts in Solitude* (New York: Farrar, Straus & Cudahy, 1958) 17 (subsequent references will be cited as "*TS*" parenthetically in the text).

[14] Thomas Merton, *Contemplative Prayer* (New York: Herder and Herder, 1969) 110 (subsequent references will be cited as "*CPr*" parenthetically in the text); see also *IE* 33–34; Thomas Merton, *Contemplation in a World of Action* (Garden City, NY: Doubleday, 1972) 99, 384 (subsequent references will be cited as "*CWA*" parenthetically in the text); *L&L* 211; Thomas Merton, *The Monastic Journey*, ed. Brother Patrick Hart (Kansas City: Sheed, Andrews and McMeel, 1977) 22 (subsequent references will be cited as "*MJ*" parenthetically in the text); *SCel* 142.

persona formed by human illusions and compulsions. It is "the uncreated Image, buried and concealed by sin in the depths of our souls" that "rises from death" through the power of the risen Jesus and the gift of the Spirit, which "becomes for us the source of a new life, a new identity and a new mode of action" (*NM* 167).[15] What is new about the new self is not some sort of different personality, or novel character traits, but a new insight into one's genuine identity and a new empowerment to be the person one really is. "It is the familiar self who dies and rises in Christ. The 'new man' is totally transformed, and yet he remains the *same person*. He is spiritualized, indeed the Fathers would say he is 'divinized' in Christ" (*LH* 60).

As the false self that must die is grounded in the illusion of a separate, self-sufficient existence, so the true self that rises from the dead knows itself "in Christ." Its identity is inseparable from the Christ who brought it to life; in a real sense, this true self *is* Christ. In the "Life in Christ" chapter of *New Seeds of Contemplation*, Merton writes, "I become a 'new man' and this new man, spiritually and mystically one identity, is at once Christ and myself. . . . Christ Himself becomes the source and principle of divine life in me. Christ himself, to use a metaphor based on Scripture, 'breathes' in me divinely by giving me His Spirit" (*NSC* 158–59).[16] A similar passage in *The New Man* makes the paschal context of this identification explicit: "Christ living in me is at the same time Himself and myself. . . . I remain the singular person that I am. But mystically and spiritually Christ lives in me from the moment that I am united to Him in His death and resurrection, by the sacrament of Baptism and by all the moments and incidents of a Christian life" (*NM* 168–69).[17]

The final sentence of this passage is perhaps not completely coherent ("from the moment that I am united . . . by all the *moments* . . ."), but it reflects a significant ambiguity concerning the realization of Christ's death and resurrection in one's own life. If on one level the Christian has already died and risen with Christ in baptism, on another level this identification with Christ is an ongoing process which develops through "all the moments and incidents of a Christian life,"

---

[15] See also *NMI* xv, 258–59.
[16] See also *L&L* 232.
[17] See also *MJ* 23; *NM* 169–70, 232.

by a series of deaths and resurrections in which the presence and effects of sin are rooted out in an ever more profound experience of dying to self and living "in Christ."[18] This is of course the fundamental pattern of the spiritual life, of becoming what one already is, of appropriating the paschal mystery, making it one's own, in a progressively more mature and complete conformation to the Lord. Thus Merton can speak of the two traditional "dark nights" of the mystical path, the night of sense and the night of spirit, as "two spiritual deaths. In the first the exterior man 'dies' to rise and become the inner man. In the second the interior man dies and rises so completely united to God that the two are one and there remains no division between them except the metaphysical distinction of natures" (*IE* 93). The entire spiritual journey, from initial awakening to the heights of contemplative union, is a passage through the cross to the fullness of divine life, through, with, and in Christ. Thus Merton can simply describe "contemplation as a sharing in the death and resurrection of Christ" (*NM* 16).[19]

The Paschal Mystery and Authentic Community

Two supremely important consequences for the spiritual life follow from an identification of the true self with the risen Christ. First of all, this identification is the basis for genuine community. The resurrection of Jesus means precisely that his presence is no longer restricted to the confines of one time or place. The life of the risen Lord is cosmic in its scope. "Rising from the dead, Jesus lived no longer merely in Himself. . . . He extends his personality to include each one of us who are united to Him by faith. . . . The primary aspect of His risen life is His life in the souls of His elect. He is now not only the natural Christ, but the mystical Christ, and as such He includes all of us who believe in Him" (*NM* 168).[20] Therefore union with Christ is at the same time communion with everyone else who is united with Christ: "our Christian life is in fact the life of the risen Christ active and fruitful within all of us" (*LH* 81). The true self has passed,

---

[18] See also *NM* 157–58.
[19] See also Thomas Merton, *The Ascent to Truth* (New York: Harcourt, Brace, 1951) 17; *NMI* 188–89.
[20] See also *IE* 38; *MJ* 22–23; *NM* 16–17; *NMI* 211.

through the cross, from isolation to communion, from alienated individualism to loving solidarity with all who share the new life of faith in the risen Lord. "After all," Merton writes, "transformation into Christ is not just an individual affair: there is only one Christ, not many. He is not divided. And for me to become Christ is to enter into the Life of the Whole Christ, the Mystical Body made up of the Head and the members, Christ and all who are incorporated in Him by His Spirit . . . so that the whole Christ is Christ and each individual is Christ" (*NSC* 156–57).[21]

Thus the identity of the true self is intrinsically social. Even in solitude there is no separation from the community of the redeemed: "Christ . . . has united us to one another in Himself. We all live together in the power of His death which overcame death. We neither suffer alone nor conquer alone nor go off to eternity alone. In Him we are inseparable: therefore, we are free to be fruitfully alone whenever we please, because wherever we go, whatever we suffer, whatever happens to us, we are united with those we love in Him because we are united with Him" (*NMI* 87).

This unity in the risen Lord is not only an identity but a vocation. Every human being is implicitly united to Christ because all share with Christ the same human nature: "we are all one with Christ, we are all in Christ by virtue of our humanity, just as we are in Adam by virtue of our humanity" (*NM* 136). Therefore the vocation of the Church as the Body of Christ is to witness to this unity of humanity in Christ, and the work of evangelization is the process of awakening others to a realization of their own share in the paschal mystery: "The whole life of the kingdom of God consists then in the gradual extension of the spiritual effects of the death and resurrection of Jesus to one soul after another until Christ lives perfectly in all whom He has called to Himself" (*NM* 154).

Paradoxically, the church and its members are called to proclaim the power of the resurrection by making visible the suffering love of the cross. Because in society, as in individual persons, the effects of the redemption are not yet fully realized, because Christ's victory

---

[21] For an earlier version of this passage, see Thomas Merton, *Seeds of Contemplation* (New York: New Directions, 1949) 95–96 (subsequent references will be cited as *SC* parenthetically in the text); see also *L&L* 192, 206; *NMI* 186–87; *NSC* 65, 70.

over sin and death will reach its fulfillment only with the final revelation of God's reign, in a certain sense Christ continues to suffer throughout the course of history: "according to Pascal," Merton writes, "Christ 'is in agony until the end of the world'" (though he immediately adds, "although he is also triumphant and in glory") (*NM* 155). Therefore, to be one with Christ is to continue to share in the cross, though always in the context of that hope grounded in experience of the risen Lord.[22] The mission of the church to make the saving power of Christ available to the world depends upon the willingness of Christians to be signs and instruments of the divine compassion: "Life in Christ is life in the mystery of the cross. It is . . . a participation in a divine mystery, a *sacred action* in which God Himself enters into time and, with the co-operation of men who have answered His call and have been united in a holy assembly, the Church, carries out the work of man's redemption" (*NSC* 163).

This cooperation in the work of redemption is simply fidelity to the divine plan and the divine will, even when they conflict with one's own plans and desires and dreams. To choose God's way rather than one's own is to deny oneself and to follow Jesus as a true disciple: "Our response to Christ means taking up our cross, and this in turn means shouldering our responsibility to seek and to do, in all things, the will of the Father. This was in fact the whole essence of Christ's earthly life, and of his death and resurrection" (*LH* 36).[23] The salvific will of God is most succinctly expressed by Jesus himself in the new commandment he gives to his disciples: "Love one another as I have loved you" (John 15:12). Every act of authentic love entails a willing self-sacrifice which manifests the presence and power of the cross. "All true love is a death and a resurrection in Christ. It has one imperious demand: that all individual members of Christ give themselves completely to one another and to the Church, lose themselves in the will of Christ and in the good of other men, in order to die to their own will and their own interests and 'rise again' as other Christs."[24] Even more challenging than the love that leads one to lay

---

[22] See Thomas Merton, *He Is Risen* (Niles, IL: Argus, 1975) 18.

[23] See also *NMI* 135; *SCel* 219.

[24] Thomas Merton, *Disputed Questions* (New York: Farrar, Straus & Cudahy, 1960) 100 (subsequent references will be cited as "*DQ*" parenthetically in the text); see also Thomas Merton, *The Living Bread* (New York: Farrar, Straus &

down one's life for one's friends is the willingness to love one's enemies even to the point of dying for them, but this too is the meaning and the mandate of Christ's cross: "We can only get to Heaven by dying for other people on the cross. And one does not die on a cross by his own unaided efforts. He needs the help of an executioner. We have to die, as Christ died, for those whose sins are to us more bitter than death—most bitter because they are just like our own" (*NMI* 212).[25] To love one's enemy in the face of such a death, whether literal or figurative, is of course possible only because the love is first Christ's own love, and the death is first Christ's own death. Their value and their meaning and their power are his first, but ours also because and insofar as we are his. This is what it means "to bear witness to the truth of Christ by laying down our lives at His bidding" (*NMI* 135).

But there is another dimension to the ongoing passion of Christ throughout history. The crucified Jesus is also to be encountered in all those who suffer, as he did, from the sins of others. "Murder, massacres, revolution, hatred, the slaughter and torture of the bodies and souls of men, the destruction of cities by fire, the starvation of millions, the annihilation of populations and finally the cosmic inhumanity of atomic war: Christ is massacred in His members, torn limb from limb; God is murdered in men" (*NSC* 71).[26] It is these least ones, the victims of injustice, the persecuted and afflicted, "with whom He has particularly identified Himself: and in whom He Himself suffers His passion until the end of time. In them He wins eternal victory over untruth, injustice, hatred and oppression."[27] Therefore to be united

---

Cudahy, 1956) xii, xvi (subsequent references will be cited as "*LB*" parenthetically in the text).

[25] See also *LB* 150.

[26] Though this focus is rightly associated particularly with the later Merton, it is already present in the original version of this passage (*SC* 54) and is actually evident even before he entered the monastery: see the journal passage for May 26, 1940, in Thomas Merton, *Run to the Mountain: The Story of a Vocation. Journals, vol. 1: 1939–1941*, ed. Patrick Hart, OCSO (San Francisco: HarperCollins, 1995) 223: "For Christ suffers in the Church; and there is nothing suffered on earth that Christ Himself does not suffer. Everything that happens to the poor, the meek, the desolate, the mourners, the despised, happens to Christ" (subsequent references will be cited as "*RM*" parenthetically in the text).

[27] Thomas Merton, Foreword to "Reflections on Love: Eight Sacred Poems" (n.p., 1966) unpaged; for the background of these poems, see William H. Shannon,

to him is to be united with them in a special way: Christian action on behalf of the poor and oppressed, in pursuit of justice and peace, has an essentially paschal character. It is rooted in the compassion of Christ which must be incarnated in the compassion of Christians.

Such action is itself a participation in the redemptive work of Christ, and as such it is governed by the norms of that work. As Christ triumphed over sin and death through the unarmed power of suffering love, so those who are "in Christ" testify to that victory by confronting evil equipped only with the gifts of the Spirit. "If the Cross is God's 'No' to worldly arrogance, then our decision for Christ must be a renunciation of all reliance on worldly power" (L&L 231). To believe in the nonviolent power of the cross is to believe that the kingdom of God, the reign of truth and justice and love, has been definitively established, and that "the Lord of truth is indeed risen and reigning over his Kingdom."[28] It is to believe that the vocation of the Christian community is to make that reign visible and tangible here and now: "The great historical event, the coming of the Kingdom, is made clear and is 'realized' in proportion as Christians themselves live the life of the Kingdom in their own space and time" (FV 16). One lives the life of the kingdom not by avoiding or evading darkness and death, but by holding fast to the hope at the center of the paschal mystery: "From the darkness comes light. From death, life. From the abyss there comes, unaccountably, the mysterious gift of the Spirit sent by God to make all things new, to transform the created and redeemed world, and to re-establish all things in Christ" (CPr 28).

The Paschal Mystery and Contemplative Union

If identification with Christ crucified and resurrected is the basis for human community, it is also the basis for union with God. This is the second important consequence of discovering the true self in

---

Silent Lamp: The Thomas Merton Story (New York: Crossroad, 1992) 234–38; for an analysis, see Patrick F. O'Connell, "Eight Freedom Songs: Thomas Merton's Cycle of Liberation," *The Merton Annual* 4 (1994) 87–128.

[28] Thomas Merton, *Faith and Violence: Christian Teaching and Christian Practice* (Notre Dame, IN: University of Notre Dame Press, 1968) 18 (subsequent references will be cited as "*FV*" parenthetically in the text).

Christ. Merton writes, "But if my true spiritual identity is found in my identification with Christ, then to know myself fully, I must know Christ. . . . The beginning of self-realization in the fullest Christian sense is therefore a sharing in the orientation which directs Christ, as Word, entirely to his Father" (*NM* 170). To know God, in other words, is to enter into the mystery of trinitarian love, to be one with the Father through grace as the Son is one with the Father by nature, in the Holy Spirit who is the mutual love of Father and Son. Such knowledge is a direct result of participation in the paschal mystery. One enters into God with and in the risen Jesus because one has left behind the self that cannot know God, the sinful self which has been put to death with Christ.

This passing over into God is experienced in two forms, eternal salvation and personal transformation—the ultimate act of self-surrender and self-transcendence in physical, temporal death; and the foretaste of eternal life in the mystical death of contemplative union with God. For the true self, death is simply the ultimate ratification of the choice to die and live with Christ, the last in the series of paschal surrenders: "When the sinful *Dasein* is aware of itself as understood mercifully and as 'seen' full of mercy by the Creator and Redeemer, then the evil of sin, the curse of death, are 'forgotten utterly.' . . . Not that we do not die: but death itself becomes the crowning event of a saved life and the door to spirit, being, and truth in the Cross of Christ" (*L&L* 206).[29] Only in union with the death of Christ does death become the doorway to life. "The Christian hope that is 'not seen' is a communion in the agony of Christ. It is the identification of our own *agonia* with the *agonia* of the God who has emptied Himself and become obedient unto death. It is the acceptance of life in the midst of death, not because we have courage, or light, or wisdom to accept, but because by some miracle the God of Life Himself accepts to live, in us, at the very moment when we descend into death" (*NM* 5). The death of Christ transforms the meaning of death or, rather, gives meaning to what is otherwise meaningless and absurd. The linkage between sin and death is broken; the cross makes death a liberation from sin, that is, from the self-absorbed isolation and self-divided alienation which is, quite literally, a hell.

---

[29] See also *NMI* 79, 234, 262–63.

> For a Christian, this sublimation of death by freedom and love can only be the result of a free gift of God in which our personal death is united with the mystery of Christ's death on the cross. The death of Christ is not simply the juridical payment of an incomprehensible ransom which somehow makes us acceptable at the gate of heaven. It has radically transformed the sinful death of man into a liberating and victorious death, a supreme act of faith and love, because it also transforms man's life by faith and love. The obedience of Christ transforms the death of man into an act of glad acceptance and of love which transcends death and carries him over into eternal life with the Risen Christ. (*L&L* 103)[30]

This eternal life is not merely immortality but God's own life, the fullness of life that had no beginning and will have no end, the life that the Son shares with the Father, and that all the redeemed experience because they are identified with the Son.

But this eternal life, "to know you the only true God, and Jesus Christ whom you have sent" (John 17:3), does not begin with physical death but with "the Christian's *metanoia*, his participation in the death and resurrection of Christ. . . . This death to the 'old self' and new life in the spirit sent by Christ 'from the Father' means not only a juridical salvation 'in heaven' and 'in the hereafter' but much more a new dimension of one's present life" (*L&L* 192). Contemplation is the full experiential awareness of this new dimension, of God's own life. "Christian contemplation gives a certain intuitive appreciation or savor of the divine inner life in so far as it is a personal participation, by grace, in that life itself" (*CWA* 179). That is, in the traditional phrase, we become by grace what Christ is by nature, a transformation that is brought about by the redemptive power of the cross. "We recognize the unseen Father in so far as we are sons, in and with Christ. The Spirit utters in us the cry of recognition that we are sons in the Son (Romans 8:15). This cry of admiration, of love, of praise, of everlasting joy is at once a cry of glad self-annihilation on the part of our transient ego, and an exalted shout of victory of the New Man raised from the dead in Christ by the Spirit who raised Christ himself from the dead" (*CWA* 179). It is this new person, the true self, who is able to pray,

---

[30] See also *NM* 5, 191.

> Father, I love You Whom I do not know, and I embrace you Whom I do not see, and I abandon myself to You Whom I have offended, because You love in me Your only begotten Son. You see Him in me, You embrace Him in me, because He has willed to identify Himself completely with me by that love which brought Him to death, for me, on the Cross. . . . You have willed to see me only in Him, but in willing this You have willed to see me more really as I am. (*TS* 71–72)

In the fullness of divine union, the true self in Christ is drawn into an experience of the life of God that transcends language and thought. Wordless, imageless contemplation, which does not concentrate on the figure of Christ, is not for that reason less but more Christ-centered, as one puts on the mind of Christ and with Christ loves and lives in the Father.[31] This culminating experience of reality, of authentic selfhood grounded in God, is both theocentric and Christocentric because it is deeply trinitarian: "The Father, dwelling in the depths of all things and in my own depths, communicates to me His Word and His Spirit. Receiving them I am drawn into His own life and know God in His own Love, being one with Him in His own Son" (*NSC* 40–41).[32] It is both theocentric and Christocentric because it is at root paschal: "Christian contemplation, in one vivid blaze of love and illumination, apprehends at once the reality of God as the totally other and the unknown, as a dynamism of reality, realization and ecstasy, as incarnate in Jesus Christ, as given to us entirely in the Spirit, as taking us entirely to Himself in the death and resurrection of Christ" (*CWA* 179). The entire creation is encountered in its divine ground; unity with other persons is caught up into union with God in Christ. The true self that experiences contemplative union, the "inner 'I' who is always alone, is always universal: for in this inmost 'I' my own solitude meets the solitude of every other man and the solitude of God. Hence it is beyond division, beyond limitation, beyond selfish affirmation. It is only this inmost and solitary 'I' that truly loves with the love and the spirit of Christ. This 'I' is Christ Himself, living in us; and we, in Him living in the Father" (*DQ* 207).

---

[31] See also *NSC* 157 (*SC* 96–97).
[32] Compare the earlier version of this passage (*SC* 23), which lacks the final clarifying phrase.

The Paschal Mystery as Integrating Factor

Just as Merton presents the paschal mystery as the indispensable event that unites the true self in Christ with the human community and with the triune God, so he finds it as well to be the common factor that integrates different dimensions of the Christian life. First of all, it allows for a synthesis of doctrine and experience. It is clear from what has already been said that the framework of Merton's spiritual teaching is constituted by the central Christian dogmas of the Trinity, the incarnation, and the redemption. It is equally clear that these traditional doctrines are not simply to be accepted as truths to be believed. For their full significance to be appreciated, they must be appropriated, made one's own, experienced in a deeply personal way. The goal of contemplation, the goal of the Christian life itself, is not merely to know about God but to know God, to enter into a relationship of mutual love and personal commitment. Contemplation for Merton is "Not something general and abstract, but something on the contrary as concrete, particular and 'existential' as it can possibly be" (*IE* 34). It calls, in Cardinal Newman's terms, not just for notional assent but for real assent, a "yes" to God that involves not only the mind but the heart, the whole person. Merton is heir to the tradition of monastic theology which his friend Jean Leclercq described as being based not on the familiar phrase *"Credo ut intelligam"* ("I believe, that I might understand") but *"Credo ut experiar"* ("I believe, that I might experience").[33] "Christian faith," according to Merton, "is not just a habit by which we are inclined to give assent to certain dogmatic information; it is a conversion of our whole being, a surrender of the entire person to Christ in His Church" (*L&L* 230). It requires not just a change of beliefs but a change of identity, which is effected by the cross: "our knowledge of God through Christ depends on our spiritual union with Christ in the central mystery of our Redemption—His death and resurrection. This is not only a truth which we accept as historical, not only a dogma which we believe: it is a redemptive fact which we must make the center of our own

---

[33] See the distinction between scholastic and monastic theology in Jean Leclercq, OSB, "Saint Bernard and the Monastic Theology of the Twelfth Century" in *Saint Bernard, Theologian*, 2 vols. (Berryville, VA: Our Lady of the Holy Cross Abbey, 1961) 1.6–7.

spiritual life" (*NM* 232). This is in no way a devaluation of the dogmatic dimension of Christianity; it is rather a proper valuing of doctrine not as dead letter but as life-giving spirit: dogmatic formulations are not substitutes for an experience of God, but ways of articulating that experience so that others may also participate in it.

In a similar way, the liturgical and sacramental life and the contemplative life are for Merton not alternative but complementary ways to God, because both are part of the same process of drawing the Christian into the paschal mystery: "in order to enter fully into the communion with the life brought to us by Christ we must in some sense—sacramentally, ascetically, mystically—die with Christ and rise with Him from the dead" (*NM* 154). Thus the eucharistic liturgy is to be understood not merely as a formal act of worship, not as a ritual commemoration of a past event, but as a privileged locus of encounter with the events of the redemption: "our life in Christ comes from our participation in His death and resurrection. But the Cross and Resurrection of Christ are something more than a historical memory. They are a present fact, mystically actualized by the Liturgy, or the 'sacred action' which we call the mass" (*MJ* 8–9).[34] The fundamentally paschal character of the liturgy extends to all the sacraments. "The faithful die and rise with Christ in all their sacramental contacts with the risen Savior" (*NM* 233),[35] especially in baptism and the Eucharist. According to Merton, "Our life of grace is the life of the Risen Christ in us. We are buried together with Him by baptism in death that as Christ is risen from the dead so also we may walk in newness of life" (*SCel* 66).[36] Likewise, the "most sanctifying action a Christian can perform is to receive Christ in the Eucharistic mystery, thus mystically participating in His death and resurrection, and becoming one with him in spirit and in truth" (*LH* 78).[37] Liturgy and sacraments, then, are the normal way in which Christians are brought into contact with the crucified and risen Lord.[38]

---

[34] See also *LB* 14, 138; *MJ* 58; *NM* 233; *NSC* 164, 165; *RM* 342; *SCel* 133; Merton develops the paschal implications of Lent in *SCel* 113–16, 122; of the Easter Vigil in *NM* 238; of Easter in *SCel* 144–46.

[35] See also *NM* 202.

[36] See also *NM* 157, 200, 203; *NMI* 81–82, 90–91, 178.

[37] See also *IE* 62.

[38] For the paschal dimension of the priesthood, see *NMI* 142–43.

But they do not operate in isolation from the rest of the Christian life. The effects of the Mass and the sacraments on the lives of Christians "will never be complete unless they prolong these liturgical contacts by private prayer, meditation, asceticism and works of charity. The grace of the sacraments is given not merely to be enjoyed but used" (*NM* 233). The "*Pascha Christi* (the death and resurrection of Christ)," which "takes place beyond experience and beyond psychology in the work of the Sacraments and in our objective sharing of the Church's life," must be internalized and actualized by a "contemplative and meditative discipline . . . of struggle, of self-emptying, 'self-naughting,' of letting go and of subsequent recovery in peace and grace on a new level" (*CWA* 163). Responding to "our vocation to die with Christ in order to rise with him" is a lifelong process: "It is perfectly true that we die with him in Baptism and rise from the dead: but this in only the beginning of a series of deaths and resurrections. We are not 'converted' only once in our life but many times, and this endless series of large and small 'conversions,' inner revolutions, leads finally to our transformation in Christ" (*LH* 158–59). Conversely, liturgy and sacraments are in danger of degenerating into sterile routine unless the worshiper brings to the celebration a lived experience of the meaning of the cross.

> The whole liturgy is animated by the movement of descent and ascent which is that of the Christian Pasch, the Easter Mystery of our death and resurrection with Christ. Unless the Christian participates to some degree in the dread, the sense of loss, the anguish, the dereliction and the destitution of the Crucified, he cannot really enter into the mystery of the liturgy. He can neither understand the rites and prayers, nor appreciate the sacramental signs and enter deeply into the grace they mediate. (*CPr* 133)[39]

Thus liturgy and sacraments must have a contemplative dimension to be meaningful, while contemplative union with God in Christ is the completion, the full personal actualization, of the paschal mystery encountered liturgically and sacramentally.

The paschal focus of Merton's thought can plausibly be considered as one of the principal reasons why his writings on the monastic life

---

[39] See also *L&L* 159.

have been found relevant by readers who are not monks. By considering monasticism as one way in which the cross and resurrection of Christ are appropriated, Merton situates the monastic life in the context of the Christian spiritual life as a whole, and thus implicitly, and at times even explicitly, presents the monk as exemplary for all Christians, a paradigm of the quest for the true self in Christ. In his "Notes on the Future of Monasticism," Merton defines the monk not by what differentiates him from other Christians, but as one who commits himself to the Christian project with single-minded intensity:

> the monk is a person who in traditional language "seeks God" or seeks by *metanoia* and inner revolution to deepen his consciousness and awareness in such a way that he "experiences" something of the ultimate ground of being and to [sic] the saving power of the Spirit, and witnesses to this in some way. In Christian terms this means of course a life of "death and resurrection in Christ," in the fullest sense a life "in the Spirit," a life of charismatic freedom, humility, peace, surrender, transformation and joy—a life of Love in terms of the Gospel and the Kingdom of God. (*CWA* 218–19)

He goes on to point out that monasticism is not "the *only* Christian vocation or even necessarily the *best* way to be a Christian," and interestingly—in view of his distinct lack of enthusiasm for the U.S. space program[40]—compares the monk to "a spaceman [who] undergoes certain experimental tests and develops certain skills" (*CWA* 219); that is, like the astronaut, the monk is a kind of explorer[41] whose work will have an impact even on those who are no more likely to enter a monastery than to walk in space.

---

[40] See Merton's poem "Why Some Look Up to Planets and Heroes" (Thomas Merton, *Emblems of a Season of Fury* [New York: New Directions, 1963] 3–5; Thomas Merton, *The Collected Poems of Thomas Merton* [New York: New Directions, 1977] 305–7); see also *CGB* 48–49, an expansion of the original journal entry of February 3, 1961 (Thomas Merton, *Turning Toward the World: The Pivotal Years. Journals, vol. 4: 1960–1963*, ed. Victor A. Kramer [San Francisco: HarperCollins, 1996] 92); but see also Merton's later reflections from mid- to late 1965 (Thomas Merton, *Dancing in the Water of Life: Seeking Peace in the Hermitage. Journals, vol. 5: 1963–1965*, ed. Robert E. Daggy [San Francisco: HarperCollins, 1997] 258, 260, 321, 324–25).

[41] See Merton's famous image of the solitary explorer in "A Letter on the Contemplative Life" (*MJ* 171–72).

The specific regimen of a monk's life is simply a particular way of entering into the mystery of Christ. Merton tells his brother monks, "We have to reproduce in our life the cross of Christ so that having died sacramentally to sin in baptism and penance, we may also put to death sin in our flesh by restraining our evil desires and bad tendencies. This is the basis for our life of monastic asceticism" (*MJ* 24).[42] Thus monastic obedience, for example, is properly understood as a means of deepening the realization of the true self in Christ: "the discipline involved here is that of a crucifixion which eliminates a superficial and selfish kind of experience and opens to us the freedom of a life that is not dominated by egoism, vanity, wilfullness, passion, aggressiveness, jealousy, greed" (*CWA* 114).[43] Monastic prayer, "accomplished in silence, in nakedness of spirit, in emptiness, in humility . . . is a participation in the saving death and resurrection of Christ" (*CPr* 28).[44] The monk, like all Christians, is called "to die completely to our old life and to our old self, and become new men in Christ . . . in a word to 'become Christ' (quoting Gal 2:19–21)" (*LV* 306–7) in order "to enter into the infinite and unending circuit of love that is the very life of the Three Divine Persons, in which each gives all to the other and receives all again in His gift" (*LV* 69).

What is unique about monasticism is its visible and public detachment from the routines of secular existence, a death to the expectations and compulsions of society: "The pattern of the monastic life is a real death and resurrection, and for us especially there is this element of a real death to the world, to the ordinary life that we would otherwise be living as Christians or as active apostles. Whatever we call our life, cloistered or contemplative or monastic, it does imply a real break and therefore a real liberation, by a kind of death, from the claims and demands of a highly distracted and confused life in the

---

[42] See also *CPr* 25–26.

[43] In his conferences on the vow of obedience, Merton tells his novices: "*Our obedience is a union of our will with the will of Christ dying on the Cross for love.* By obeying we unite ourselves with the great act of freedom and truth, the supreme manifestation of love in the world" (Thomas Merton, *The Life of the Vows: Initiation into the Monastic Tradition* 6, ed. Patrick F. O'Connell, Monastic Wisdom [MW], vol. 30 [Collegeville, MN: Cistercian Publications, 2012] 249) (subsequent references will be cited as "*LV*" parenthetically in the text).

[44] See also *CPr* 40; *MJ* 95.

world" (*CWA* 381). But even here the monk stands as a salutary sign of contradiction, a warning to all Christians that they too must die to the world insofar as it makes absolute claims on their loyalty. Ultimately the life of the monk is not simply for his own salvation but serves as a witness to the entire church: "His loneliness had a prophetic and mysterious quality, something almost in the nature of a sacramental sign, because it was a particular charismatic way of participating in the death and resurrection of Christ. What is lonelier than death? To confront the emptiness, the void, the apparent hopelessness of this desert and to encounter there the miracle of new life in Christ, the joy of eschatological hope already fulfilled in mystery—this was the monastic vocation" (*CWA* 239).[45]

The paschal mystery even has a contribution to make to interreligious dialogue. Merton is clear, first of all, that there is a paschal dimension to every life of authentic self-realization, whether or not a person is aware of the person and presence of Christ: "for Christian theology, death 'in Christ' is not merely a matter of external forms but of interior grace, and this grace can be and is given to every man, Christian or not, whose death is, in fact, the last free culminating gift in a fruitful life oriented to ultimate truth in God (whether known or unknown, but at least implicitly loved and sought)" (*L&L* 103). On the level of dialogue, Merton finds significant analogies between the Christian paschal experience and, for example, certain central insights of Buddhism, so that the significance of another tradition is illuminated by comparison with one's own: "Just as the Buddha's 'Fire Sermon' radically transforms the Buddhist's awareness of all that is around him, so the 'word of the Cross' in very much the same way gives the Christian a radically new consciousness of the meaning of his life and of his relationship with other men and with the world around him" (*ZBA* 51). Paradoxically, the converse can also be true, as the Buddhist emphasis on immediate experience and existential liberation can actually sharpen an appreciation of the dynamism of Christian transformation: "Suffering, as both Christianity and Buddhism see, each in its own way, is part of our very ego-identity and empirical existence, and the only thing to do about it is to plunge right into the middle of contradiction and confusion in order to be

---

[45] See also *SCel* 207.

transformed by what Zen calls the 'Great Death' and Christianity calls 'dying and rising with Christ'" (*ZBA* 51). The emphasis in Zen on direct experience is a salutary reminder that what is of the utmost importance in Christianity as well is not objective knowledge but intuitive, immediate participation in the fullness of reality.

Merton believed strongly that interreligious dialogue at the present stage of development needed to operate not primarily on the level of concepts and doctrinal systems but on the level of spiritual experience. But for him this did not exclude the paschal mystery, but recognized its central importance. It is surely significant that one of the last and certainly one of the most fully developed statements Merton ever made concerning the paschal character of the Christian life came in the context of a discussion of Zen, where he emphasizes that "it is essential to remember that for a Christian 'the word of the Cross' is nothing theoretical, but a stark and existential experience of union with Christ in His death in order to share in His resurrection." It is not simply an "assent to the dogmatic proposition Christ died for our sins" but a relinquishing, a crucifixion, of the self-centered ego as "the principle of our deepest actions, which now proceed from Christ living in us." Here he quotes once again the key verse from Galatians 2, "I live, now not I, but Christ lives in me!" and joins to it the reference in Philippians 2 to *kenosis*, "a self-emptying . . . in union with the self-emptying of Christ 'obedient unto death!'" (Phil 2:5–11). He concludes: "It is essential to true Christianity that this experience of the Cross and of self-emptying be central in the life of the Christian so that he may fully receive the Holy Spirit and know (again by experience) all the riches of God in and through Christ" (an uncited allusion to Colossians 2:2) (*ZBA* 55–56).

For Thomas Merton, the paschal mystery of participation in the redemptive death and resurrection of Jesus is indeed "central in the life of the Christian" and central to his own holistic spiritual vision. It is the key to understanding and, more important, to experiencing the discovery of the true self, the reality of human spiritual communion, the fullness of union with God. It integrates doctrine with experience, liturgy and sacraments with contemplation, monasticism with other forms of Christian life, even to some degree, Christian with non-Christian religious experience. It synthesizes theocentric and Christocentric perspectives in a dynamism that is incarnational in its origin and trinitarian in its consummation. The paschal heart of Merton's spirituality is, finally, the paschal heart of Jesus himself, a heart filled with the love and compassion by which Jesus identified fully with broken, suffering, sinful humanity in order that, identified with him, all people might enter into the fullness of God's own life. It is the paschal heart of which Merton himself spoke in prayer: "Father, I come to You in your own Son's self, for it is His Sacred Heart that has taken possession of me and destroyed my sins and it is He Who presents me to You. And where? In the sanctuary of His own Heart which is your palace and the temple where the saints adore You in Heaven" (*TS* 72).

4

Wisdom and Prophecy:
The Two Poles of Merton's Spirituality

If we had to select a single quality that would explain Thomas Merton's undiminished influence and significance more than a half-century after his death, we would do well, as we have already seen, to recognize his catholicity as at least a leading candidate. By this I refer not to his confessional adherence to Roman Catholicism, as deep and strong as that was, but to the third of the four marks of the church, the universality, the breadth of vision, of which Merton writes in *Conjectures of a Guilty Bystander*:

> the more I am able to affirm others, to say "yes" to them in myself, by discovering them in myself and myself in them, the more real I am. I am fully real if my own heart says *yes* to *everyone*. I will be a better Catholic, not if I can *refute* every shade of Protestantism, but if I can affirm the truth in it and still go further. So, too, with the Muslims, the Hindus, the Buddhists, etc. . . . There is much that one cannot "affirm" and "accept," but first one must say "yes" where one really can. If I affirm myself as a Catholic merely by denying all that is Muslim, Jewish, Protestant, Hindu, Buddhist, etc., in the end I will find that there is not much left for me to affirm as a Catholic; and certainly no breath of the Spirit with which to affirm it.[1]

---

[1] Thomas Merton, *Conjectures of a Guilty Bystander* (Garden City, NY: Doubleday, 1966) 129 (subsequent references will be cited as *"CGB"* parenthetically in the text).

In a world where particularism, fragmentation, and a narrow, often exclusive, identification with one's own national, ethnic, racial, religious, or gender group all too often overcome an awareness and acceptance of our shared humanity, such a holistic perspective is more necessary than ever.

I believe Merton's gift and challenge to the church of the twenty-first century is the summons to become more catholic in this sense, which means precisely to become more ecumenical as well. He exemplifies what has been called the "both/and" approach that characterizes Catholicism at its best—an attitude that takes into account both matter and spirit, both faith and reason, both grace and nature, both church and world, both contemplation and action, both the uniqueness of Jesus and the ubiquity of divine revelation. It is a perspective that is comfortable with, though never complacent about, paradox, as befits a faith that believes in a savior who is both fully human and fully divine, that affirms, in Merton's words, "the Incarnation of the Logos and man's Redemption and Divinization as the supreme manifestation of wisdom and of the 'attunement of conflicting opposites.'"[2] It is an incarnational, sacramental vision, which seeks and finds the gracious presence of God within the world of space and time, which discovers in creation and in history signs of the Creator who nonetheless infinitely transcends them, which recognizes that the same mystery of being that has its definitive manifestation in the person and work of Christ is also disclosed in many different forms in the sacrament of the created world, the cosmic revelation available to all people.

This ability to perceive the sacredness of the ordinary, the unity of the disparate, is regularly associated by Merton, especially in the last decade of his life, with the gift of wisdom. In his essay "Gandhi and the One-Eyed Giant," he describes wisdom as a way of knowing "which transcends and unites . . . which dwells in body and soul together and which, more by means of myth, of rite, of contemplation, than by scientific experiment, opens the door to a life in which the individual is not lost in the cosmos and in society but found in

---

[2] Thomas Merton, *The Behavior of Titans* (New York: New Directions, 1961) 81–82.

them."³ This sapiential or sophianic consciousness responds to the world not as a detached, objective observer, but with an intuitive, participatory awareness of the "hidden wholeness"⁴ of all reality, and with a willingness to allow this "transfigured, spiritualized and divinized cosmos" to become aware of itself and to "[utter] its praise of the Creator"⁵ in and through oneself, a vocation shared particularly by the contemplative and the poet.

But wisdom itself can be seen as part of a "both/and" pairing: just as in the scriptures the wisdom books are complemented by the prophetic writings, so in Merton's mature spirituality the sapiential is balanced by the prophetic. If wisdom recognizes how creation already manifests the presence of God, prophecy calls attention to the gaps between divine design and human realization, the personal and social failures and consequent brokenness that obscure or interfere with the unfolding of God's will for the creation. Hence Merton's attentiveness to the ruptured bonds between creation and Creator, the alienation and isolation caused by the rejection of wisdom, the violation of the divine image through violence and war, racial and religious prejudice, and the exploitation of the poor. But for Merton, as for Jeremiah, the prophetic calling is not just to "root up and to tear down" but "to build and to plant" (cf. Jer 1:10), not just denunciation but annunciation, a bringing of the future into the present, a call to model God's covenantal love and justice here and now.

For Merton, the dimensions of wisdom and prophecy must complement and interpenetrate one another. Without the leaven of prophecy, wisdom might tend to overlook the problems and contradictions of the concrete human condition; receptivity could decay into inertia and quietism: "what we seek is really the truth that we

---

³ Thomas Merton, ed., *Gandhi on Non-Violence: Selected Texts from Non-Violence in Peace and War* (New York: New Directions, 1965) 1 (subsequent references will be cited as "*GNV*" parenthetically in the text).

⁴ "*Hagia Sophia*" in Thomas Merton, *Emblems of a Season of Fury* (New York: New Directions, 1963) 61 (subsequent references will be cited as "*ESF*" parenthetically in the text); *The Collected Poems of Thomas Merton* (New York: New Directions, 1977) 363 (subsequent references will be cited as "*CP*" parenthetically in the text).

⁵ Thomas Merton, *Disputed Questions* (New York: Farrar, Straus & Cudahy, 1960) 20–21 (subsequent references will be cited as "*DQ*" parenthetically in the text).

already possess," Merton writes, but adds, "yet to take life thoughtlessly, passively as it comes, is to renounce the struggle and purification which are necessary" (*CGB* 166). Conversely, without the grounding of wisdom, prophecy could become shrill, harsh, and self-righteous: it could degenerate into what Merton calls the "frenzy of the activist" which "destroys the fruitfulness of his own work, because it kills the root of inner wisdom which makes work fruitful" (*CGB* 73). But by articulating a dynamic balance between a sapiential perception of the fullness of the divine revelation and a prophetic awareness of the incompleteness of the human response, Merton recognizes and creatively engages the two dimensions of reality as sacrament, the "already" and the "not yet."

He is able to do justice simultaneously to an appreciation of the primordial unity of creation, to be accepted and cherished as a gift, and to the obligation to incarnate that unity, to make it visible and tangible, in a world rent by fragmentation and alienation. Such a dialectic is of course simply the application, on the social and even the cosmic level, of the basic call to realize, to actualize, one's true identity. The prophet calls the individual, the community, the entire creation to become what according to the sage they already are on the deepest level of their being: epiphanies of the divine, signs and instruments—sacraments—of God's creative and redemptive love. A reflective consideration of some of Merton's central ideas about wisdom and prophecy brings us close to the heart of this holistic, catholic vision, and suggests some of the reasons why his writings continue to energize and to challenge people at the dawn of a new millennium.

Wisdom becomes an increasingly important category for Merton's thought in the last decade of his life for at least four reasons: it firmly roots him in his own Christian contemplative tradition; it serves as a point of contact and dialogue with the great traditions of the East; it provides a theological grounding for a sacramental view of creation; and it provides an alternative perspective to the analytical, quantitative, exploitative approach characteristic of scientific rationalism. Each of these themes contributes an essential element to Merton's spiritual teaching.

At its highest level, wisdom is synonymous with contemplative realization, as Merton indicates, for example, when he distinguishes the approach of the medieval university to truth through "*scientia*, intellectual knowledge" from that of the monastery through "*sapientia*, or mystical contemplation."[6] While he never stops using the term "contemplation," of course, often in his later writings he seems to find the word "wisdom" more evocative, and perhaps less misleading. He is aware of the somewhat problematic connotations which "contemplation" sometimes carries, what he calls the "unfortunate resonances" of "the philosophic elitism of Plato and Plotinus."[7] In classical Greek thought, "contemplation was definitely aristocratic and intellectual . . . the privilege of a philosophical minority, for whom it was a matter of study and reflection rather than of prayer."[8] While Merton emphasizes that such "intellectual hedonism" certainly does not characterize authentic Christian contemplation, which is rooted in the paschal mystery of dying and rising with Christ, the word can retain certain equivocal suggestions of a life of "ease, aestheticism, and speculation" (*IE* 33).

An entirely different set of connotations attaches to the scriptural term wisdom (*sophia*, *sapientia*). While Merton is certainly familiar with the association of wisdom with maxims of practical behavior such as those found in the Book of Proverbs, his customary use of the term is based on other biblical texts and contexts: wisdom as the first and, particularly in the Cistercian tradition, the most exalted of the seven gifts of the Holy Spirit listed in Isaiah 11, the Pauline contrast between human and divine wisdom in 1 Corinthians, and especially the personified figure of Wisdom as the creative agent of God in Proverbs 8 and the Wisdom of Solomon, a figure that is identified implicitly in the New Testament and explicitly by the church fathers with the Logos of John's gospel, the preexistent Word of God through whom all things were made and who takes on human nature in the person of Jesus.

---

[6] Thomas Merton, *Love and Living*, ed. Naomi Burton Stone and Brother Patrick Hart (New York: Farrar, Straus, Giroux, 1979) 7.

[7] Thomas Merton, *Contemplation in a World of Action* (Garden City, NY: Doubleday, 1971) 158.

[8] Thomas Merton, *The Inner Experience: Notes on Contemplation*, ed. William H. Shannon (San Francisco: HarperCollins, 2003) 32 (subsequent references will be cited as "*IE*" parenthetically in the text).

From this standpoint, growth in wisdom is a process of more and more complete conformation to Christ, divine wisdom incarnate, through sharing in the paschal mystery, "the wisdom given by His Spirit to those who have left all things to follow Him—the wisdom of the Cross";[9] it culminates in "an experience of God, an existential communion in His own intimate life which is Love Itself."[10] It is also the consummate attainment of personal identity, the human capacity to image the divine: "It is the ultimate in man's self-realization, for when it is perfected, man not only discovers his true self, but finds himself to be mystically one with the God by Whom he has been elevated and transformed" (*NM* 48).

This "essentially theological, Christological, and mystical"[11] conception of Christian wisdom persists throughout Merton's monastic life. It can be found as early as *The Spirit of Simplicity* of 1948, in which Merton draws on the Cistercian tradition, which relates *sapientia* to *sapere*, to know by tasting, and defines wisdom as "the knowledge of God by the experience of (tasting) His infinite goodness."[12] It continues through *Faith and Violence*, published in the final year of his life, in which he describes "Contemplative wisdom" as "a living contact with the Infinite Source of all being, a contact not only of minds and hearts, not only of 'I and thou,' but a transcendent union of consciousness in which man and God become, according to the expression of St. Paul, 'one spirit.'"[13]

A further advantage of the term "wisdom" as found in the tradition is its flexibility—it can be used to refer to the whole process of development of the receptive, contemplative dimension of the person, not just its highest reaches, as St. Bernard in the opening sermon on the Song of Songs shows how the Christian progresses from the wisdom

---

[9] Thomas Merton, *Silence in Heaven: A Book of the Monastic Life* (New York: Crowell, 1956) 20.

[10] Thomas Merton, *The New Man* (New York: Farrar, Straus & Cudahy, 1961) 109 (subsequent references will be cited as "*NM*" parenthetically in the text).

[11] Thomas Merton, *The Literary Essays of Thomas Merton*, ed. Brother Patrick Hart (New York: New Directions, 1981) 101 (subsequent references will be cited as "*LE*" parenthetically in the text).

[12] Thomas Merton, *The Spirit of Simplicity* (Trappist, KY: Abbey of Gethsemani, 1948) 85.

[13] Thomas Merton, *Faith and Violence: Christian Teaching and Christian Practice* (Notre Dame, IN: University of Notre Dame Press, 1968) 222 (subsequent references will be cited as "*FV*" parenthetically in the text).

of Ecclesiastes, a recognition and rejection of the vanities of the world, to the wisdom of Proverbs, the reformation of conduct through ascetic discipline, to the ultimate wisdom of the Song of Songs, the enjoyment of the divine embrace.[14] In discussing the "salt of wisdom" placed on the tongue at baptism, Merton himself writes, " 'Wisdom' here of course implies an experience of the things of God, a deep knowledge of the ways of the Lord. It is perhaps not strictly the same as the contemplative gift [of wisdom] described by St. Thomas. It has no doubt practical connotations which imply the prudent conduct of one's life, more than the repose of contemplation, but in the end one cannot escape the fact that the gift is conceived by the Church as in some sense mystical" (*NM* 217–18). Thus the terminology of wisdom stresses the spiritual life as a continuum, a process of conformation to Christ that reaches from the humblest efforts to avoid sin to the heights of mystical union. It undermines any notion of elitism, and suggests that all are participants in the same spiritual journey, and that all are called to an ever-deepening experience of divine wisdom. "The true spiritual life," Merton writes in *New Seeds of Contemplation*, "is a life of wisdom, a life of sophianic love. . . . When St. Paul said that Love was the fulfillment of the Law and that Love had delivered man from the Law, he meant that by the Spirit of Christ we were incorporated into Christ, Himself the 'power and wisdom of God,' so that Christ Himself thenceforth became our own life, and light and love and wisdom. Our full spiritual life is life in wisdom, life in Christ."[15]

Without in any way relinquishing or compromising this explicitly Christian, and Christocentric, view of wisdom, Merton gradually comes to recognize a similar process operative in non-Christian contemplation. He writes:

> in all religions it is more or less generally recognized that this profound "sapiential" experience, call it gnosis, contemplation, "mysticism," "prophecy," or what you will, represents the deepest and most authentic fruit of the religion itself. . . . To put it in grossly oversimplified language, all religions aspire to a

---

[14] Bernard of Clairvaux, *On the Song of Songs 1*, trans. Kilian Walsh, OCSO (Kalamazoo, MI: Cistercian Publications, 1976) 1–7.

[15] Thomas Merton, *New Seeds of Contemplation* (New York: New Directions, 1961) 141 (subsequent references will be cited as "*NSC*" parenthetically in the text).

"union with God" in some way or other, and in each case this union is described in terms which have very definite analogies with the contemplative and mystical experiences in the Christian, and particularly the Catholic, tradition.[16]

This discovery of a comparable focus, especially in the religions of the East, on a concrete, intuitive, existential illumination that is at once perfect self-realization and a union beyond subject and object with the ground of all reality, opens the way to a fruitful dialogue focused not on abstract concepts and conflicting doctrines, but on contemplative experience. Thus Merton finds wisdom terminology particularly useful for articulating some of the common or at least analogous elements found in diverse traditions. While sensitive to the particular nuances of the various forms of Eastern thought, and careful to point out their differences with Christianity and among themselves, Merton is able to show how a sapiential orientation is invariably present in all authentic spiritual paths.

For example, Confucianism, though focused on the ethical rather than the ontological dimension of life, is described by Merton as "much more than a philosophy: it is a *wisdom*, that is to say, it is not a doctrine, but a *way of life* impregnated with truth" (*MZM* 59).[17] In particular, the one who has attained the highest of the four virtues, "Chih, or wisdom, has learned spontaneous inner obedience to Heaven, and is no longer governed merely by external standards."[18] Likewise the Taoist master "knows the unknown not by intellectual penetration, or by a science that wrests for itself the secrets of heaven, but by the wisdom of 'littleness' and silence which knows how to receive in secret a word that cannot be uttered except in an enigma. This enigma is not a verbal riddle but the existential mystery of life itself" (*MZM* 73).

---

[16] Thomas Merton, *Mystics and Zen Masters* (New York: Farrar, Straus and Giroux, 1967) 204–5 (subsequent references will be cited as "*MZM*" parenthetically in the text).

[17] For further discussion see Patrick F. O'Connell, "'A Way of Life Impregnated with Truth': Did Thomas Merton Undervalue Confucianism?" in Patrick F. O'Connell, ed., *Merton & Confucianism: Rites, Righteousness and Integral Humanity* (Louisville, KY: Fons Vitae, 2021) 267–90.

[18] Thomas Merton, *The Way of Chuang Tzu* (New York: New Directions, 1965) 19.

It is with Buddhism, and specifically with Zen, that the fruitfulness of Merton's method of correlation becomes most apparent, though the enlightenment experience itself resists description even more than in Christian mysticism, which never loses its personalistic dimension, so that we are particularly aware that the sapiential language is suggestive rather than definitive. It is nonetheless quite helpful: "the true purpose of Zen [is] awakening a deep ontological awareness, a wisdom-intuition (*Prajna*) in the ground of the being of the one awakened."[19] *Prajna*, the "mature grasp of the primordial emptiness in which all things are one" (*ZBA* 68), is variously translated as "enlightenment, contemplation, wisdom" (*MZM* 31), is equated with the Tao (*MZM* 224), and in one passage is even assimilated to Merton's two favorite terms for wisdom: "a transcendent Self . . . in Christian terms, is metaphysically distinct from the Self of God and yet perfectly identified with that Self by love and freedom, so that there appears to be but one Self. Experience of this is what we here call 'transcendent experience' or the illumination of wisdom (*Sapientia, Sophia, Prajna*)" (*ZBA* 71–72). This passage suggests the sort of cross-fertilization that takes place in the course of Merton's studies of Eastern thought, by which insights from Zen enrich his description of Christian wisdom even as the Christian sapiential tradition provides a point of entry for dialogue with Zen.

While the use of wisdom terminology has distinct advantages as a bridge between East and West, it also raises questions about the intrinsic relationship, if any, between Christian and non-Christian wisdom. Is there some univocal meaning to the word as applied to the contemplative experiences of diverse traditions, beyond a rather tenuous analogy in method or discipline? Is there any basis for equating *prajna*, for example, with *sophia*, or the Tao with the Logos? Can the Christian identification of wisdom with Christ be reconciled with the oriental perception of wisdom? Though he is clear that there are significant differences in experience and articulation between Christian and non-Christian wisdom, Merton's whole approach to the issue suggests that these questions can be answered affirmatively.

---

[19] Thomas Merton, *Zen and the Birds of Appetite* (New York: New Directions, 1968) 48 (subsequent references will be cited as "*ZBA*" parenthetically in the text).

His response concentrates on the experiential level, but also contains, at least implicitly, a theological dimension, which depends, I believe, on the third of his four central themes, creation as a manifestation of divine wisdom. For Merton, the very existence, order, life, and beauty of the universe, and of each creature within it, reflects the image of the Logos, the divine Wisdom who made it: "The forms and individual characters of living and growing things, of inanimate beings, of animals and flowers and all nature, constitute their holiness in the sight of God. Their inscape is their sanctity. It is the imprint of His wisdom and His reality in them" (*NSC* 30). This is the aspect of wisdom that Merton eventually liked to call the sophianic, the epiphany of wisdom in creation and the corresponding human response, "the central wisdom that comes in tune with the divine and cosmic music" (*CGB* 3). Thus there is a pattern of order, a revelatory dimension, within the structure of reality itself, prior to but in harmony with the positive revelation of Scripture and incarnation: "For wisdom is the full epiphany of God the Logos, or Tao, in man and the world of which man is a little exemplar."[20]

This cosmic revelation is the theme of Merton's beautiful prose-poem *"Hagia Sophia"* ("Holy Wisdom"), but it is also a key for integrating explicitly Christian wisdom with that not only of Eastern religions but of pre-Christian Western thought and even of artists who may not be Christian but who share a fundamental sapiential consciousness. Merton's understanding of wisdom unites a deeply Christocentric, incarnational faith with an openness to insights from all sources, a true catholicity, for the same mystery of being that finds its definitive manifestation in Christ is also disclosed in many different forms through the natural or cosmic revelation available to all. This basically sacramental approach to created reality leads not only to *theoria physike* (as already noted in chapter 2), but to the contempla-

---

[20] Thomas Merton, *The Hidden Ground of Love: Letters on Religious Experience and Social Concerns*, ed. William H. Shannon (New York: Farrar, Straus, Giroux, 1985) 543 [12/13/61 letter to Bruno Paul Schlesinger] (subsequent references will be cited as "HGL" parenthetically in the text); also found in Thomas Merton, *Seeds of Destruction* (New York: Farrar, Straus and Giroux, 1964) 249 (subsequent references will be cited as "SD" parenthetically in the text) and Thomas Merton, *Cold War Letters*, ed. Christine M. Bochen and William H. Shannon (Maryknoll, NY: Orbis, 2006) 22 (subsequent references will be cited as "CWL" parenthetically in the text).

tive appreciation of creation,[21] to the validation of "natural" human experience of the transcendent, since the human person above all is "in some mysterious sense, an epiphany of the divine wisdom" (*HGL* 541; *SD* 245; *CWL* 22).

From this Christian humanist perspective, all authentic human insight into reality is intrinsically related to Christ, for all truth participates in the infinite wisdom of the Logos who became flesh in Jesus. Such a stance, Merton himself points out, is in harmony with the approach of the Greek Fathers: quoting Clement of Alexandria's statement that Pythagoras and Plato were aided by God in their search for truth, Merton affirms that "In fact, there is a relation between all 'wisdoms,'" and agrees with Clement's hint "that all wisdom opened out upon true religion" (*LE* 100). He quotes with approval John Wu's translation of the first line of John's gospel as "In the beginning was the Tao" (*ZBA* 33) and elsewhere calls attention to "the sapiential awareness of the hidden patterns of life which, in Taoism, foreshadowed their fulfillment in the Gospel of Christ" (*MZM* 70). After describing Zen as "not Kerygma but realization, not revelation but consciousness, not news from the Father who sends His Son into this world, but awareness of the ontological ground of our own being here and now, right in the midst of the world," he adds that "the supernatural Kerygma and the metaphysical intuition of the ground of being are far from being incompatible. One may be said to prepare the way for the other" (*ZBA* 47). Likewise, he finds in a "secular" writer such as William Faulkner a "natural sapiential outlook" (*LE* 101), and comments that Faulkner's story "The Bear" reveals "the inner meaning of the wilderness as an epiphany of the cosmic mystery" (*LE* 104), an awareness coming from "the primitive wisdom of the American Indian" (*LE* 105), "a kind of knowledge by identification, an intersubjective knowledge, a communion in cosmic awareness and in nature . . . a wisdom based on love" (*LE* 108).

As important as this transcultural, transconfessional communion in wisdom is for Merton, in and of itself, it assumes even greater significance in light of the present critical state of human development.

---

[21] See Thomas Merton, *The Ascent to Truth* (New York: Harcourt, Brace, 1951) 27–28; *IE* 67–68; and Thomas Merton, *An Introduction to Christian Mysticism: Initiation into the Monastic Tradition 3*, ed. Patrick F. O'Connell (Kalamazoo, MI: Cistercian Publications, 2008) 121–36.

One aspect of wisdom to which Merton returns again and again is the figure of Wisdom "at play" in creation, from Proverbs 8.[22] He describes her memorably in "*Hagia Sophia*": "Sophia, the feminine child, is playing in the world, obvious and unseen, playing at all times before the Creator. Her delights are to be with the children of men. She is their sister. The core of life that exists in all things is tenderness, mercy, virginity, the Light, the Life considered as passive, as received, as given, as taken, as inexhaustibly renewed by the Gift of God. Sophia is Gift, is Spirit, *Donum Dei*. She is God-given and God Himself as Gift" (*ESF* 66; *CP* 368). This association of wisdom with play and with the feminine is contrasted with the deadly seriousness of a pragmatic, utilitarian, "masculine" approach to life, in which everything is to have a clearly defined purpose. Wisdom celebrates the realm of delight, spontaneity, joy, freedom. It is completely "useless," gratuitous, like the rain in Merton's essay "Rain and the Rhinoceros," which could not be possessed, quantified, bought, or sold, which "reminds me again and again that the whole world runs by rhythms I have not yet learned to recognize, rhythms that are not those of the engineer."[23] Wisdom is pure gift, the antithesis of personal achievement, as Merton notes in describing theologian Karl Barth's love of Mozart in the opening pages of *Conjectures of a Guilty Bystander*, suggesting that Barth may have been "unconsciously seeking to awaken, perhaps, the hidden sophianic Mozart in himself, the central wisdom that comes in tune with the divine and cosmic music and is saved by love, yes, even by *eros*" (*CGB* 3).[24]

---

[22] For the central importance of this dimension of the wisdom theme in Merton's mature thought, as expressed particularly in "*Hagia Sophia*," and its roots in the sophiology of the Russian mystical tradition, see the magisterial work of Christopher Pramuk, *Sophia: The Hidden Christ of Thomas Merton* (Collegeville, MN: Liturgical Press, 2009); see also Christopher Pramuk, *At Play in Creation: Merton's Awakening to the Feminine Divine* (Collegeville, MN: Liturgical Press, 2015).

[23] Thomas Merton, *Raids on the Unspeakable* (New York: New Directions, 1966) 9.

[24] See also the earlier version of this passage in Thomas Merton, *Turning Toward the World: The Pivotal Years. Journals, vol. 4: 1960–1963*, ed. Victor A. Kramer (San Francisco: HarperCollins, 1996) 49–50 [9/17/60] (subsequent references will be cited as "*TTW*" parenthetically in the text).

But to become attuned to this divine and cosmic music, one must stop listening to another kind of wisdom, a pseudo-wisdom that tries to force the cosmos to conform to its rhythms. Merton traces the distinction back to St. Paul's contrast of two kinds of wisdom:

> one which consists in the knowledge of words and statements, a rational, dialectical wisdom, and another which is at once a matter of paradox and of experience, and goes beyond the reach of reason. To attain to this spiritual wisdom, one must first be liberated from servile dependence on the "wisdom of speech." (1 Cor 1:17) This liberation is effected by the "word of the Cross," which makes no sense to those who cling to their own familiar views and habits of thought and is a means by which God "destroys the wisdom of the wise." (1 Cor 1:18-23). . . . On the other hand, he who can accept this paradoxical "foolishness" experiences in himself a secret and mysterious power, which is the power of Christ living in him as the ground of a totally new life and a new being. (*ZBA* 55)

This distinction is later developed by St. Augustine as the difference between *scientia* and *sapientia*, science and wisdom, a standard topos throughout medieval literature and one that Merton sees as supremely relevant to contemporary technological society. Scientific knowledge, which is basically objective, analytical, abstract, and quantitative, has a legitimate, indeed indispensable, role to play in human life. When it is properly balanced with wisdom, there is personal, social, and cosmic harmony. The problem comes when science usurps the role of wisdom and claims to have all the answers, or rather declares the questions raised by a sapiential perspective to be meaningless. This is of course no new problem. Merton himself traces it back to the Fall, because of which Adam

> mentally reconstructed the whole universe in his own image and likeness. That is the painful and useless labor which has been inherited by his descendants—the labor of science without wisdom; the mental toil that pieces together fragments that never manage to coalesce in one completely integrated whole: the labor of action without contemplation, that never ends in peace or satisfaction, since no task is finished without opening the way to ten more tasks that have to be done. (*NM* 117–18)

This spiritual disorientation and restlessness has always been an inescapable part of the human condition, but in traditional societies it has been held in check by the respect accorded to the sapiential dimension. But modern Western technological society has tended to erode or even actively suppress such respect, to emphasize control over rather than appreciation of and unity with what is known. Knowledge becomes a mode of power and power the primary motive for knowledge. Merton writes:

> Science and technology are indeed admirable in many respects and if they fulfill their promises they can do much for man. But they can never solve his deepest problems. On the contrary, without wisdom, without the intuition and freedom that enable man to return to the root of his being, science can only precipitate him still further into the centrifugal flight that flings him, in all his compact and uncomprehending isolation, into the darkness of outer space without purpose and without objective. (*FV* 224)

Hence the urgent need to draw on all available resources of wisdom to counteract the distorted and dangerous preeminence of manipulative, self-aggrandizing knowledge. The recovery of the sapiential dimension of life therefore involves virtually every aspect of Merton's mature thought. It informs not only his interest in contemplative renewal and interreligious dialogue but his commitment to nonviolence, exemplified above all by Gandhi, whose "religio-political action was based on an ancient metaphysic of man, a philosophical wisdom which is common to Hinduism, Buddhism, Islam, Judaism, and Christianity: that 'truth is the inner law of our being'" (*SD* 231).[25]

Awareness of and commitment to this wisdom common to the great religious traditions, the presence of truth and love at the core of our being and at the heart of the universe, is of course characteristic of Merton's vision as well. The sapiential, sophianic dimension is never far beneath the surface of any of his mature work. In his late essay, "The Contemplative Life in the Modern World," Merton may well have definitively expressed the full implications of this perspective:

---

[25] See also *GNV* 10–11.

> I believe the reason for the inner confusion of Western man is that our technological society has no longer any place in it for wisdom that seeks truth for its own sake, that seeks the fullness of being, that seeks to rest in an intuition of the very ground of all being. Without wisdom, the apparent opposition of action and contemplation, of work and rest, of involvement and detachment, can never be resolved. Ancient and traditional societies, whether of Asia or of the West, always specifically recognized "the way" of the wise, the way of spiritual discipline in which there was at once wisdom and method, and by which, whether in art, in philosophy, in religion, or in the monastic life, some men would attain to the inner meaning of being, they would experience this meaning for all their brothers, they would so to speak bring together in themselves the divisions or complications that confused the life of their fellows. By healing the divisions in themselves they would help heal the divisions of the whole world. (*FV* 217–18)[26]

In this presentation of the holistic scope of wisdom, which has the capacity to transcend polarities and to reconcile inner and outer divisions, we also recognize that there is an intrinsic prophetic dimension to authentic wisdom: it is both a sign of contradiction to an ethos of power and exploitation and an instrument of hope and healing for those seeking reintegration.

If there is a certain prophetic character already present in wisdom, Merton would attribute it to the fact that biblical prophecy is rooted in the sapiential, contemplative vocation of Israel, the covenant intimacy offered at Sinai with "the austere, unseen yet ever-present and all merciful Lord of the desert" (*DQ* 224). The role of the prophet was less to foretell the future than to recall the past, "the age of Israel's nuptials with the Lord" (*DQ* 224), and to summon the people of God back to their true identity and vocation. As the Lord had liberated the enslaved Israelites from the tyranny of their Egyptian taskmasters

---

[26] For an earlier version of this passage, see Thomas Merton, "*Honorable Reader*": *Reflections on My Work*, ed. Robert E. Daggy (New York: Crossroad, 1989) 86.

and led the ragtag community into the wilderness, in the words of Hosea, "to speak to her heart" (Hos 2:14; cf. *DQ* 225), so the mission of the prophets was to liberate Israel from the temptations of power, comfort, inequity, complacency, which enslaved some spiritually and oppressed others materially. "The great prophets of Israel," Merton writes, "were men of God, divine instruments, whose function it was to keep alive the spirit of equality, theocratic independence and spiritual autonomy which had characterized the life of Israel in the desert" (*DQ* 224). The prophetic summons to an Israel easily seduced by the ready availability of the gods of the Canaanites was consistently a call to rediscover its roots, to recommit itself to the covenant made in the wilderness with its demands for fidelity, justice, and steadfast love. The prophetic message was unvarying in its core meaning: "return to the spirit of your days in the desert! Recovery of the spirit of the desert meant a return to fidelity, to charity, to fraternal union; it meant the destruction of the inequalities and oppressions dividing rich and poor; conversion to justice and equity meant the return to the true sabbath. For the law of the desert was the law of the sabbath, of peace, direct dependence on the Lord, silence and trust, forgiveness of debts, restoration of unity, purity of worship" (*DQ* 224–25). It is a call to reintegration, to wholeness, a recovery of unity with the Lord, with one another, with creation—a program that corresponds perfectly with the sapiential life.

But prophecy is a desert vocation in another sense as well. For Merton, the prophet is above all a witness, who "shoulders the 'burden' of vision that God lays upon him. He bows under the truth and the judgments of God, sometimes the concrete, definite historical judgment pronounced on a given age, sometimes only the manifestation of God's transcendent and secret holiness, which is denied and opposed by sin in general. But above all the prophet is one who bears the burden of the divine mercy—a burden which is a gift to mankind, but which remains a burden to the prophet in so far as no one will take it from him" (*DQ* 222–23). Though his message is one of life, it is threatening to those who prefer the illusion of life that they have constructed for themselves. In calling the community to accountability and repentance, the prophet sets his face against the prevailing ethos, speaks the truth to power, and is often ignored or ridiculed or rejected or persecuted. He is, almost perforce, a solitary, a desert figure, a voice crying in the wilderness. "In the Old Testament," Merton points out, "what happens to Elijah the prophet? He has to stand completely alone against the whole structure. . . . Something similar happens to Saint Francis. For him, too, there's a radical break with the world into a prophetic and free life where he made his own choices."[27] The "burden" of prophecy, then, is paradoxically a liberation from the constrictions of artificial and alienating social norms and expectations: "the prophets in Scripture," Merton says, "are called away from their people to stand on a different ground where they can choose freely before God, where they can make choices not predetermined by society" (*SpC* 134). But because the prophet is essentially a witness, this freedom is never for the sake of the individual prophet alone, but for the very people he has been called away from, to testify to a different way of life, a different source and goal, "to be to them a sign of contradiction which reminds them of a freedom they've forfeited" (*SpC* 134).

Merton finds that this prophetic tradition, like so much else in the Old Testament, culminates in the person and work of Jesus, who is led by the Spirit into the wilderness to confront the power of evil, who preaches good news to the poor and liberation to captives, and who is finally rejected and led outside the city to be executed by religious and political authorities. "Look at the Gospel of Mark," Merton advises, "which scholars say is a desert gospel. The idea of the temptation in the desert runs all through this gospel. It's a prelude to the Passion, making the whole Gospel of one piece. Remember that the temptation in the desert centers on power, among other things. 'I will give you all these kingdoms *if* . . .' The real reply to that is the Crucifixion. The prophetic struggle with the world is the struggle of the Cross against worldly power" (*SpC* 81). It is a struggle which is engaged not by turning the weapons of worldly power against the world, but by enduring the worst that the forces of evil can inflict and emerging from the grave to witness that the forces of life and freedom are more powerful than death and oppression. Incorporation in Christ, then, means sharing in this prophetic mission. "A prophet

---

[27] Thomas Merton, *The Springs of Contemplation: A Retreat at the Abbey of Gethsemani*, ed. Jane Marie Richardson (New York: Farrar, Straus, Giroux, 1992), 132–33 (subsequent references will be cited as "*SpC*" parenthetically in the text).

is one who lives in direct submission to the Holy Spirit in order that, by his life, actions and words, he may at all times be a sign of God in the world of men. Christ the Incarnate Word was of course the supreme Prophet, and all sanctity participates in this prophetic quality" (*DQ* 223). Prophecy, therefore, is not a relic of the past but a responsibility of the present: it is a participation in the identity and mission of Jesus, an intrinsic dimension of what it means to be sealed with the Spirit at baptism, given the name of Christian, called to a life of discipleship.

Merton conceives the essential role of prophecy in the contemporary world to be essentially what it was in the biblical world: the identification and denunciation of idolatry. If anything, the need for prophets is greater today because the false gods in which people place their faith and their hopes are more insidious, less easily recognized as idols, yet no less divinized and worshiped, and no less enslaving. The Latin word translated as "idol," Merton notes, is "*simulacrum* which has implications of a mask-like deceptiveness, of intellectual cheating, of an ideological shell-game. The word *simulacrum*, it seems to me, presents itself as a very suggestive one to describe an advertisement, or an over-inflated political presence, or that face on the TV screen" (*FV* 152). Such images represent all the forces in society that claim to mediate meaning, but instead manipulate people for their own advantage, with people's own at least implicit acquiescence, as in any confidence game. They are held captive by illusions, mistaking the image for the reality, the relative for the absolute:

> if, in fact, we live in a society which is par excellence that of the *simulacrum*, we are the champion idolators of all history. . . . The things that we do, the things that make our news, the things that are contemporary, are abominations of superstition, of idolatry, proceeding from minds that are full of myths, distortions, half-truths, prejudices, evasions, illusions, lies: in a word—*simulacra*. Ideas and conceptions that look good but aren't. Ideals that claim to be humane and prove themselves, in their effects, to be callous, cruel, cynical, sometimes even criminal. (*FV* 152–53)

Here Merton condemns not only worship of wealth and comfort and material possessions and political or even religious power, but a more insidious appeal to concepts such as patriotism or freedom or justice which, however valid they may be in the abstract, are frequently disguises for self-serving and oppressive policies in actual practice. Ideologies easily become gods to which people offer their time, devotion, and unquestioning loyalty, and to which they are all too often willing to sacrifice the lives of others, especially those who worship comparable idols at different shrines: "We have no trouble at all detecting all this in the ideologies of *other* nations, other social groups. . . . Until we admit that we are subject to the same risks and the same follies, the same evils and the same fanaticisms, only in different forms, under different appearances (*simulacra*) we will continue to propose solutions that make our problems insoluble" (*FV* 154).

The first task of the prophet, then, is to see reality as it actually is, to distinguish substance from illusion. "To live prophetically you've got to be questioning and looking at factors behind the facts. You've got to be aware that there are contradictions. In a certain sense, our prophetic vocation consists in hurting from the contradictions in society. This is a real cross in our lives today. For we ourselves are partly responsible" (*SpC* 157). Note that for Merton authentic prophecy does not involve self-righteousness, a condemnation of others which is simultaneously an assertion of one's own innocence. The prophet must begin by recognizing and exorcising his or her own illusions and idolatries, his or her own complicity in acquiescing to, perhaps even promoting, a social structure built on deception and oppression. Prophets recognize their own liberation as a gift, a grace, which becomes the substance of their witness. True prophecy is founded not in arrogance but in humility.

It is precisely this humility, rooted in the recognition of God's presence, which gives the prophet the courage to speak and act prophetically. Prophecy for Merton is simply the recovery of one's true identity as grounded in Christ and filled with the Spirit: what one says or does to challenge the powers and principalities is simply the logical consequence of being one's authentic self. "We just let Christ be faithful to us. If we live with that kind of mind, we are prophetic. We become prophetic when we live in such a way that our life is an experience of the infallible fidelity of God. That's the kind of prophecy we are called to, not the business of being able to smell the latest fashion coming ten years before it happens. It is simply being in tune with God's mercy and will" (*SpC* 73). The witness of prophecy is a matter of presence before it is a matter of words; its testimony is made by the orientation of one's entire life: "Prophecy is not a technique, it is not about telling someone else what to do. If we are completely open to the Holy Spirit, then the Spirit will be able to lead us where God wants us to go. Going along that line, our lives will be prophetic" (*SpC* 74).

Merton realizes, of course, that "going along that line" will inevitably bring one into conflict with a society that demands conformity and is heading in a different direction. When the wisdom implanted in the created world had been obscured and distorted by efforts to exploit creation, and particularly other human beings, for selfish purposes, those who share the prophetic vocation of Christ are called to be signs of contradiction: "the real challenge to Christianity today is . . . above all the recovery of a creative and prophetic iconoclasm over against the idols of power, mystification and super-control. . . . Wherever idols, religious or secular, are set up as absolutes, as necessary, as final, the human and valid response is an affirmation of man in his concreteness, his limitation, his openness, his potentiality for development" (*FV* 255–56). Prophecy refutes by its very exercise of freedom the deterministic presumptions of a totalitarian mindset. Furthermore, the prophet thereby exposes the illusions of freedom in a conformist society. "One of the central issues in the prophetic life is that a person rocks the boat, not by telling slaves to be free, but by telling people who *think* they're free that they're slaves. That's an unacceptable message. There's nothing new about telling the blacks that they're having a rough time. The prophetic thing in this country is to tell white people that they need the blacks to be free *so they'll be liberated themselves*. Few people say this" (*SpC* 133). Likewise to point to the restrictions on freedom in the Soviet Union while glossing over the less blatant restrictions of a consumerist mass society "organized for profit and for marketing" (*SpC* 129) is not prophecy but self-justification.

The freedom of the prophet is also exercised by standing with those who are not free, by "actual human solidarity and communion" with those victimized by idolatries of race and class and power and money and comfort.

> Against the mass brutality of war and police oppression, solidarity with the victims of that oppression. Against the inhumanity of organized affluence, solidarity with those who are excluded from any participation in the benefits of almost unlimited plenty. Where "the world" means in fact "military power," "wealth," "greed," then the Christian remains against it. When the world means those who are concretely victims of these demonic abstractions (and even the rich and mighty are their victims too) then the Christian must be for it and in it and with it. (*FV* 256)

Thus the first task of prophecy is denunciation, a clear-sighted critique of various forms of illusory meaning, for the sake of a defense of the human person as made in the image of God and therefore possessed of an inalienable dignity and liberty.

But the prophetic charism is not only denunciation, but annunciation, the proclamation of the good news that the idols are indeed illusions, phantoms, and that the true Lord is a God of love and justice and liberation. The prophet is called not merely to predict what will happen in the future, but to live God's plan for the future here and now. "This way of living is prophetic, not in the sense of sudden illuminations as to what is going to happen at some future moment, but in the sense that we are so one with the Holy Spirit that we are already going in the direction the Spirit is going" (*SpC* 49). The prophetic charism is to live out the reign of God, to be sign and instrument of *shalom* and justice and love, in the midst of a world of hatred and oppression and division. The prophet is so committed to the vision of God's kingdom that God's rule becomes visible, incarnate, in his or her own life. "The great historical event, the coming of the Kingdom, is made clear and is 'realized' in proportion as Christians themselves live the life of the Kingdom in the circumstances of their own place and time" (*FV* 16). This is the authentic prophetic charism, to allow the present moment at once to recapitulate the past, the redemptive events of Christ's life, death, and resurrection, and to anticipate the future, the completion of the drama of salvation. It is because it carries this eschatological character that nonviolence is for Merton not peripheral but central to the life of Christian discipleship: "Nonviolence is not for power but for truth. It is not pragmatic but prophetic. It is not aimed at immediate political results, but at the manifestation of fundamental and crucially important truth.

Nonviolence is not primarily the language of efficacy, but the language of *kairos*. It does not say 'We shall overcome' so much as 'This is the day of the Lord, and whatever may happen to us, *He* shall overcome" (*LE* 28).[28] Surely this is the heart of the prophetic annunciation of the Good News.

Merton suggests, then, that the prophetic charism is to recognize and reveal the *kairos*, the acceptable time, the time of decision, the time of the inbreaking of God's reign. But this is properly understood as the gift and responsibility of the Christian community as a whole. "Not just individuals but the community itself should be prophetic. That's an ideal, of course. But that's our task: not to produce prophetic individuals who could simply end up as a headache, but to be a prophetic community" (*SpC* 134). It is the task of the church, as the Body of Christ and thus the heir to the prophets, to counter the "claim to complete autonomy," to self-constituted meaning, which passes for a value system in the contemporary world. "Christianity sees that a society that justifies its behavior and bases its existence on this supposed autonomy of man does, in fact, devote to destruction and death the very resources and energies which it claims to be using for the affirmation and improvement of life. . . . It was the task of the prophets . . . to discover this kind of meaning in the events of the history of Israel. And it remains the prophetic task of the Church to interpret events of our own time in this same kind of way" (*CGB* 100). The church is called both to affirm what is authentic and good in human aspirations and to dissociate herself from all that can degrade and undermine these aspirations: "The Church has an obligation *not* to join in the incantation of political slogans and in the concoction of pseudo-events, *but to cut clear through the deviousness and ambiguity of both slogans and events by her simplicity and her love*" (*FV* 161). The burden of prophecy is not an option but an obligation for Christians today, who must either "face the anguish of being a true prophet" or "enjoy the carrion comfort of acceptance in the society of the deluded by becoming a false prophet and participating in their delusions" (*FV* 68). Prophetic witness is central to the very identity and vocation

---

[28] Also in Thomas Merton, *The Nonviolent Alternative*, ed. Gordon C. Zahn (New York: Farrar, Straus, Giroux, 1980) 75.

of the church, which is to model and promote the unity God intended for all humanity.

Yet the church, like Israel, may abdicate its responsibilities and settle for acceptance of the status quo. It may become implicated in the very illusions it is called to witness against. In such cases fidelity to the church demands of its members the same prophetic critique delivered to the wider society. "Such criticism is not a disloyalty. On the contrary, fidelity to truth and to God demands it. One of the most important aspects of our current biblical-existentialist theology is precisely the prophetic consciousness of a duty to question the claims of any religious practice that collaborates with the 'process of leveling' and alienation" (*MZM* 273). When the larger community compromises the truth, the prophetic role may devolve upon the few who remain faithful, like Franz Jägerstätter, the (recently beatified) "solitary witness" who was executed for refusing to fight in Hitler's war. Such examples, like those of the Old Testament prophets, keep alive in dark times the true meaning of the covenant: "The real question raised by the Jägerstätter story is not merely that of the individual Catholic's right to conscientious objection . . . but the question of the Church's own mission of protest and prophecy in the gravest spiritual crisis man has ever known" (*FV* 75). It may also be that those outside the institutional confines of the church, the poor and marginalized themselves, the artists and the poets, may at times speak with a more authentic prophetic voice than professed Christians, because they too have access to the truth revealed in creation and experience, the wisdom which contains seeds of the prophetic. Merton continually reminds himself and his readers of the necessity not only to speak but to listen, because the voice of the Spirit, with its consolations and its challenges, may be communicated through the most surprising instruments: "Those with ears to hear, let them hear" (Mark 4:9).

For those with the patience and the courage to listen, this *kairos*, the sapiential, prophetic announcement of once and future wholeness, is being continuously revealed. "Here," Merton writes in *Conjectures*, "is an unspeakable secret: paradise is all around us and we do not understand. It is wide open. The sword is taken away, but we do not know it: we are off 'one to his farm and another to his merchandise.' Lights on. Clocks ticking. Thermostats working. Stoves cooking.

Electric shavers filling radios with static. 'Wisdom,' cries the dawn deacon, but we do not attend" (*CGB* 118).[29] But such inattention is not inevitable: to be still, to recollect ourselves, to leave our busyness and diversions behind makes possible a vision of renewal, allows us to awaken "from a dream of separateness," as Merton describes it in the Fourth and Walnut passage of *Conjectures* (140).[30] It is of such an awakening that Merton speaks in "*Hagia Sophia*" when he says: "I am like all mankind awakening from all the dreams that ever were dreamed in all the nights of the world. It is like the One Christ awakening in all the separate selves that ever were separate and isolated and alone in all the lands of the earth. It is like all minds coming back together into awareness from all distractions, cross-purposes and confusions, into unity of love. . . . It is like being awakened by Eve. It is like being awakened by the Blessed Virgin. It is like coming forth from primordial nothingness and standing in clarity, in Paradise" (*CP* 363).[31] Here is Merton's catholicity, his holistic vision, in all its purity and power.

While Thomas Merton never laid special claim to the mantle of sage or prophet for himself, his reflections on wisdom and prophecy have in them an authenticity and authority that may encourage us to hope that if we do attend, we may hear with him the "dawn deacon" crowing "Wisdom," may learn the unspeakable secret, may discover that on the summit of the seven-storied mount of Purgatory the gates of paradise, of the world as designed by the Creator and restored by the Redeemer, are indeed open, and that we have been invited to enter.

---

[29] See also the earlier version of this passage: *TTW* 7 [6/5/60].

[30] See also the earlier version of this passage: Thomas Merton, *A Search for Solitude: Pursuing the Monk's True Life. Journals, vol. 3: 1952–1960*, ed. Lawrence S. Cunningham (San Francisco: HarperCollins, 1996) 181–82 [3/19/58].

[31] See also the original journal entry for this passage: *TTW* 17–18 [7/2/60].

Awakening in Eden:
Merton and the Recovery of Paradise

In the lovely opening passage of "The Night Spirit and the Dawn Air," the third section of his journal *Conjectures of a Guilty Bystander*,[1] Thomas Merton describes the emergence of a new day out of the silence and darkness of the Kentucky countryside surrounding his monastery. He focuses on what he calls the *"point vierge,"* that "moment of awe and inexpressible innocence" when the birds wake up and ask "if it is time for them to 'be.'" This "virginal point" at which they are drawn back into life, restored to their authentic identity and activity, is a kind of epiphany, a revelation of the creative Love that calls into existence all that is: "the most wonderful moment of the day is that when creation in its innocence asks permission to 'be' once again, as it did on the first morning that ever was." But such awareness, this glimpse of an unfallen world, is frustrated, Merton says, by human desires to control reality, by sheer inattentiveness and

---

[1] Thomas Merton, *Conjectures of a Guilty Bystander* (New York: Doubleday, 1966) 117–18 (subsequent references will be cited as *"CGB"* parenthetically in the text). *Conjectures* is a much expanded, reordered, and rewritten version of journal entries from the late 1950s and early 1960s. A comparison of this entry with the original version, from June 5, 1960 (Pentecost Sunday), provides a good example of Merton's revising; see Thomas Merton, *Turning Toward the World: The Pivotal Years. Journals, vol. 4: 1960–1963*, ed. Victor A. Kramer (San Francisco: HarperCollins, 1996) 7 (subsequent references will be cited as *"TTW"* parenthetically in the text). For the background of this passage in Islamic mysticism, see David M. Odorisio, "'We Bump. We Burst into Secrets': Thomas Merton's Sufi Spirituality in California—Making Our 'Yes' to Life," *The Merton Seasonal* 50.3 (Fall 2025) 12–13.

self-absorption, by alienation from creation that is also estrangement from the Creator and from one's own authentic self. This, for Merton, is the meaning of sin, the preference for illusion over reality, for the busyness of doing over the stillness and receptivity of being. He concludes the passage, "Here is an unspeakable secret: paradise is all around us and we do not understand. It is wide open. The sword is taken away, but we do not know it: we are off 'one to his farm and another to his merchandise.' Lights on. Clocks ticking. Thermostats working. Stoves cooking. Electric shavers filling radios with static. 'Wisdom,' cries the dawn deacon, but we do not attend."

A central aim of all Merton's writing is to articulate this "unspeakable secret," to direct attention to this proclamation of a "wisdom which transcends and unites, wisdom which dwells in body and soul together and which, more by means of myth, of rite, of contemplation, than by scientific experiment, opens the door to a life in which the individual is not lost in the cosmos and in society but found in them."[2] Among the myths—the imaginative patterns that convey a truth transcending literal facts—that Merton finds most powerful in conveying this wisdom is the one at the heart of the dawn passage in *Conjectures*: the return to paradise.[3] Salvation is imaged as the restoration of that primordial unity and harmony of all creation in God that had been shattered by the fruitless quest for a spurious autonomy and betrayed by the resulting compulsion to treat what is not the self as possessions to be controlled or threats to be overcome, rather than as gifts to be accepted with respect and gratitude. It is this traditional image of the mysterious journey forward to the beginning, the reversal of the Fall, that Merton repeatedly invokes in his efforts to describe what it means to be a genuine Christian, an au-

---

[2] Thomas Merton, ed., *Gandhi on Non-Violence: Selected Texts from Non-Violence in Peace and War* (New York: New Directions, 1965) 1.

[3] It is noteworthy that the revised version of William H. Shannon's classic work, *Thomas Merton's Dark Path: The Inner Experience of a Contemplative* (New York: Farrar, Straus, Giroux, 1982) is entitled *Thomas Merton's Paradise Journey: Writings on Contemplation* (Cincinnati: St. Anthony Messenger Press, 2000). Shannon comments that this "is an appropriate title, as 'paradise' is a favorite theme in Merton's writings about contemplation. . . . The human story after the fall is the long arduous journey back to paradise. The way of that journey is contemplation" (3).

thentic contemplative, a true monk, a perceptive writer—an authentic human being.

For Merton, the Genesis story of Creation and Fall is to be understood not as factual history but as "a poetic and symbolic revelation, a completely *true*, though not literal, revelation of God's view of the universe and of His intentions for man. The point of these beautiful chapters is that God made the world as a garden in which He himself took delight. He made man and gave to man the task of sharing in His own divine care for created things."[4] But by usurping the role of God rather than participating in it, by the futile desire to substitute himself for God as the center of his own being and of his world, Adam denied his own deepest identity as formed in the image of God, as well as his vocation to participate in the creative work of God. His refusal to accept his own contingency, his denial of his radical dependence upon his Creator, led him to prefer the illusion of autonomy to the reality of grace, the gift of unmerited and unlimited love. It was, in Merton's familiar terminology, the preference for the false self of egotistical desires over the true self loved into being by God. Thus sin is not just a specific immoral action but a state of self-division and alienation from reality. It rejects the unity designed by God for a life of division and conflict, a life of estrangement not only from God but from the rest of creation made by God, from other people made in the divine image, and from one's own deepest self: "man is created for peace, delight, and the highest spiritual happiness. . . . But man's weakness and superficiality, his inordinate love of a self metaphysically wounded with contingency, makes the Paradise life impossible."[5]

But the salvation brought by Christ reverses of the effects of the Fall. For Merton, following St. Paul (see Rom 5:15–21; 1 Cor 15:20–23, 42–50), redemption is to be understood as a restoration through

---

[4] Thomas Merton, *New Seeds of Contemplation* (New York: New Directions, 1961) 290–91 (subsequent references will be cited as "*NSC*" parenthetically in the text).

[5] Thomas Merton, *The Literary Essays of Thomas Merton*, ed. Brother Patrick Hart (New York: New Directions, 1981) 254 (subsequent references will be cited as "*LE*" parenthetically in the text).

Christ, the new Adam, of the paradisal unity disrupted by the first Adam's act of self-glorification, which was simultaneously an act of self-alienation. In *The New Man*, the work in which he explores this theme most extensively, he writes,

> The first Adam, by the irresponsible misuse of his freedom, by the act of original pride in which he substituted self-assertion for self-realization, had brought death, illusion, error, destruction into the life of man by awakening inordinate desire. The second Adam, by the perfect use of His freedom in obedience to the Truth, reintegrated man into the reality of the spiritual order. He restored man to his original existential communion with God, the source of life, and thus opened again to him the closed gate of Paradise.[6]

It is a movement from division, a dualistic perspective that separates and divides, to a unified, holistic vision. "In the beginning, Adam was 'one man.' The Fall had divided him into 'a multitude.' Christ had restored man to unity in Himself. The Mystical Christ was the 'New Adam' and in Him all men could return to unity, to innocence, to purity, and become 'one man.' *Omnes in Christo unum*."[7] This return to unity is of course possible only if one is willing to let go of one's self-created, self-centered identity by entering into the mystery of the cross. The false self must be surrendered to death in order for the true self to live in Christ. "This meant, of course, living not by one's own will, one's own ego, one's own limited and selfish spirit, but being 'one spirit' with Christ. . . . The individual has 'died' with Christ to his 'old man,' his exterior, egotistical self, and 'risen' in Christ to the new man, a selfless and divine being, who is the one Christ, the same who is 'all in all'" (*ZBA* 117). By being one with Christ, one returns with Christ to the unity of God's original design for creation. Like the good thief, one hears the words of Christ, "This day you shall be with me in paradise" (Luke 23:43). To be in paradise, Merton writes,

---

[6] Thomas Merton, *The New Man* (New York: Farrar, Straus & Cudahy, 1961) 151 (subsequent references will be cited as "*NM*" parenthetically in the text).

[7] Thomas Merton, *Zen and the Birds of Appetite* (New York: New Directions, 1968) 117 (subsequent references will be cited as "*ZBA*" parenthetically in the text).

is to recover one's true self, to find oneself in Christ by losing oneself in Christ: "Paradise is simply the person, the self, but the radical self in its uninhibited freedom. The self no longer clothed with an ego."[8] The inner division symbolized by the dualistic "knowledge of good and evil" is healed by the gift of a wisdom that is able to experience "the recovery of that 'purity' or 'emptiness' which for the early Fathers was union with the divine light, not considered as an 'object' or 'thing' but as the 'divine purity' which enriches and transforms us in its own innocence" (*ZBA* 102). This emptying of self, the *kenosis* of which Paul speaks in Philippians 2, is actually the fullness of the divine presence. In a sense, Merton says, we do not merely "reenter" paradise. We *become* the new paradise, the dwelling place of God with humanity: "We see that we ourselves are Adam, we ourselves are Christ, and that we are all dwelling in one another, by virtue of the unity of the divine image reformed by grace, in a way that is analogous to the circumincession of the Three Divine Persons in the Holy Trinity. God Himself dwells in us and we in Him. We are His new Paradise. And in the midst of that Paradise stands Christ Himself, the Tree of life" (*NM* 161). Inner reintegration, therefore, is inseparable from the reformation of community. Union with the risen Christ is communion with all humanity, indeed all creation, that shares in the new life brought by Christ's victory over the divisions of sin and death. In Christ the " 'mirror' of the divine nature," which "was shattered into millions of fragments by that original sin which alienated each man from God, from other men and from himself . . . becomes once again a perfectly united image of God in the union of those who are one in Christ" (*NM* 149). Likewise, the power of the Resurrection extends "not only into man's spirit but also, ultimately, into all the material creation as well" (*NM* 150).

Merton makes clear that this paradise is not the final destination of humanity. It is a foretaste of eternal life but not its full fruition. "Paradise is not 'heaven.' Paradise is a state, or indeed a place, on earth. Paradise belongs more properly to the present than to the future life. In some sense it belongs to both. It is the state in which man

---

[8] Thomas Merton, *Love and Living*, ed. Naomi Burton Stone and Brother Patrick Hart (New York: Farrar, Straus, Giroux, 1979) (subsequent references will be cited as "*L&L*" parenthetically in the text).

was originally created to live on earth" (*ZBA* 116). But it is nevertheless an experience of oneness not only with creation but with the Creator, because it is not merely a return to the state of the first Adam but a participation in the infinitely richer life of the new Adam, the risen Christ who has ascended to the Father: "For in my soul and in your soul I find the same Christ Who is our Life, and He finds Himself in our love, and together we all find Paradise, which is the sharing of His Love for His Father in the Person of Their Spirit" (*NSC* 66).[9]

The realization of such an awareness is of course not automatic or instantaneous—the journey to Eden is a lifetime process of becoming what one is, of actualizing this recognition of renewed creation and living it out—of claiming the unity one has been given in Christ: "the recovery of this paradise, which is always hidden within us at least as a possibility, is a matter of great practical difficulty . . . a way of temptation and struggle" (*ZBA* 123–24). The process of conformation to the new Adam and rejection of the old is undertaken by the series of deaths and resurrections that make up the life project of the Christian. One is simultaneously in paradise and in the desert, already saved and still working out one's salvation in fear and trembling. Yet paradoxically, Merton maintains, simply by accepting the desert, the state of emptiness, of dependence, of selflessness, one becomes aware that one has been in paradise all the while: "The desert becomes a paradise when it is accepted as a desert. The desert can never be anything but a desert, if we are trying to escape from it. But once we accept the desert, it becomes a paradise if it's fully accepted, [along] with the Passion of Christ."[10] The struggle is simply the effort required to trust enough to accept paradise as a totally undeserved divine gift. The temptation is to reject the freedom of Eden for the security of a comfortable servitude to the habits and customs of the unredeemed self in a fallen but familiar world.

---

[9] This passage is already found in *Seeds of Contemplation*, the original 1949 version of this work revised in 1961 as *New Seeds*: see Thomas Merton, *Seeds of Contemplation* (New York: New Directions, 1949) 49.

[10] Thomas Merton, *Thomas Merton in California: The Redwoods Conferences & Letters*, ed. David Odorisio (Collegeville, MN: Liturgical Press, 2024) 268 (subsequent references will be cited as "*TMC*" parenthetically in the text).

This trust and this freedom are discovered, according to Merton, in contemplation. To be a contemplative is to share in the vocation of Adam, whose "whole being . . . gathered up in the purity of a contemplation that was at the same time effortless and supreme, sang to God with the realization that he was full of God and thus became aware of himself and of the world as God's paradise" (*NM* 56). To be a contemplative is to realize that the gates of paradise have been reopened; it is to enter into the new creation, to know the new life brought by Christ not just by report but by experience. Contemplation is the immediate awareness of the loving presence of God that is simultaneously an awareness of oneself as the image of God, so intimately united with its divine source and goal that God and self are experienced as one. The contemplative is the one who realizes the fundamental truth that apart from God one has nothing, one is nothing. Contemplation is the state of utter and complete receptivity to divine life. Merton writes,

> The situation of the soul in contemplation is something like the situation of Adam and Eve in Paradise. Everything is yours, but on one infinitely important condition: it is all *given*. There is nothing that you can claim, nothing that you can demand, nothing that you can *take*. And as soon as you try to take something as if it were your own—you lose your Eden. The angel with the flaming sword stands armed against all selfhood that is small and particular, against the "I" that can say "I want . . ." "I need . . ." "I demand . . ." No individual enters Paradise, only the integrity of the *Person*. (*NSC* 229)

Contemplation is therefore a liberation, a release from enslavement to idols—above all, the idol of self. Freed from obsession with the narrow concerns of a particular individual, the contemplative is likewise free from the desire to control and exploit others, free to see them as they are seen by God and to love them as they are loved by God: "the contemplative, who had restored in his own soul the image of God, was the truly free man: for he alone could walk with God, as Adam had walked with Him in Paradise. He alone could stand and speak freely to God His Father, with complete confidence."[11]

---

[11] Thomas Merton, *The Inner Experience: Notes on Contemplation*, ed. William H. Shannon (San Francisco: HarperCollins, 2003) 154.

Contemplation, as Merton explains it, transcends all dualisms: between God and self, between the natural and the supernatural, between action and rest. "The Recovery of Paradise . . . is the recovery of man's lost likeness to God in pure, undivided simplicity" (*ZBA* 102). In this context, contemplation is not opposed to action. Purifying activity leads to contemplation, and contemplation overflows into activity that is a participation in the creative work of God. Knowing the good by doing good leads to knowing God as the source and fullness of all goodness: "By turning away from the experiential knowledge of moral evil, by seeking only that existential knowledge of good which is the exclusive right of those who know good by doing it, we reenter the spiritual paradise of God and prepare ourselves to realize His presence within us by contemplation" (*NM* 185). The action that leads to contemplation is complemented by the action that springs from contemplation: "In Paradise there was no opposition between action and contemplation. We too, if we recover, in Christ, the paradisiacal life of Adam which He has restored to us, are supposed to discover that the opposition between them vanishes at last." Adam's work had "an essentially contemplative character, since it was entirely impregnated with light and significance by his union with God." Because his vocation was "to act as God's instrument in cultivating and developing the natural creation . . . Adam's work was an important aspect of his existential communion with the reality of nature and of the supernatural by which he was surrounded" (*NM* 77–79).

From this perspective, the return to paradise is not an escape from the world of space and time but the acceptance of a responsibility to share in God's continuing creative and redemptive work in and for the world. It is to become a sign and instrument of the unity intended by God and restored by Christ. To dwell in Eden is to be a sign of contradiction and a sign of attraction to a world that is largely unaware of its true form. It is to be energized by the Spirit of God to renew the face of the earth. The contemplative recognizes and affirms the unity of all humanity and the dignity of every human being. "If we instinctively seek a paradisiacal and special place on earth," Merton writes, "it is because we know in our inmost hearts that the earth was given us in order that we might find meaning, order, truth, and salvation in it. . . . Paradise symbolizes this freedom and creativity, but in reality this must be worked out in the human and personal encounter with the stranger seen as our other self."[12] There is no paradise that is selective and exclusive, no matter how often people try to pretend that there is. The notion, for example, of America as an earthly paradise, a place of renewed innocence based on separation from the guilt of the old world of Europe, is considered by Merton not "a valid and creative myth" (*CGB* 24) but a sterile daydream, an evasion, a culpable refusal to acknowledge the ways in which this image is built on the exclusion and oppression of those who did not belong—the indigenous Native American, the imported African slave. An authentic paradise consciousness cannot coexist with an acceptance of division: "There is no lost island merely for the individual. We are all pieces of the paradise isle . . . the paradise which is Christ and His Bride, God, man, and Church"; we are truly in paradise, Merton says, when we "see that the stranger we meet there is no other than ourselves—which is the same as saying that we find Christ in him" (*MZM* 112). Identification with the marginalized, those considered expendable or insignificant, is the mark of the true contemplative, who has transcended all divisions in the Christ who fills all in all.

Likewise, a respect for the created world as "sacrament," a revelation of God's creative love, is evidence of an authentically contemplative awareness. Writing of the great fourteenth-century English mystics, Julian of Norwich and her contemporaries, Merton finds in them "a 'paradise spirituality' which recovers in Christ the innocence and joy of the first beginnings and sees the world—the lovely world of moors and wolds, midland forests, rivers and farms—in the light of Paradise, as it first came from the hand of God" (*MZM* 152). The recovery of such an awareness is particularly important in the present age, when the power of technology and the profitability of exploiting natural resources make the recovery of a holistic appreciation of the natural world a matter of utmost urgency. Paradise consciousness is ecological consciousness, and the work of paradise is the protection of creation. In his letter to the author Rachel Carson after reading

---

[12] Thomas Merton, *Mystics and Zen Masters* (New York: Farrar, Straus and Giroux, 1967) 111–12 (subsequent references will be cited as "*MZM*" parenthetically in the text).

Silent Spring, Merton writes: "the whole world itself, to religious thinkers, has always appeared as a transparent manifestation of the love of God, as a 'paradise' of His wisdom, manifested in all His creatures, down to the tiniest, and in the most wonderful interrelationship between them." The Fall has blinded humanity to this interrelationship by reducing creation to a merely utilitarian resource to be disposed of for private pleasure or gain. "The 'vocation' of modern man," Merton declares, is to rejoin technology and wisdom "in a supreme humility which will result in a totally self-forgetful creativity and service."¹³ The contemplative is the person who is in the best position to bring the "cosmic perspective" of wisdom to this task because the contemplative experiences not only the world as it is but also the world as God intends it to be.

As someone who has made a professed commitment to a life of contemplation, the monk is a person whose vocation it is to dwell in this restored paradise—not of course in an exclusive but in a representative way. "The monk is a man of paradise who consecrates himself to God by a solemn and perpetual vow in order to spend his entire life in cultivating the spiritual Eden, the 'new creation' of space and light marvellously effected by God through the Incarnation, Passion and Resurrection of His Son."¹⁴ This association is evident from the outset of Merton's career as a writer. The title of his autobiography, *The Seven Storey Mountain*,¹⁵ is of course a reference to Dante's mountain of Purgatory, with its successive levels on which the penitent is healed of the scars of the seven deadly sins. Located at the summit of the mountain is the Garden of Eden, which the purified soul, restored to original innocence, enters at the completion of the ascent. Though the connection is never explicitly made in the autobiography, the identification of the Abbey of Gethsemani with

---

¹³ Thomas Merton, *Witness to Freedom: Letters in Times of Crisis*, ed. William H. Shannon (New York: Farrar, Straus, Giroux, 1994) 71.
¹⁴ Thomas Merton, *Seasons of Celebration* (New York: Farrar, Straus and Giroux, 1965) 207.
¹⁵ Thomas Merton, *The Seven Storey Mountain* (New York: Harcourt, Brace, 1948) (subsequent references will be cited as "*SSM*" parenthetically in the text).

Dante's earthly paradise atop the seven-storey mountain is logically consistent with the overall pattern of the story. Yet Merton would certainly never claim that by entering the monastery he had completed the process of purgatorial purification.

The solution to this anomaly had actually already been given by Merton in his journal account of his initial visit to Gethsemani during Holy Week of 1941. He wrote there: "Abbeys are paradises, but in two different senses—and that the abbey is at the same time an earthly and a heavenly paradise is a paradox: especially because it is both only because it is also a purgatory."[16] The monk's self-denial and disciplined work make it a purgatory, a process of purification from sin and its effects, but the freedom with which it is undertaken make it a paradise as well:

> Behind the strictness of the Trappist's discipline is this complete metaphysical freedom from physical necessity that makes it, ontologically speaking, a kind of play. This use of work as play to save the monk's soul results, indirectly, in the abbey being an earthly paradise—because work necessarily produces results, and the results, in this case, are a perfect community, a marvelous farm, beautiful gardens, a lovely chapel, woods, the cleanest guest house in the world, wonderful bread, cheese, butter—all things make this abbey the only really excellent community of any kind, political, religious, or anything, in the whole country. (*RM* 336)

Two days later he is less analytical and even more straightforwardly enthusiastic in his response:

> I have not written what a paradise this place is [though of course he has, at length!], on purpose. I think it is more beautiful than any place I ever went to for its beauty—anyway, it is the most beautiful place in America. I never saw anything like the country. A very wide valley—full of rolling and dipping land, woods, cedars, dark green fields—maybe young wheat. The monastery barns—vineyards. The knoll with the statue of St. Joseph in the

---

[16] Thomas Merton, *Run to the Mountain: The Story of a Vocation. Journals, vol. 1: 1939–1941*, ed. Patrick Hart (San Francisco: HarperCollins, 1995) 334 (subsequent references will be cited as "*RM*" parenthetically in the text).

middle of a great field where the road goes through a shallow cut towards the village—and the station on the line from Louisville to Atlanta. And in the window comes the good smell of full fields—*agri pieni*. (RM 347)

Thus from his first acquaintance with the monastery he associates it with a restored paradise.

Merton heads these reflections on the abbey as paradise and purgatory "*Paradisus Claustralis*," which can be translated both as "enclosed garden" and as "paradise of the cloister." His use of the traditional phrase,[17] which indicates that he is already aware that his comparison is not original, is repeated as the title of the final chapter of his history of the Cistercian Order, *The Waters of Siloe*, written shortly after *The Seven Storey Mountain*. Here the application of the image of paradise to the monastic life is stated with full force:

> What a transformation is worked in a community of men by the marvelous power of charity and contemplation, by the power of that pure, disinterested love which is a created participation in the sublime life of God! It turns monasteries into Edens where men recover the lost innocence of their father Adam. It turns the cloister into a Paradise where the monks begin, even on earth, to imitate the contemplation and praise of the nine choirs of angels—and the angels, remember, are cenobites. One of the greatest joys of monastic life, as of heaven itself, is the consciousness that all this happy contemplation is *shared*.[18]

Here the emphasis is on the common life as the central element in the restoration of paradise—the community images the healing of the inner and outer divisions that were brought about by the Fall. The harmony of the monks' voices in choir symbolizes the harmony of restored humanity. This rather romantic and idealized vision of the monastic community as *paradisus claustralis* gives way, over the course of time, to a more chastened yet more realistic recognition that the same struggles to incarnate this redeemed identity with the New Adam go on inside as well as outside the monastery. Even in *The*

---

[17] See also *TMC* 268.
[18] Thomas Merton, *The Waters of Siloe* (New York: Harcourt, Brace, 1949) 347.

Seven Storey Mountain itself there are some hints of dissatisfaction with the busyness of the Trappist routine[19] and an indication of attraction to the more solitary life of the Carthusians,[20] more ordered toward contemplation (which Merton became acquainted with particularly through a book entitled *Le Paradis Blanc!*[21])—an attraction that would lead to recurring thoughts of switching orders in the late 1940s and early 1950s.[22] While there is a continuity in Merton's association of monasticism and paradise throughout his career as monk and writer, there is a shift of emphasis in his use of the image from monastic community to monastic solitude. It is significant that in his next book on monasticism, *The Silent Life* (1957), he associates the recovery of paradise first with the Christian life generally but then with monastic solitude in particular:

> Through Christ man returns to the original perfection intended for human nature by God. The Christian life is therefore a return to "paradise," a partial restoration of the joy and peace of Adam's contemplative life in Eden. In saving man, the passion of Christ has also healed his body and all its faculties, and indeed the sanctifying power of the Cross has poured itself out upon the whole world, and man is once again able to find God in himself and in everything else. . . . This "return to paradise," this return to the perfection of charity in which man was created by God, is the true end of the monastic life. And in all the great Rules, and all the traditional documents of the great monks of the past, this return is seen as an ascent to divine contemplation. Just as Moses in the solitude of Mount Horeb led his flocks into the inner parts of the desert, and there saw the burning bush, and heard the Voice that spoke, and learned, from the Voice, the unutterable and Holy Name of God, so too the monk penetrates into the wilderness by silence and perfect solitude.[23]

---

[19] See *SSM* 420.

[20] See *SSM* 327–28, 383–84.

[21] See Thomas Merton, *Entering the Silence: Becoming a Monk and Writer. Journals, vol. 2: 1941–1952*, ed. Jonathan Montaldo (San Francisco: HarperCollins, 1996) 43 (subsequent references will be cited as "*ES*" parenthetically in the text).

[22] See, for example, *ES* 124, 147, 237, 247, 338.

[23] Thomas Merton, *The Silent Life* (New York: Farrar, Straus & Cudahy, 1957) 169–70.

In the pamphlet "Monastic Peace," published the following year, he does describe the monastery as a kind of sacrament of renewed life: "The monastery remains in the world, but not of the world, as a vision of peace, a window opening on the perspectives of an utterly different realm, a new creation, an earthly paradise in which God once again dwells with men and is almost visibly their God, their peace and their consolation."[24] But he immediately goes on to warn against any kind of posturing or self-dramatization on the part of the community or individual monks:

> Of course, the monastic community could not perfectly achieve this end if it were to remain too conscious of itself. . . . It is vain and absurd merely to retail the observances and customs of monks, and worse still to dramatize their essentially undramatic solitude, in order to arouse the curiosity or admiration of the world. Such talk would be contrary to the very spirit of the monastic vocation which loses all its justification as soon as the attention of men is drawn to the monks themselves, instead of being led, beyond them, to God. (*MJ* 47)

There is no guarantee, Merton has come to realize, that the monastic institution will foster an environment with an authentically "paradisal" awareness. Looking back at the decay of monasticism in the Middle Ages, he notes that it gave in to the temptation to reduce the person to a cog in a well-oiled institutional machine: "The 'person' was only what he was in the eyes of the institution because the institution was, for all intents and purposes, Paradise, the domain of God, and indeed God himself. To be in Paradise, then, consisted in being defined by the paradisic community" (*L&L* 9). But despite, or perhaps because of, his incisive critique of the perils inherent in expecting monastic structures and routines to preserve this paradise consciousness, Merton never wavers from the conviction that the monastic charism is to serve as a kind of icon of redeemed humanity, restored to unity with God, with creation and with one's own authentic identity. In his essays on monastic renewal, he emphasizes that it is adherence to this holistic vision that is essential:

---

[24] Thomas Merton, *The Monastic Journey*, ed. Brother Patrick Hart (Kansas City: Sheed, Andrews and McMeel, 1977) 43 (subsequent references will be cited as "*MJ*" parenthetically in the text).

the renewal of monasticism cannot have any real meaning until it is seen as a renewal of the *wholeness* of monasticism in its *charismatic* authenticity. Instead of concentrating on this or that means, we need first of all to look more attentively at the end. . . . The charism of the monastic life is the freedom and peace of a wilderness existence, a return to the desert that is also a recovery of (inner) paradise. This is the secret of monastic "renunciation of the world." Not a denunciation, not a denigration, not a precipitous flight, a resentful withdrawal, but a liberation, a kind of permanent "vacation" in the original sense of "emptying." The monk simply discards the useless and tedious baggage of vain concerns and devotes himself henceforth to the one thing really necessary—the one thing that he really wants: the quest for *meaning* and for *love*, the quest for his own identity, his secret name promised him by God.[25]

It is in this context that monastic community, "the communal charism of brotherhood in pilgrimage and in hope" (*CWA* 17), is properly understood and accepted. The monastic life becomes a kind of eschatological sign, a witness to the fullness of redemption already given but not yet fully realized. "The monk . . . sees and experiences the Kingdom of Promise as already fulfilled. The monastic life is at once a recovery of paradisal simplicity, of wilderness obedience and trust, and an anticipated completion in blessed light. Monastic 'contemplation' is not merely reposeful consideration of eternal verities but a grasp of the whole content of revelation, albeit obscurely, in the deep experience of a fully lived faith" (*CWA* 188).

Certainly it is this experience of faith that Merton sought to live out in his hermitage, not on the basis of any personal righteousness but due to the continuing revelation of divine mercy. In his essay *Day of a Stranger*, written shortly before he moved permanently to the hermitage, he meditates on the call to solitude as an invitation to recognize and embrace the Love hidden in the depth of all that is real, to "marry the silence of the forest" and hear "the secret that is heard only in silence." This secret is the same "unspeakable secret" revealed in the dawn passage in *Conjectures*, "the virginal point of

---

[25] Thomas Merton, *Contemplation in a World of Action* (Garden City, NY: Doubleday, 1971) 16 (subsequent references will be cited as "*CWA*" parenthetically in the text).

pure nothingness which is at the center of all other loves," an awareness that each particular love, insofar as it is authentic, shares in the one all-encompassing Love, that all particular surrenders are concrete ways of participating in the primal and primary surrender of self to Absolute Reality, which is to embrace "the most rare of all the trees in the garden, at once the primordial paradise tree, the *axis mundi*, the cosmic axle, and the Cross."[26]

One of the discoveries Merton made in his engagement with the wisdom of other religious traditions was a recognition that awareness of this "primordial paradise tree" in the midst of the garden is not restricted to professed Christians. Paradise consciousness, an intuitive experience of the unity of all that is, transcends confessional boundaries, and while interpretations are not identical, they form a valid basis for dialogue and mutual appreciation. For example, some of Merton's own most salient comments on the return to paradise are found in the context of his dialogue with the Zen scholar D. T. Suzuki on the sayings of the Desert Fathers, in which it was Suzuki who introduced the topic of the Fall and recovery of paradise as a framework for understanding the lives and words of these early Egyptian hermits. Merton comments,

> what is most fascinating about this particular essay is that the Zen concepts of "emptiness," "discrimination," etc., are evaluated in terms of the Biblical story of the Fall of Adam. . . . It is certainly a matter of very great significance that Dr. Suzuki should choose, as the best and most obvious common ground for a dialogue between East and West . . . the most primitive and most archetypal fact of all Judaeo-Christian spirituality: the narrative of the Creation and Fall of man in the Book of Genesis. (*ZBA* 102–103)

In concluding the dialogue, he remarks, "I feel that in talking to him I am talking to a 'fellow citizen,' to one who, though his beliefs in

---

[26] Thomas Merton, *Day of a Stranger* (Salt Lake City: Gibbs M. Smith, 1981) 49; it is noteworthy that in the preliminary draft of this essay, this passage about the tree of paradise is included twice, both in the middle of the essay, as here, and at its very end: see Thomas Merton, *Dancing in the Water of Life: Seeking Peace in the Hermitage. Journals, vol. 5: 1963–1965*, ed. Robert E. Daggy (San Francisco: HarperCollins, 1997) 240, 242 (subsequent references will be cited as "*DWL*" parenthetically in the text).

many respects differ from mine, shares a common spiritual climate" (*ZBA* 138). It would not, I think, be inaccurate to say that this climate is the climate of paradise, of an innocence that the Christian would say has been restored by Christ and that the Buddhist would say was there, unrecognized, all the time (an idea that Merton considers, if properly interpreted, to be consistent with Christianity as well, since the separation from Christ that exiled humanity from paradise is based on an illusion of autonomy that has no ontological justification, since to be separated from the divine ground is to cease to be[27]). Likewise Merton's attraction to Chuang Tzu is bound up with the early Chinese Taoist master's "edenic" sensibility:

> Chuang Tzu's Taoism is nostalgic for the primordial climate of paradise in which there was no differentiation, in which man was utterly simple, unaware of himself, living at peace with himself, with Tao, and with all other creatures. But for Chuang this paradise is not something that has been irrevocably lost by sin and cannot be regained except by redemption. It is still ours, but we do not know it, since the effect of life in society is to complicate and confuse our existence, making us forget who we really are by causing us to become obsessed with what we are not.[28]

Merton does not attempt to reconcile these divergent views theologically, for instance by considering how the grace of Christ the eternal Logos is present even when it is not recognized, a point that he does make elsewhere.[29] He is content to call attention to and appreciate the analogies.

The intuition of paradise is also a bond that unites the contemplative and the poet. Intrinsic to the vocation of the literary artist is the "Edenic office of the poet" (*LE* 29), the responsibility to call things

---

[27] See Merton's letter to Suzuki in Thomas Merton, *The Hidden Ground of Love: Letters on Religious Experience and Social Concerns*, ed. William H. Shannon (New York: Farrar, Straus, Giroux, 1985) 563–64.

[28] Thomas Merton, *The Way of Chuang Tzu* (New York: New Directions, 1965) 17.

[29] See, for example, *MZM* 70, *ZBA* 47, *LE* 101–4.

by their right names and so to affirm the goodness and unity of reality, as well as to protest against the violation and denial and rejection of that unity. "All really valid poetry (poetry that is fully alive and asserts its reality by its power to generate imaginative life) is a kind of recovery of paradise," Merton claims. "Not that the poet comes up with a report that he, an unusual man, has found his way back into Eden: but the living line and the generative association, the new sound, the music, the structure, are somehow grounded in a renewal of vision and hearing so that he who reads and understands recognizes that here is a new start, a new creation. Here the world gets another chance" (*LE* 128).

Thus it is not surprising that some of Merton's own most effective poetry takes as its subject the return to Eden.[30] For example, in his poem "In the Rain and the Sun," from his 1949 volume *The Tears of the Blind Lions*,[31] a storm brings "Dogs and lions. . . to my tame home . . . my Cistercian jungle" (ll. 22–23) and makes the "Songs of the lions and whales" audible in his verse: "With my pen between my fingers / Making the waterworld sing!" (ll. 26–28). Thus a kind of return to Eden is experienced, in which "Adam and Eve walk down my coast / Praising the tears of the treasurer sun" (ll. 43–44). "Dry Places," also from *The Tears of the Blind Lions* (*TBL* 25–26; *CP* 215–17), pictures an abandoned mining town as a contemporary equivalent to the demon-haunted deserts of monastic Egypt, literally a "ghost town," where the bones of the dead try to seize the souls of the living; the scene by metonymy suggests the fallen world *in toto*, contrasted with the remembrance of "Adam our Father's old grass farm," the paradisial world for which "Christ was promised first without scars

---

[30] For a helpful discussion of what he terms Merton's "poetry of Paradise consciousness," see George A. Kilcourse, *Ace of Freedoms: Thomas Merton's Christ* (Notre Dame, IN: University of Notre Dame Press, 1993) 66–76. For a discussion of this theme in Merton's *Eighteen Poems*, the series of lyrics written for the nurse with whom he had a brief but intense relationship in 1966, see Bonnie Thurston, "Human Love and the Love of God in *Eighteen Poems*" in Paul M. Pearson, Danny Sullivan, and Ian Thompson, eds., *Thomas Merton: Poet, Monk, Prophet* (Abergavenny, Wales: Three Peaks Press, 1998) 68–79.

[31] Thomas Merton, *The Tears of the Blind Lions* (New York: New Directions, 1949) 23–24 (subsequent references will be cited as "*TBL*" parenthetically in the text); Thomas Merton, *The Collected Poems of Thomas Merton* (New York: New Directions, 1977) 214–15 (subsequent references will be cited as "*CP*" parenthetically in the text).

[a clear expression of Merton's Scotist belief that the incarnation was not exclusively a consequence of the Fall] / When all God's larks called out to Him / In their wild orchard" (ll. 35–37). "A Psalm," a third poem from the same volume (*TBL* 30–31; *CP* 220–21), describes the progression from the singing of the divine office, "When psalms surprise me with their music" (l. 1), through a resultant experience of the harmony of all creation, as "Choirs of all creatures sing the tunes / Your Spirit played in Eden" (ll. 9–10), to a deep contemplative silence and emptiness in which "God sings by Himself in acres of night" (l. 28); this poem foreshadows a vein that Merton will explore in many of the poems of the 1950s and 1960s.[32]

Probably the best known of Merton's "paradise poems" is "Grace's House," from *Emblems of a Season of Fury* (1963),[33] based on a drawing by a young girl (appropriately named Grace) sent to Merton by her father; it describes the "child's world" as a "Paradise . . . / Where all the grass lives / And all the animals are aware" (ll. 37–39) and concludes with the rueful recognition that for those who have lost their innocence, "Alas, there is no road to Grace's house!" (l. 50). In the same volume, "The Fall" (*ESF* 52–53; *CP* 354–55) contrasts the total self-emptying, the surrender of all self-created identification, which brings about a return to paradise, with the exile from Eden in a world of organized routines and recorded identities, concluding that only those who have been liberated from oppressive social identities are truly able to live in the social world creatively because "They bear with them in the center of nowhere the unborn flower of nothing, / . . . the paradise tree" (ll. 22–23).[34]

Perhaps the most beautiful expression of Merton's paradise consciousness, and an appropriate conclusion to this chapter, is the prose-poem "*Hagia Sophia*" ("Holy Wisdom"), also from *Emblems of a Season*

---

[32] For a detailed discussion of these poems, see Patrick F. O'Connell, "Thomas Merton and the 'Edenic Office of the Poet': Three Poems from *The Tears of the Blind Lions*," *The Merton Annual* 32 (2019) 183–204.

[33] Thomas Merton, *Emblems of a Season of Fury* (New York: New Directions, 1963) 28–29 (subsequent references will be cited as "*ESF*" parenthetically in the text); *CP* 330–31.

[34] For detailed discussions of these two poems, see Patrick F. O'Connell, "'The Surest Home Is Pointless': A Pathless Path through Merton's Poetic Corpus," *CrossCurrents* 58.4 (2008) 526–34, 538–42.

of Fury (*ESF* 61–69; *CP* 363–71).³⁵ As the poem begins, the speaker is in the hospital and is awakened at dawn by the gentle hand of a nurse.³⁶ This experience is successively described as the awakening

---

³⁵ On the importance of this work for Merton's mature spirituality, see Christopher Pramuk, *Sophia: The Hidden Christ of Thomas Merton* (Collegeville, MN: Liturgical Press, 2009), and Christopher Pramuk, *At Play in Creation: Merton's Awakening to the Feminine Divine* (Collegeville, MN: Liturgical Press, 2015).

³⁶ Note that this poem was written about seven years before Merton fell in love with the student nurse in the spring of 1966. Merton himself would make this connection in his journal entry for September 10, 1966: "(She was born just about two months before I came through Cincinnati on my way to Gethsemani! And I walked through Cincinnati station with the words of Proverbs 8 in my mind: 'And my delights were to be with the children of men!'—I have never forgotten this; it struck me so forcefully then! Strange connection in my deepest heart—between M. and the 'Wisdom' figure—and Mary—and the Feminine in the Bible—Eve etc.—Paradise—wisdom. Most mysterious, haunting, deep, lovely, moving, transforming!)" (Thomas Merton, *Learning to Love: Exploring Solitude and Freedom. Journals, vol. 6: 1966–1967*, ed. Christine M. Bochen [San Francisco: HarperCollins, 1997] 130–31 [subsequent references will be cited as "*LL*" parenthetically in the text]). The details of this relationship are found particularly in Part II: "'Daring to Love': April 1966–September 1966" (*LL* 35–126), with further references in later sections (see *LL* 130–31, 141, 143–44, 151, 154–57, 161–62, 172–73, 176–77, 181–82, 192–93, 204, 208, 222, 227, 232–33, 237, 260, 269), and in Appendix A: "'A Midsummer Diary for M.': June 1966" (*LL* 301–48). For extended discussion, see editor Christine M. Bochen's Introduction (*LL* xiii–xxiii) and her entry "*Learning to Love*" in William H. Shannon, Christine M. Bochen, and Patrick F. O'Connell, *The Thomas Merton Encyclopedia* (Maryknoll, NY: Orbis, 2002) 250–54 (subsequent references will be cited as "*Encyclopedia*" parenthetically in the text); see also Michael Mott, *The Seven Mountains of Thomas Merton* (Boston: Houghton Mifflin, 1984) 435–54, 461–62; Jim Forest, *Living with Wisdom: A Life of Thomas Merton*, rev. ed. (Maryknoll, NY: Orbis, 2008) 193–203, with its suggestive chapter title: "A Proverb Named Margie"; John Howard Griffin, *Follow the Ecstasy: Thomas Merton, The Hermitage Years, 1965–1968* (Fort Worth, TX: Latitudes Press, 1983) 77–131. For an overview of Merton's poems to and for M., see Patrick F. O'Connell, "*Eighteen Poems*" (*Encyclopedia* 128–32); see also Douglas Burton-Christie, "Rediscovering Love's World: Thomas Merton's Love Poems and the Language of Ecstasy," *CrossCurrents* 39.1 (Spring 1989) 64–82; Bonnie Thurston, "Human Love and the Love of God in *Eighteen Poems*" in Paul M. Pearson, Danny Sullivan, and Ian Thompson, eds., *Thomas Merton: Poet, Monk, Prophet* (Abergavenny, Wales: Three Peaks Press, 1998) 68–79; Robert Waldron, *Thomas Merton—The Exquisite Risk of Love: The Chronicle of a Monastic Romance* (London: Darton, Longman, Todd, 2012). The poems were published in a limited edition of 250 copies: Thomas Merton, *Eighteen Poems* (New York: New Directions, 1985); three had already been published in *CP* (447–48, 615–18, 801–802); five more are found in journal entries (*LL* 52–54, 56–57, 59–61, 64–65, 131–33; thirteen have been included in Thomas Merton, *In the Dark before Dawn: New Selected Poems*, ed. Lynn R. Szabo (New York: New Directions, 2005) 188–219.

of humanity from dreams to reality, of a fragmented human race to the unity of love in the One Christ, of Adam to the first morning of life in Eden, of the world to the final morning of eschatological restoration. The gentleness and mercy of the nurse who calls the speaker back into consciousness is likened to being awakened by Eve or by the Virgin Mary: it is an experience of paradise and of a redeemed world. It is given above all to the least ones, represented by the man in the hospital, a man in need of healing, a man who in his vulnerable state is summoned to trust, to give up defensiveness and self-assertion. In the context of Merton's ongoing reflections on the theme of the return to the original unity of all reality in God, it is clear that to accept this invitation to come back to life is to attend to the "dawn deacon" of *Conjectures*: it is to respond to the "hidden wholeness" of Wisdom; it is, indeed, to awaken in Eden.

Merton's Vision of the Kingdom

"The time is fulfilled, and the Kingdom of God is at hand; repent and believe in the good news" (Mark 1:15). These first words spoken by Jesus in the Gospel of Mark, the proclamation inaugurating his ministry, situate the kingdom, or reign, of God at the very heart of the gospel message. They suggest that in order to accept Jesus' invitation to follow him, it is essential to appreciate the significance of this revelation of God's reign for Jesus' life and work and for the ongoing witness of the church. Yet too often in discussions of Christian life, this enigmatic image is given little attention, and misleading or incomplete interpretations can sometimes blunt its impact or obscure its importance. For this, as for so many other fundamental aspects of Christian faith and practice, the work of Thomas Merton can serve as a particularly valuable resource. While the image of the kingdom is not mentioned with any frequency or examined in any depth in Merton's earlier works,[1] his writings during the final decade of his life draw repeatedly on the language of the kingdom to explore what it means to be a faithful disciple of Christ in the second half of the

---

[1] For early comments on the kingdom in Merton's journals, see Thomas Merton, *Entering the Silence: Becoming a Monk and Writer. Journals, vol. 2: 1941–1952,* ed. Jonathan Montaldo (San Francisco: HarperCollins, 1996) 63, 81, 132, 142, 143, 293, 417, 471, and Thomas Merton, *A Search for Solitude: Pursuing the Monk's True Life. Journals, vol. 3: 1952–1960,* ed. Lawrence S. Cunningham (San Francisco: HarperCollins, 1996) 49, 61, 212 (subsequent references will be cited as "SS" parenthetically in the text).

twentieth century. It is particularly noteworthy that consideration of the kingdom and its import recurs across a broad spectrum of Merton's writings: it is a motif that helps to weave together meditations on the meaning of redemption, reflections on the mission of the church, essays on the need for contemplative awareness, and calls to prophetic action on behalf of peace. The kingdom of God emerges as a key factor contributing to the underlying holistic vision refracted in so many apparently disparate directions in Merton's later work, while his insights into this rich and powerful, yet mysterious, symbol illuminate its crucial significance for contemporary Christianity.

For Merton, the kingdom of God must first of all be recognized as an intrinsic component of the life and mission of Jesus: in his birth, in his preaching of good news to the poor, and above all in his death and resurrection, the transforming power of God's reign is released into the world. With the incarnation, the kingdom itself takes on concrete human features: it becomes enfleshed in the person of Jesus. "The Gospel of the Nativity," Merton writes, "is a solemn proclamation of an event which is the turning point of all history: the coming of the Messiah, the Anointed King and Son of God, the Word-made-Flesh, pitching his tent among us, not merely to seek and save that which was lost, but to establish his kingdom, the eschatological kingdom, the manifestation of the fullness of time and the completion of history."[2] The full actualization of the potential for freedom and life that is the true and authentic destiny of every human being as created in the divine image is the gift offered by the advent of Christ: in Jesus the contradiction between the dynamism of human nature as it was meant to be, "oriented toward a perfection of life that is to be achieved only in total self-giving," and human life as it is in fact lived, in which "this unlimited natural possibility is, to our anguish, discovered in actual experience to be so limited, so restricted, so frustrated, and so

---

[2] Thomas Merton, *Love and Living*, ed. Naomi Burton Stone and Brother Patrick Hart (New York: Farrar, Straus, Giroux, 1979) 223 (subsequent references will be cited as "*L&L*" parenthetically in the text); see also Thomas Merton, *Seasons of Celebration* (New York: Farrar, Straus and Giroux, 1965) 108 (subsequent references will be cited as "*SCel*" parenthetically in the text).

ambiguous as to produce not hope but only despair" (*L&L* 224), is resolved by the appearance of a human being who not only models authentic human existence but empowers others to share in this restored and fulfilled humanity. The birth of Jesus ushers in the reign of God because in Jesus the will of God, the divine plan for creation, is fully present in an absolutely faithful human being: "in Christ we therefore see man as he is intended to be: a child of God, capable of growth in God, a child for whom growth as man is growth to find himself in God" (*L&L* 225). Thus the coming of Christ makes possible not simply the healing and redeeming of individuals but the renewal of all humanity: the incarnation is the turning point of all history because it is a new beginning that already contains within itself the ultimate fulfillment of creation; in the birth of Jesus the "end" of history, both its goal and its completion, is already anticipated and assured: "the message of Christmas is eschatological: it is the revelation and celebration of the new age in which we live, in which our humanity has been restored to us untrammeled and disentangled, in Christ" (*L&L* 225).

Such a transformation, of course, is not brought about without conflict. The ministry of Jesus, particularly as depicted in the Synoptic Gospels, is marked by the confrontation of the vision of the kingdom as preached and lived by Jesus with the actual state of human affairs, the reign of sin symbolized on one level by demonic possession and represented on another by all-too-human oppressors who fear a challenge to their comfort and control. In proclaiming to the poor the good news that the reign of God is theirs, Jesus reveals the kingdom to be a sign of contradiction to the illusory perception that wealth or social status or political power confers or connotes superiority before God. In Merton's view, "the sign *par excellence*" of the presence of the kingdom is Jesus' identification with the outcast, the lowly, the insignificant: "the prophetic message of salvation, the fulfillment of the divine promises is now formally announced to the *anawim*, to those who hungered and thirsted for the Kingdom because they had no hope but the Lord" (*SCel* 98). That hope is fulfilled because God's compassionate love is made present to "the least of these" in Jesus: "Christ has appeared in the midst of the poor as one of them, and has taken them to Himself so that they are, in a most special way, Himself. What happens to them happens, in a very particular way, to Him. . . . The Last Days have come not merely because the poor have *heard about* Christ but because they 'are' Christ" (*SCel* 98). Thus the reign of God overturns the value system complacently accepted by the world, a reversal that has profound consequences for everyone, since the "poor themselves now become an eschatological sign of Christ, a sign by which other men are judged" (*SCel* 98), inasmuch as what is done to them has been done to him.

The consequences of this challenge to the prevailing order of Jesus' own time are that he is indeed treated as the poor and the expendable have always been treated: because he has interfered with the smooth running of the system, he is eliminated. His arrest, torture, and execution are an attempt to silence and discredit the proclamation of the reign of God, an attempt proven futile by Jesus' divine vindication, his triumph over the forces of sin and death. It is above all in the crucifixion and resurrection of the Lord that the disclosure of the kingdom of God reaches its climax. In the risen Jesus the kingdom is fully revealed. "The Paschal Mystery," according to Merton, "is above all the mystery of life, in which the Church, by celebrating the death and resurrection of Christ, enters into the Kingdom of Life which He established once for all by His definitive victory over sin and death" (*SCel* 113). Because Christ is already risen, sin has already been defeated, and the kingdom has already become present: "For with the death and resurrection of Christ we are in a new world, a new age. The fulness of time has come. The history of the world has achieved an entirely new orientation. We are living in the messianic Kingdom."[3] It is through the gift of the Holy Spirit, sent by the glorified Christ, that the disciples of Jesus are empowered to share in the risen life of Jesus and so to participate in the present reality of the kingdom. "The new world which is called the Kingdom of God, the world in which God reigns in man by His divine Spirit, the world of the Second Adam is, in fact, the Eon of the resurrection—the new age that begins to dawn with the rising of Christ from the dead, which reaches out

---

[3] Thomas Merton, *The New Man* (New York: Farrar, Straus & Cudahy, 1961) 148 (subsequent references will be cited as "*NM*" parenthetically in the text); see also *SCel* 64, 66, and Thomas Merton, *Faith and Violence: Christian Teaching and Christian Practice* (Notre Dame, IN: University of Notre Dame Press, 1968) 18 (subsequent references will be cited as "*FV*" parenthetically in the text).

to touch, with the pure spiritual light of that dawning, each soul newly incorporated into the Risen Christ" (*NM* 152).[4]

Such an understanding of the kingdom as a present reality is, on the face of it, preposterous. Violence and hatred remain pervasive; the forces of evil and death, according to the evidence of experience, continue to control individual lives and the course of history. The claim to be living in the kingdom of God, the "new creation," appears to be a sign of pathetic foolishness or culpable blindness to the ways of the world. Yet Merton maintains such a belief even as he refuses to avert his gaze from the destructive and oppressive forces of war and genocide and racial injustice and exploitation of the poor that mark his era of history. For Merton the contemporary disciple of Christ is one who is able to perceive with the eyes of faith "the victory of Christ and the reality of his Kingdom in the world even now, in all the confusion, the chaos and the risk of this historical and revolutionary time of crisis which we call the atomic age."[5] Christian life is situated precisely in that tension between affirmation of the kingdom of God present in the risen Jesus and awareness of its absence both in society and in individual lives:

> The Body of Adam which should be transfigured with light, is a Body of obscurity and untruth. That which should be One in love is divided into millions of frenzied and murderous hostilities. Yet the fact remains: Christ the King of Peace has come into the world and saved it. He has saved Man. He has established His Kingdom, and His kingdom is the Kingdom of Peace. Furthermore, *we* are His Kingdom. Yet we have devised a power capable of destroying not cities, not nations, but *Man*. (*SCel* 96)

There are ways of easing this tension by situating the kingdom on another plane than that of present human experience: by making it

---

[4] See also the discussion of the "life of the Kingdom of God" as brought about by participation in the paschal mystery, in which "we . . . die with Christ and rise with Him from the dead" (*NM* 154).

[5] Thomas Merton, *Contemplation in a World of Action* (Garden City, NY: Doubleday, 1971) 180 (subsequent references will be cited as "*CWA*" parenthetically in the text); see also Thomas Merton, *Seeds of Destruction* (New York: Farrar, Straus and Giroux, 1964) 129–30 (subsequent references will be cited as "*SD*" parenthetically in the text).

a transcendent realm, "the kingdom of heaven," contrasted with the earthly reign of sin and death; or a future realm, the kingdom to be established at Christ's return in glory, when the kingdoms of this world are to be cast down; or an interior kingdom, the "reign of God within," a spiritual kingdom of light in contrast with the outer realm of darkness. While Merton recognizes that the kingdom has a transcendent, and a future, and an interior dimension,[6] he refuses to absolutize any or all of these and so relinquish a belief that the reign of God must be available to be experienced and manifested here and now.[7] Unless the kingdom is in some way concretely present, the entire Christian message is called into question: "Are you He Who is to come, or look we for another?" (*SCel* 96). The kingdom should be the definitive sign that the powers of death did not and will not triumph, but if it "is so 'spiritual' that it has absolutely no visible or meaningful effect in contemporary society, we might as well admit it has no meaning that our contemporaries are likely to be interested in" (*SCel* 93). The key recognition for Merton is that "*we* are His Kingdom"—or putting the emphasis on the verb, as he does elsewhere, "we *are* His Kingdom" (*SCel* 92). Christians are not called to observe the kingdom but to incarnate it: the same reality definitively manifested in Jesus must be made visible and tangible in those who claim to be his followers. The christological question, "Are you he who is to come . . . ?" is transposed into a discipleship question: "Are *you* the kingdom of Christ Who is come, the Prince of Peace, the Just One, the Messiah who comes to bring unity and peace to the divided world of man?" (*SCel* 93).[8]

---

[6] For Merton's awareness of the early Christians' expectation of an imminent *parousia*, see Thomas Merton, *Zen and the Birds of Appetite* (New York: New Directions, 1968) 18 (subsequent references will be cited as "*ZBA*" parenthetically in the text); see also his discussion of the "Recovery of Paradise" as "the discovery of the 'Kingdom of God within us'" (*ZBA* 102).

[7] See the discussion of "the great importance of the concept of 'realized eschatology'" as "the heart of genuine Christian humanism" in Thomas Merton, *Dancing in the Water of Life: Seeking Peace in the Hermitage. Journals, vol. 5: 1963–1965*, ed. Robert E. Daggy (San Francisco: HarperCollins, 1997) 87 (subsequent references will be cited as "*DWL*" parenthetically in the text).

[8] See also the discussion of the petition of the Lord's Prayer, "Thy Kingdom Come" in Thomas Merton, *Conjectures of a Guilty Bystander* (Garden City, NY: Doubleday, 1966) 108–9 (subsequent references will be cited as "*CGB*" parenthetically in the text).

In Merton's view, answering this question in such a way that the message of Christ is illumined rather than obscured is the essential task of the Christian in the world, the central meaning of discipleship. In and for a world where Christ's victory over evil and death often seems invisible, the Christian vocation is to witness to the presence and power of the kingdom here and now. The persuasiveness of the Christian message is directly related to the fidelity with which the Christian community and its individual members live out the good news of the kingdom by identifying and resisting the powers of sin and death in themselves and in their society, and by identifying with the greater powers of compassionate love and eschatological joy lived by Christ and given by the Spirit. In perhaps his most impassioned and effective reflection on the meaning of the kingdom, Merton writes, "The great historical event, the coming of the Kingdom, is made clear and is 'realized' in proportion as Christians themselves live the life of the Kingdom in the circumstances of their own place and time" (*FV* 16). By serving as a sign of contradiction to the power of sin and death and a sign of invitation to the fullness of human life, which is ultimately the fullness of divine life, Christians resolve the tension between commitment to the present reality of the kingdom and recognition of the continuing power of darkness and division: "The saving grace of God in the Lord Jesus is proclaimed to man existentially in the love, the openness, the simplicity, the humility and the self-sacrifice of Christians. By their example of a truly Christian understanding of the world, expressed in a living and active application of the Christian faith to the human problems of their own time, Christians manifest the love of Christ for men (John 13:35, 17:21), and by that fact make him visibly present in the world" (*FV* 16).[9] This perception of the crucial importance of the kingdom for Christian living has profound implications for Merton's conception of the church, his understanding of contemplation both within and beyond monastic life, and his theory and practice of Christian action for justice and peace.

---

[9] See also Merton's comments on the "fantastic and humanly impossible belief" that Christians participate in the building of the kingdom (*NM* 5–6).

From Merton's perspective, the relationship of the church to the kingdom of God is intrinsic but dynamic. He rejects the static view of the kingdom predominant in the Middle Ages that simply identified it with the church and with Christian society.[10] In this view, "the Kingdom of God on earth is the Church as a sociological entity, an established institution with a divine mandate to guide the destinies of culture, science, politics, etc., as well as religion" (*CGB* 41–42). Such an interpretation not only fosters complacency and triumphalism but also postulates a neat division between church and world that excludes from the kingdom anyone and anything not formally incorporated within the ecclesial institution. It encourages a crusading mentality when the church is dominant in society and a fortress mentality when it is not. Merton cites the view of Otto of Friesing, a Cistercian historian of the twelfth century, who saw the conversion of Constantine as fusing the kingdom of God with the Roman Empire: "When the Emperor became Catholic, then Christendom = the Kingdom of God, i.e. the Christian politico-religious world is the kingdom of God"; the consequence of such an identification has all too often become evident in the history of the church: "there is no more to be done, but to preserve the status quo of the kingdom, if necessary by violent repression, coercion rather than apostolate. The apostolate of united coercion!!"[11] Any perspective that questioned this total identification, that pointed out limitations or flaws in the social organization of the church or of Christian society, would be resisted and even suppressed by "thrusting them outside the 'city' where their evolution became distorted and unhealthy" (*TTW* 274), thus ensuring the

---

[10] See his comment that "*Christendom* is not *Christianity* . . . not 'the Kingdom' and . . . not the Mystical Christ" (*SCel* 91); see also his discussion of Dietrich Bonhoeffer's recognition of the danger of the church preaching itself rather than witnessing to the kingdom (*L&L* 44–45).

[11] Thomas Merton, *Turning Toward the World: The Pivotal Years. Journals, vol. 4: 1960–1963*, ed. Victor A. Kramer (San Francisco: HarperCollins, 1996) 273 (subsequent references will be cited as "*TTW*" parenthetically in the text); see also his critique of what he calls "the Carolingian world view" in which "the Empire has become, provisionally at least, holy. As figure of the eschatological kingdom, worldly power consecrated to Christ becomes Christ's reign on earth" (*CWA* 146–47).

self-fulfilling prophecy that such movements were hostile to the church and thus to the faith.[12]

If Merton rejects this equation of church and kingdom, he also refuses to endorse two alternative positions; he is somewhat sympathetic to the motives and ideals of those who, in their disillusion with the church's historical failure to incarnate the gospel, look to other movements and ideologies to accomplish what the church could not, but he is profoundly skeptical of their conclusion, the perception that "the progressives and revolutionaries of 'the world' have unconsciously hit upon the right answers and are building the Kingdom of God where the Church has failed to do so" (*CGB* 42).[13] According to this "false Christian optimism which tries to 'experience' the Kingdom in what is not the Kingdom" (*DWL* 27), the duty of a modern Christian is to embrace the revolutionary agenda in the hope that the church will be allowed a place in the new age. The problem with this discovery of the kingdom in secular garb, of course, (besides its complete subsuming of the religious into the political) is that it simply substitutes another institution or social movement, one with perhaps a much less developed moral sensitivity, for the church, with the result that the same self-righteousness, the same justification of coercion, appears in a new guise. Merton looks askance at those, including some Catholics, whose critique of "western capitalism" leads them to turn east, "to dream of a Constantine in Moscow and a new Muscovite Christian Kingdom of God! As if," Merton sardonically notes, "this were a *new* dream!" (*TTW* 274). He is equally unconvinced by the much more common, albeit unformulated, assumption that "the 'Western' realm of America [is] the heir of the Holy Roman Empire" (*TTW* 273), the latest embodiment of the kingdom: any such attempt to identify God's reign with human structures

---

[12] See also Merton's endorsement of Rudolf Bultmann's emphasis on grace (*DWL* 59), where he rejects the hope "that the Church will become once again a world power and a dominant institution" in favor of the hope that "the Spirit will shake the world when Christians have lost what they held on to and have entered into the eschatological kingdom—where in fact they already are!" For a somewhat expanded version of this passage, see Thomas Merton, *A Vow of Conversation: Journals 1964–1965*, ed. Naomi Burton Stone (New York: Farrar, Straus, Giroux, 1988) 9–10.

[13] See also *CGB* 108–9, *FV* 69.

and institutions, whether it be "holy Russia" or an American "City on a Hill," is ultimately an expression of idolatrous confusion—a temptation to glorify, even worship, the work of human hands.

But Merton is equally critical of those whose recognition of the church's shortcomings posits a disjunction between church and kingdom by simply excluding the kingdom from space and time or turning it into a purely private reign of God over the individual human soul. This attitude fosters its own type of complacency, since it releases Christians from any obligation to make the kingdom incarnate in their own lives. If one way "to evade the responsibilities of a Christian in history" is "by saying that the kingdom has arrived and medieval Christendom is/was the kingdom," another way "to do the same" is "by saying the kingdom will arrive only at the end of, or outside of time" (*TTW* 274). If this were the case, one would enter the kingdom only by transcending the world of history, a world irremediably tainted by sin, in order to be drawn into a timeless supernatural sphere, whether imaged as heavenly immortality or as the innermost recesses of the heart where God already reigns. Such views are based, Merton maintains, on a radically inadequate understanding of the gospel message of the kingdom. While "the genuine Christian spirit must *necessarily* resist the identification of the Kingdom of God with a limited human society" (*TTW* 274), it must also recognize and affirm that the vocation of the Christian community and each of its members is to be an epiphany of the kingdom, a sign of the kingdom's transforming presence and an instrument of its further unfolding. While the church cannot be simply identified with the kingdom, the kingdom, the full expression of God's will for creation, is both its origin and its goal. The church in its concrete existence is always an incomplete and inadequate manifestation of the kingdom, but it is called to recommit itself continually to witnessing to the truth of Jesus' proclamation that the reign of God is at hand. The church affirms both the immanence of the kingdom, its present reality, and the eschatological character of the kingdom, its future fulfillment.[14] The church participates in the identity of the kingdom, which nonetheless always transcends the confines of the church. Thus the

---

[14] For the fruitful tension between present and future dimensions of the kingdom, see *SCel* 48, 61.

Christian community cannot rest in a static, complacent claim to embody the kingdom but is continually summoned to move with humility and with confidence toward an ever deeper yet never perfected incarnation of the essential values that constitute God's reign, to model the love and peace and unity that are God's will for history.[15]

Christians are empowered to be signs and instruments of the kingdom through the gift of the Holy Spirit sent by the risen and glorified Jesus. According to Merton the fundamental (though by no means the exclusive) way in which the Spirit is encountered and received is through the liturgical and sacramental life of the church, which draws the believer into the mystery of Christ's death and resurrection. "The idea of 'rebirth' out of life as a 'new man in Christ, in the Spirit,' of a 'new life' in the Mystery of Christ, or in the Kingdom of God, is fundamental to Christian theology and practice—it is, after all, the whole meaning of baptism" (*CWA* 206).[16] By dying to the old, sinful self and putting on Christ, one experiences the present reality of the kingdom and is commissioned, simply by the way one lives one's life, to make the reign of God available to others. This of course is not the mission of individuals but of the community of faith, for in baptism one becomes a member of the Body of Christ. What is surrendered in baptism is a "delusive, individual autonomy" and what is given in its stead is the realization that one's deepest identity is Christ, an identity shared by all who have made the same profession of faith. The fundamental hope of the Christian, Merton affirms, is "that by His Spirit, which is the Spirit and Life of His Church, He will live and act in me, and, having become one with Him, having found my true identity in Him, I will act only as a member of His Body and a faithful citizen of His Kingdom" (*CGB* 100). One of the principal fruits of contemporary liturgical renewal, in Merton's view, is a restored awareness of this communal and "political" (in the

---

[15] For a discussion of the "dynamism of patient and secret growth" of the kingdom in the gospels and the early church, see *FV* 17–18, and for an "active and dynamic view of the Kingdom of Christ," see *NM* 155.

[16] See also the discussion of baptism as entering into "the mystery of Christ—the Kingdom of God" in Thomas Merton, *Life and Holiness* (New York: Herder and Herder, 1963) 78 (subsequent references will be cited as "*LH*" parenthetically in the text).

broadest sense) dimension of Christian faith. Baptism must be seen not merely as an individualistic cleansing from the effects of sin but as a response "to the personal vocation, the call of Christ to enter into the Christian *polis* and to labor together with the other members of the Church to establish the reign of Christ's holiness, of the Holy Spirit, upon the earth, and to strive to bring all other men together with himself into eternal life" (*SCel* 7–8).

It is this commitment that is, or should be, renewed whenever Christians assemble to proclaim their faith and honor their Lord. "Liturgy," Merton writes, "is the celebration of our unity in the Redemptive Love and Mystery of Christ. It is the expression of the self-awareness of a redeemed people. If the people themselves are not aware of their status and of their nobility as sons of God in Christ, how can they convincingly affirm and exercise their full spiritual rights as citizens in the Kingdom of God?" (*SCel* 2–3). Thus liturgy properly heightens the community's awareness of its oneness in and through Christ, in order that it can make the love on which that unity is founded active and effective in the wider world.

Liturgy, Merton insists, is a fundamentally public activity. The Eucharist, above all, is the event in which the present reality of the kingdom is celebrated and the responsibility to spread the good news of the kingdom is reaffirmed. The Eucharist is fundamentally the work of Christ, a re-presentation of the salvific work of cross and resurrection: "It is the mystery in which Christ Himself, invisibly present in the midst of His faithful, spontaneously assisted by their free and sanctified love, and acclaimed by their unanimous consent, accomplishes His work of Redemption, announcing the full establishment of His Kingdom and sharing with all the fruits of salvation" (*SCel* 8). To receive communion is to participate fully in the paschal victory that definitively establishes God's reign: "Liturgy is a ritual participation in the death of Christ (by which all our sins are expiated) and in His glorious Resurrection (by which His divine life is made our own) and in His Ascension (by which we enter with Him into heaven and sit at the right hand of the Father). We who offer the Holy Sacrifice and who receive into our hearts the Body and Blood of the Savior are building the Kingdom of Heaven on earth and in history" (*SCel* 133). While the kingdom remains hidden, "possessed only in the darkness of faith and hope" (*SCel* 133), the vocation of those who become Christ's body by sharing Christ's body is to bring what is hidden to light, "to enter into the confusion of the world bearing something of the light of Truth in our hearts, and . . . exercising something of the mysterious, transforming power of the Cross, of love and of sacrifice" (*SCel* 132).

Merton is not so naïve, of course, as to think that the Christian community has been or will be completely faithful to this mission. The community and its members are called to an ongoing conversion, a recognition and confession of failure to live as citizens of the new creation, a death to self on ever deeper levels of one's being.[17] "The call to 'do penance' is based not on the fact that penance will keep us in trim, but on the fact that 'the Kingdom of Heaven is at hand.' Our penance—*metanoia*—is our response to the proclamation of the Gospel message, the *Kerygma* which announces our salvation if we will hear God and not harden our hearts" (*SCel* 130). This repentance must not be envisioned simply as a way of removing guilt and avoiding judgment but as an empowerment "to obey the will of God commanding us to take our place in time, in history and in the work of building His Kingdom of Love and Truth" (*SCel* 138).

Thus the whole liturgical and sacramental life of the church is fundamentally oriented toward the proclamation and experience of the reign of God. This does not mean that Merton would restrict the working of the Spirit, and so the presence of the kingdom, to the formal activity of the church: "the objective immensity and power of the Kingdom that is established, in mystery" may be glimpsed beyond the boundaries of the church, for God's Spirit blows where it wills. There is a "great unknown liturgy that goes up to God from the darkness of the world in which the Kingdom is denied. Its citizens perhaps do not even know for sure of what Kingdom they are citizens, yet they suffer for God and the Word triumphs in them, and through them man will once again be, in Christ, the perfect Ikon of god [*sic*]" (*SS* 143). In his own experience of "simple and human dialogue with Pasternak and a few others like him," even those with no affiliation

---

[17] For a discussion of the history of the church as filled with failures to witness to the kingdom, see *SCel* 100, and Thomas Merton, *Disputed Questions* (New York: Farrar, Straus & Cudahy, 1960) 141 (subsequent references will be cited as "*DQ*" parenthetically in the text).

with the Christian church, Merton claims to have experienced "the true Kingdom of God, which is still so clearly, and evidently, 'in the midst of us'" (*SS* 225). Yet encounters with the kingdom beyond the boundaries of the church do not lessen the responsibility of those within the church to serve as the primary witnesses of the good news that the reign of God is at hand, and to call the world to conversion and fidelity by their own faithfulness to the message they proclaim.

For Merton, the reality of the kingdom is at the heart of both the contemplative and the active dimensions of the Christian life. As an experience of the divine presence and a foretaste of eternal union with God, contemplation is a way of participating in the kingdom: "because my faith is eschatological," Merton writes in his journal, "it is *also* contemplative, for I am even now in the Kingdom and I can even now see something of the glory of the Kingdom and praise Him who is King" (*DWL* 182).[18] It is through the presence of the Holy Spirit that this "union of contemplation and eschatology" is brought about, for in the Spirit, the firstfruits of resurrected life, "that Truth which is the end" is already disclosed: "we are already fully and eternally alive. Contemplation is the loving sense of this life and this presence and this eternity." While contemplative realization does not exclude the desire to be plunged ever more deeply into the infinite spring of trinitarian love, by providing a taste of that supreme reality, a "realization and 'experience' of the lifegiving Spirit in Whom the Father is present to us through the Son, our way, truth, and life" (*DWL* 182), it serves as a corrective to all attempts to domesticate the Spirit and co-opt the vision and language of the kingdom for limited and transitory goals. "Without contemplation and interior prayer the Church . . . will be reduced to being the servant of cynical and worldly powers, no matter how hard her faithful may protest that they are fighting for the Kingdom of God" (*CPr* 144). Contemplation provides the discernment that keeps present action from substituting its own ends

---

[18] For association of the kingdom with New Testament teaching on prayer, see *LH* 105; for entry into the kingdom through "fidelity to meditation," see Thomas Merton, *Contemplative Prayer* (New York: Herder and Herder, 1969) 40–41 (subsequent references will he cited as "*CPr*" parenthetically in the text).

for those of God's reign. Without "deep, powerful and pure" prayer, "filled at all times with the spirit of contemplation," Merton believes, "Christian apostolic activity" will be riddled with compromises and marred by self-interest and self-deception; it will be motivated by fear of failure, or by a desire for measurable results, rather than by selfless love. But contemplation not only serves as a guard against false or inadequate expressions of the kingdom but acts as invitation and encouragement for authentic incarnation of the kingdom. "The most important need in the Christian world today," Merton writes, "is this inner truth nourished by this Spirit of contemplation: the praise and love of God, the longing for the coming of Christ, the thirst for the manifestation of God's glory, his truth, his justice, his Kingdom in the world. These are all characteristically 'contemplative' and eschatological aspirations of the Christian heart" (*CPr* 144).[19]

Merton goes on to add that these aspirations "are the very essence of monastic prayer" (*CPr* 144). The purpose of monastic life is to serve as a privileged, though by no means exclusive, witness to the contemplative and eschatological dynamism of the church as a whole. "The monastic life," when it is truly faithful to its essential charism, "is alive with the eschatological mystery of the kingdom already shared and realized in the lives of those who have heard the Word of God and have surrendered unconditionally to its demands in a vocation that (even when communal) has a distinctly 'desert' quality" (*CWA* 199).[20] As with the church as a whole, the monastery will not fulfill this role as eschatological sign simply by its institutional functioning. It too must have a dynamic rather than a static relationship to the kingdom: "The monastic community does not effectively act as a sign of God's presence and of His kingdom merely by the fulfillment of certain symbolic functions" (*CWA* 207). Whenever the charismatic freedom of the contemplative is replaced by "an organizational

---

[19] See also Merton's discussion of the "eschatological" dimension of final or "transcultural" human integration: "The rebirth of man and of society on a transcultural level is a rebirth into the transformed and redeemed time, the time of the Kingdom, the time of the Spirit, the time of 'the end'" (*CWA* 216). For further discussion, see chapter 9 below.

[20] See also *SD* 219, *CWA* 201, 219.

mystique, so that in effect it is the institution itself that becomes definitive," there is a danger of confusing means with ends, of considering the structures or rules "as the incarnation of God's definitive truth, as the practical realization of the Kingdom" (*CWA* 193). But this is to try to possess and control what by its very nature remains perpetually a gift, a grace that can only be fruitful when it is received with wonder and humility and gratitude. If the monk is one who "sees and experiences the Kingdom of Promise as already fulfilled" (*CWA* 188), it is not due to formal arrangements, for example, those which "keep the monks strictly enclosed and remote from all external activity—this does not by itself constitute a sign of the eschatological kingdom" (*CWA* 207-8); rather, it is the spiritual gift of charismatic solitude that makes possible "a recovery of paradisal simplicity, of wilderness obedience and trust, and an anticipated completion in blessed light" (*CWA* 188).[21] It is this dynamic, indefinable "eschatological gift" that Merton associates with his own life in the hermitage: "I have never before really seen what it means to live in the new creation and in the Kingdom. Impossible to explain it. If I tried I would be unfaithful to the grace of it—for I would be setting limits to it. It is *limitless*, without determination, without definition. It is what you make of it each day, in response to the Holy Spirit" (*DWL* 276).[22] If such a "kingdom existence" cannot be defined or explained, the terms Merton associates with it—gift, grace, limitless, Holy Spirit—nevertheless reveal its essential qualities.

If in contemplation the kingdom as gift is experienced, Christian action carries out the responsibility of discipleship to make the reality of the kingdom more evident in the world: "The Kingdom is already established; the Kingdom is a present reality. But there is still work to be done. Christ calls us to work together in building his Kingdom. We cooperate with him in bringing it to perfection."[23] In what does

---

[21] See also Merton's discussion of the witness of the eremitical life as contributing to others' "awareness that the Kingdom of Christ is in the midst of us" (*CWA* 250).

[22] See also *TTW* 108, *DWL* 335.

[23] Thomas Merton, *He Is Risen* (Niles, IL: Argus, 1975) 9; see also *DQ* 141–42, *LH* 112.

this work consist? Merton looks to the great judgment scene of Matthew 25 for the most concise and meaningful answer: "Those who have fed the hungry and given drink to the thirsty, given shelter to the stranger, visited the sick and the prisoner, are taken into the kingdom, for they did all these things to Christ himself" (*LH* 115). To see and serve Christ in, and to be Christ for, other people, particularly those who are most neglected and despised, is to live the will of God for humanity, to allow God to reign on earth as in heaven. It is to counter the alienation and fragmentation of the human family in its fallen state with a commitment to model and extend the unity and solidarity intended by God. To live in the kingdom of God is to live the redeemed life here and now and so to make evident to all the salvation won by Christ. For Merton, "The task of the Christian in our time is the same as it has always been: to build the Kingdom of God in the world. To manifest Christ in individuals and in society—or rather to allow the Savior to manifest His hidden presence in the world by the charity and unity, in one Body, of those He came to save" (*DQ* 127).[24] The fact that the Christian community has all too often been unfaithful to this charge is no reason to question its validity: it is rather an invitation to continued repentance, deeper reliance on the working of the Spirit, and renewed commitment to act as God's instruments in the ongoing task of transforming the world.

While the kingdom has been definitively established in the life, death, and resurrection of Jesus, in its temporal, human dimension it is always partial and provisional: "the earthly manifestation of the Kingdom of God is still only a shadow of the eternal Kingdom that is to come" (*DQ* 127).[25] But the realization that the perfection of God's reign will come only in God's good time "cannot be made into a pretext for ignoring the temporal happiness and welfare of man in the present life" (*DQ* 127); whatever protects and enhances the essential dignity of human beings, made in the divine image, conforms

---

[24] See also the discussion of the purpose of love as "not merely . . . 'saving man's soul' as an individual" but as "establishing in time the eternal kingdom of God" (*DQ* 99).

[25] See also the discussion of the expectation of "the full revelation of the Glory and the Reign of Christ" (*CGB* 112) and Merton's comments, in connection with his reading of Karl Barth, on the necessity to "wait patiently for the Kingdom" (*CGB* 311).

to God's will for creation and therefore contributes to the revelation of God's reign. To identify the kingdom of God as "a society that is based entirely on freedom and love . . . founded on respect for the individual person" (*DQ* 142), or as "the unity of all men in peace, creativity and love" (*DQ* xii), is to see that modeling, defending, and extending these values, and resisting all forces that deny or restrict them, constitutes action on behalf of the kingdom.[26] Belief in the present reality of the kingdom is not a naïvely optimistic refusal to acknowledge the power and pervasiveness of evil in the world, but a willingness to confront the power of evil, of hatred and oppression and injustice and death, with the power of Christ's redemptive love, which in his passion endured the utmost that human sinfulness could inflict, and in his resurrection proved that life and love are the ultimate reality. To witness to the kingdom is "to seek some way of giving the mercy and the compassion of Christ a social, even a political, dimension." Having experienced the mercy of God themselves, Christians are called not to judge or condemn others but to witness to the possibility of conversion and transformation by remaining faithful to the way of Christ in all circumstances. Though the goal, the full revelation of the kingdom, remains in the future, the end is already present in the means: "the Kingdom of God . . . demands to be typified and prepared by such forms of heroic social witness that make Christian mercy plain and evident in the world" (*L&L* 218–19).

For this reason, a commitment to nonviolent resistance to evil becomes central to Merton's understanding of the kingdom, which is preeminently the reign of *shalom*. The first step is to accept the eschatological gift of Christ's peace as individuals and as a redeemed community. "The early Christians were filled with the conviction that since the Risen Christ had received Lordship over the whole cosmos and sent His Spirit to dwell in men (Acts 2:17) the kingdom of peace was already established in the Church" (*SD* 126). The very identity of the church depends on its members' commitment to live out the unity and mutual love of the messianic age among themselves and so to model God's will for all humanity. But the community of faith is called not only to be peaceful but to be peacemakers, to follow in the Lord's footsteps by bringing the message of reconciliation into a

---

[26] See also *NM* 48, *SD* 125, *CGB* 80, *L&L* 204.

fragmented, hostile, violent world, even, indeed especially, when that world may reject both message and messenger. This willingness to confront evil with no weapons but those of Jesus, the power of truth and love, is rooted in a profound trust that despite all evidence to the contrary, the Prince of Peace reigns: "the message of Christians [sic][27] is not that the kingdom 'might come, that peace might be established, but that the kingdom *is* come, and there *will* be peace for those who seek it'" (*TTW* 188). It is this eschatological hope, not some optimistic belief that enemies will become friends if only they are treated kindly, that is the true basis for Christian peacemaking: "Above all our confusions, our violence, our sin, God established His kingdom no matter what 'the world' may do about it" (*TTW* 188). The willingness of the nonviolent activist to affirm the dignity of all people, oppressed and oppressor alike, and to endure suffering and even death itself to defend that dignity, depends not on faith in the goodness of humanity but faith in the goodness of God, or rather faith in the potential goodness of every human being as created by and for God, even when some by their actions deny that goodness in themselves. As Jesus released the transforming power of the kingdom by fidelity to his mission of sacrificial, redemptive love, even in the face of hatred, rejection, and murderous violence, the Christian community and its members testify to the same transforming power operative in the world today by conforming to the pattern set by their Master, by taking up their crosses and following him, with no assurance of immediately observable results but with confidence of sharing in the mystery of the ultimate victory of love.

> The religious basis of Christian non-violence is this faith in Christ the redeemer and obedience to his demand to love and manifest himself in us by a certain manner of action in the world and in relation to other men. This obedience enables us to live as true citizens of the Kingdom, in which the divine mercy, the grace, favor and redeeming love of God are active in our lives. Then the Holy Spirit will indeed 'rest upon us' and act in us, not for our own good alone but for God and his Kingdom. (*FV* 16)[28]

---

[27] The reading probably should be "Christmas," as it is the journal entry for December 24.

[28] See also Merton's discussion of Christ's teaching "that war belonged to the world outside the Kingdom" (*SD* 128).

This survey of Merton's use of the scriptural image of the kingdom of God during the last decade of his life reveals it to be for him an immensely significant and effective way of articulating both the gifts and the responsibilities of life in Christ, of redeemed existence. The kingdom is a multidimensional yet unifying symbol that situates the present moment and the entire course of human history in relation to the once-for-all salvific action of Christ and the final eschatological completion of that action; it constitutes the intrinsic dynamism of the church yet cannot be controlled by, contained in, or restricted to the church; it summons Christians to contemplation and to action as complementary and mutually supportive ways of participating in and revealing its presence; it is both ineffably mysterious in its divine depths and starkly practical in its concrete demands. For Merton, as for the entire tradition of Christianity, the kingdom is the secret hidden in the heart of creation that gives meaning and direction to all that is of permanent value in human life: "The world was created without man, but the new creation which is the true Kingdom of God is to be the work of God in and through man. It is to be the great, mysterious, theandric work of the Mystical Christ, the New Adam, in whom all men as 'one Person' or one 'Son of God' will transfigure the cosmos and offer it resplendent to the Father" (*ZBA* 132).

"What I Wear Is Pants":
"Lay" Spirituality and Monastic Reform

In his correspondence with Rosemary Radford Ruether, we find Thomas Merton making some rather disconcerting comments about his life as a hermit. The solitude he had sought for years as the fulfillment of his monastic vocation now seems to be presented virtually as a repudiation of that vocation. On February 14, 1967, he writes, "I am in a position where l am practically laicized and de-institutionalized, and living like all the other old bats who live alone in the hills in this part of the country and I feel like a human being again. My hermit life is expressly a *lay* life. I never wear the habit except when at the monastery and I try to be as much on my own as I can and like the people around the country."[1] Three weeks later, he refers again to his "'secularized' existence as a hermit" and explains, "I am not only leading a more 'worldly' life (me and the rabbits), but am subtly infecting the monastery with worldly ideas" (*HGL* 505; *AHW* 38) through, he may mean, his weekly talks to the community on political and literary topics. Such remarks may be interpreted as an expression

---

[1] Thomas Merton, *The Hidden Ground of Love: Letters on Religious Experience and Social Concerns*, ed. William H. Shannon (New York: Farrar, Straus, Giroux, 1985) 501 (subsequent references will be cited as "*HGL*" parenthetically in the text); the same letter is also found in Thomas Merton and Rosemary Radford Ruether, *At Home in the World: The Letters of Thomas Merton & Rosemary Radford Ruether*, ed. Mary Tardiff (Maryknoll, NY: Orbis, 1995) 23 (subsequent references will be cited as "*AHW*" parenthetically in the text).

of Merton's disillusion with institutionalized monastic life in general and with the Gethsemani community in particular, or as a rather disingenuous, even somewhat duplicitous, attempt to justify his present vocation to a particularly fierce critic of monasticism.[2] Both of these motives are no doubt present to some extent. But underlying the disillusion and/or the defensiveness there may be a more complex, and ultimately more satisfying, explanation for Merton's use of this sort of language: his studies and his own experience had convinced him that a "lay" spirituality was not only compatible with monasticism but from a certain perspective was an integral part of monastic history and identity.

Such a proposal may initially strike one as illogical if not absurd: lay and monastic states would seem to be polar opposites, mutually exclusive, and in one sense they certainly are. By definition, and canon law, the vowed religious life is distinguished from the lay, secular state, and monks are religious par excellence. But "lay" can also be used to contrast with "clerical," a state which is by no means identical with "religious," though in popular perception they are easily confused. Merton himself makes note of the difference and

---

[2] Though Ruether's criticism of monastic "withdrawal" is intense, particularly in the early letters to Merton (see the letter of early March, 1967 [*AHW* 27–30]), in a generally overlooked article entitled "Monks and Marxists: A Look at the Catholic Left" (*Christianity and Crisis* 33:7 [April 30, 1973] 75–79; reprinted with an introduction by Patrick F. O'Connell in *The Merton Annual* 35 (2022) 71–84), she explicitly credits the "monastic spirituality of Thomas Merton" (along with Dorothy Day and the Catholic Worker movement) with being at the root of U.S. Catholic involvement in work for peace and justice; see particularly *MA* 35.77–78: "Here it was the probing mind of Thomas Merton that provided the hermeneutic for the spirituality taking place in Dan Berrigan, Jim Forest, Jim Douglas [*sic*] and others. In retreats at Gethsemane [*sic*], through his writings and voluminous correspondence, Merton helped to form a spirituality that transformed prayer into protest, contemplation into resistance to the powers and principalities of a murderous world. . . . Thus, in the monastic spirituality of Thomas Merton, traditional Christian rejection of 'this world' took on new and concrete meaning, not as a struggle against flesh and blood, but as a struggle against the powers and principalities of the great empires, with America as their most recent representative. Here monastic spirituality was reconnected with its apocalyptic root." Ruether goes on to compare this personalistic, "prophetic" stance with the more praxis-oriented, Marxist-influenced approach found in Latin America and elsewhere (what would come to be known as liberation theology), using each to critique what she perceives as the shortcomings of the other.

indicates its significance for a proper understanding of monastic life in reflecting on Dietrich Bonhoeffer's *Letters and Papers from Prison*, which he calls "very monastic in their own way." By this surprising statement he apparently means that Bonhoeffer's vision of "religionless Christianity," which does not publicly call attention to itself, has a dimension of hiddenness comparable to the "desert" quality of monasticism. "His 'worldliness,'" Merton continues, "can only be understood in the light of this 'monastic' seriousness, which is, however, not . . . a withdrawal, a denial. It is a mode of presence." He concludes his reflection by aligning monasticism with this stance rather than a more public, ecclesiastical witness: "Paradoxically, then, Bonhoeffer's mode of unnoticed presence in the world is basically monastic as opposed to the 'clerical' or 'priestly' presence, which is official, draws attention to itself and issues its formal message of institutional triumph."[3] Thus if the term "lay" is contrasted not with "religious" but with "clerical," it would seem that Merton is locating monasticism on the "lay" side of the division, where it is well situated, not incidentally, to enter into dialogue not only with the "secular" Christianity of a Bonhoeffer but with persons of other faiths, or even of no religious faith at all.

---

[3] Thomas Merton, *A Vow of Conversation: Journals 1964–1965*, ed. Naomi Burton Stone (New York: Farrar, Straus, Giroux, 1988) 65–66 (subsequent references will be cited as *"VC"* parenthetically in the text); a slightly different version of this passage is found in Thomas Merton, *Dancing in the Water of Life: Seeking Peace in the Hermitage. Journals, vol. 5: 1963–1965*, ed. Robert E. Daggy (San Francisco: HarperCollins, 1997) 129 (subsequent references will be cited as *"DWL"* parenthetically in the text). In *Contemplation in a World of Action* (Garden City, NY: Doubleday, 1971) (subsequent references will be cited as *"CWA"* parenthetically in the text), Merton relates this "monastic" dimension of Bonhoeffer's thought to his imprisonment: "Bonhoeffer, regarded as an opponent of all that monasticism stands for, himself realized the need for certain 'monastic' conditions in order to maintain a true perspective in and on the world. He developed these ideas when he was awaiting his execution in a Nazi prison" (7–8). Reflecting on Bonhoeffer's *Ethics* in his *Reading Notebook #16*, from the second half of 1965, Merton writes, "The monk originally *broke out* of the clerical 'space' of the Church. To roam in the desert, the ultimate of the world, the place relegated to the devil—to restore the desert to condition of paradise—by showing it is *not* a space belonging to the devil. This is the real spirit of Vatican II—as opposed to Vat I, etc., when this was not at all clear yet" (48).

I

The foundation for this position is not merely eccentric or idiosyncratic personal preference or practice on Merton's part. It is a conclusion grounded in his study of monastic origins. He notes, "The monk was originally a layman (priests were exceptional) who lived alone in the desert outside the framework of any institution, even of the Christian and Ecclesial institution."[4] This statement should not be taken to imply a separation from the wider church, but simply that the monk's participation in the church does not consist in fulfilling a specific organizational role.[5] "Christian solitude," Merton empha-

---

[4] CWA 239; see also Thomas Merton, *The Inner Experience: Notes on Contemplation*, ed. William H. Shannon (San Francisco: HarperCollins, 2003) 145: "the first monks of all, the Egyptian desert Fathers, the pioneers of the monastic and contemplative lives, were *lay people*." In *A History of Christian Spirituality* I: *The Spirituality of the New Testament and the Fathers* (1960; trans. Mary P. Ryan [London: Burns & Oates, 1963]), Louis Bouyer writes: "The monk was simply a Christian, and, more precisely, a devout layman, who limited himself to taking the most radical means to make his Christianity integral" (317) (subsequent references will be cited as "Bouyer, *History*" parenthetically in the text). In his authoritative history of early monasticism, *The Desert a City: An Introduction to the Study of Egyptian and Palestinian Monasticism under the Christian Empire* (Oxford: Blackwell, 1966), Derwas J. Chitty likewise refers to the lay character of early monasticism: about the first major figure of monasticism, he writes, "Antony was an illiterate layman, and the majority of the Egyptian monks were much the same" (86), and summarizes, "At the beginning of that period, the monastic movement was a new enterprise, a lay movement with no literature but Holy Scripture—a determination, in renunciation of the world, to live the full evangelical life, whether in solitude or community" (179) (subsequent references will be cited as "Chitty" parenthetically in the text). (Merton was familiar with both of these works: Bouyer is repeatedly cited in his 1961 monastic conferences: see Thomas Merton, *An Introduction to Christian Mysticism: Initiation into the Monastic Tradition* 3, ed. Patrick F. O'Connell [Kalamazoo, MI: Cistercian Publications, 2008] 26, 32, 49, 59, 67, 69–71, 98, 104; Chitty is quoted on p. 135 of *Reading Notebook #24*, from late May 1967; N.B. *contra* Chitty's reference here, it is now generally accepted that Anthony was literate and that the letters attributed to him are genuine: see *The Letters of St. Antony the Great*, trans. Derwas J. Chitty [Fairacres, Oxford, UK: SLG Press, 1975]; Samuel Rubenson, *The Letters of St. Antony: Monasticism and the Making of a Saint* [Minneapolis: Fortress, 1995]).

[5] See the opening words of the preface to Louis Bouyer's *The Meaning of the Monastic Life*, trans. Kathleen Pond (New York: P. J. Kenedy, 1955) (subsequent references will be cited as "Bouyer, *Meaning*" parenthetically in the text), a work that Merton himself called "fundamental" and "standard" (Thomas Merton, *The School of Charity: Letters on Religious Renewal and Spiritual Direction*, ed. Brother

sizes, is "essentially an expression of the mystery of the Church, even when in some sense it implies a certain freedom from institutional structures."[6] But this "freedom is never a freedom *from* the Church but always a freedom *in* the Church and a contribution to the Church's own charismatic heritage" (*CWA* 251).

This charismatic dimension, the willingness to be led, like Jesus, by the Spirit into the desert, to allow all familiar roles and usual comforts and securities to be stripped away so that God alone might be one's sole protection and a child of God one's only identity, was the hallmark of primitive monasticism. "In the earliest days of desert monasticism," Merton writes, "there were no vows, no written rules, and institutional structure was kept at a minimum. The monastic commitment was taken with extreme and passionate seriousness, but this commitment was not protected by judicial sanctions or by institutional control."[7] Monastic formation depended on personal

---

Patrick Hart [New York: Farrar, Straus, Giroux, 1990] 119, 145 [subsequent references will be cited as "*SCh*" parenthetically in the text]): "The purpose of this book is primarily to point out to monks that their vocation in the Church is not, and never has been, a special vocation. The vocation of the monk is, but is no more than, the vocation of the baptized man. But it is the vocation of the baptized man carried, I would say, to the farthest limits of its irresistible demands" (ix); see likewise: "monastic life is nothing else, no more and no less, than a Christian life whose Christianity has penetrated every part of it. It is a Christian life which is completely open, without refusal or delay, to the Word, which opens itself and abandons itself to it" (13); and: "To be a monk, then, is simply to be an integral Christian" (22). Merton himself writes, "The monk is not defined by his task, his usefulness. In a certain sense he is supposed to be 'useless' because his mission is not to *do* this or that but to *be* a man of God. He does not live in order to exercise a specific function: his business is life itself" (*CWA* 7).

[6] *CWA* 251; for Merton, "to be called to a totally different mode of existence, outside of secular categories and *outside of the religious establishment* . . . is the very heart of monasticism" (*CWA* 23).

[7] *CWA* 191–92; see also the introduction to Thomas Merton, *The Wisdom of the Desert: Sayings from the Desert Fathers of the Fourth Century* (New York: New Directions, 1960) 15: "An Abbot was not then, as now, a canonically elected superior of a community, but any monk or hermit who had been tried by years in the desert and proved himself a servant of God" (subsequent references will be cited as "*WD*" parenthetically in the text). In *History*, Bouyer writes: "Later on, the canonists would tend to see [monasticism] only as a state of life, defined once for all by the vows. But at this stage, the vows were still unknown and the monastic life seemed, on the contrary, to be a commitment to detachments and correlative ascents which were to have no end here below" (308).

authority, "the charismatic authority of wisdom, experience and love,"[8] rather than formal office, on relationships rather than regulations: "There was strict obedience on the part of the novice who sought to reproduce in his own life all the actions and thoughts of his spiritual master or 'spiritual father.' But the spiritual father had been chosen freely because of his own experience and his evident charism of renunciation and vision."[9]

Of course such a situation could not continue indefinitely, and the institutionalization of monasticism was both inevitable and necessary, as Merton himself recognized, noting that "it must be admitted that communal structures have a value that must not be underestimated."[10] But he also consistently maintained that the structure was for the sake of the charism, not vice versa. To equate monasticism simply with adherence to a rule is to confuse means with ends, for the purpose of monastic life is to serve as a solitary witness to the essentially paschal character of Christian discipleship, conformity not to a system or to an official function but to the person of Christ: "His loneliness had a prophetic and mysterious quality, something almost in the nature of a sacramental sign, because it was a particular charismatic way of participating in the death and resurrection of Christ. . . . To confront the emptiness, the void, the apparent hopelessness of this desert and to encounter there the miracle of new life

---

[8] *WD* 5; in *Contemplation in a World of Action*, Merton cites the teaching of Anthony: "There was nothing to which they had to 'conform' except the secret, hidden, inscrutable will of God. . . . It is very significant that . . . the authority of St. Anthony is adduced for what is the basic principle of desert life: that God is the authority and that apart from His manifest will there are few or no principles" (6–7).

[9] *CWA* 192 (see also 271); in *History*, Bouyer writes: "In the beginning . . . the superior, or more precisely, the 'abbot,' that is, the spiritual father, was not a personage endowed with an official function: he was simply the perfected spiritual man. The anchorite whose anchoritism had been fruitful, so to say, made no difficulties about allowing other men to join him and consented willingly to communicate to them everything he had received in solitude. The 'abbots,' whose sayings and the examples that illustrate them are collected in the *Apophthegms*, were precisely this" (321).

[10] Thomas Merton, *Contemplative Prayer* (New York: Herder and Herder, 1969) 30–31(subsequent references will be cited as "*CPr*" parenthetically in the text); see also *CWA* 17, 25.

in Christ, the joy of eschatological hope already fulfilled in mystery—this was the monastic vocation" (*CWA* 239; see also *CWA* 10).

As he considered the history of religious life, Merton discovered repeated instances of a return to this more charismatic, lay-oriented approach, typically associated with a more eremitic style of life. The eleventh-century hermit movement is an impressive example of this renewal of the primitive monastic vision, which arose, as it would have to, outside the confines of institutional monasticism: "Lay people or secular clerics began to withdraw directly into solitude without passing through a period of monastic formation. Living in the woods and developing as best they could their own mode of life, they remained in rather close contact with the poor (that is, generally speaking, with their own class), with outlaws and outcasts and with the itinerants who were always numerous in the Middle Ages."[11] By their very withdrawal from the accepted roles of society, whether civil or ecclesial, these solitaries were paradoxically united in solidarity with those marginalized by the prevailing social structure: "Closely identified as the hermits were with the underprivileged, the oppressed and those for whom the official institutions of society showed little real concern, the nonmonastic hermitage quickly became a place of refuge for the desperately perplexed who sought guidance and hope—if not also a hiding place and physical safety. Thus the nonmonastic hermit by the very fact of his isolation from the world became open to the world in a new and special way" (*CWA* 261). Though the movement was "tamed," as it were, by the thirteenth century,[12] and "absorbed back into monasticism," its spirit continued to remain alive in such forms as the early Cistercian lay brotherhood, which "had something of an eremitical as well as a distinctly 'lay'

---

[11] *CWA* 261; Merton specifically mentions "the very significant lay-hermit movement in the eleventh-century—lay solitaries who were also itinerant preachers to the poor and to the outcasts who had no one to preach to them" in his March 9, 1967 letter to Ruether (*HGL* 504; *AHW* 37). Paradoxically, Merton notes in a February 26, 1966 entry in his *Reading Notebook* #17 that the hermit movement eventually became a catalyst for monastic ordination: "Historical point ordination of monks to priesthood became very common in 11th–12th centuries precisely in view of hermit life. Priest-hermit considered his mass primarily as the perfect means of uniting his sacrifice-passion with the Passion of Christ" (88).

[12] But see Merton's comments on the nonmonastic hermits of fourteenth-century England, of whom Richard Rolle is the most famous example (*CWA* 302).

character" (*CWA* 262), especially for those brothers who spent long periods of time in solitude on monastic lands outside the enclosure. But the most significant heirs of this charism were the early Franciscans, "nonmonastic and completely open to the world of the poor and outcast" (*CWA* 263), who were nevertheless, in Merton's judgment, the genuine exemplars in the Middle Ages of "the authentic freedom of early monasticism" (*CWA* 358). Merton suggests "that actually the ideal of St. Francis was more purely *monastic* in the true original primitive sense than the life lived by the big Benedictine and Cistercian communities of the thirteenth century where everything was so highly organized behind walls" (*CWA* 358). It is worth noting in this connection that Francis and many of his first followers were never ordained priests, that they claimed no name but Christian and no status but *fratres minores*, lesser brothers.

Thus when Merton refers to himself offhandedly in a letter to Ruether as "a tramp and not much else" (*HGL* 501; *AHW* 24) he is actually laying claim to a rich heritage of witness to the priority of gospel to law. When he tells the fellows at the Center for the Study of Democratic Institutions, just before departing for Asia, that "the monk should not be a priest," and even says, "I should not be a priest," adding, "I didn't want to be a priest, but it was part of the system, so I became one,"[13] this should be interpreted, I think, not as a rejection or denigration of his own priesthood,[14] which continued

---

[13] Thomas Merton, *Preview of the Asian Journey*, ed. Walter H. Capps (New York: Crossroad, 1989) 49 (subsequent references will be cited as "*PAJ*" parenthetically in the text); see also the reference to the "Primitive Benedictine" foundations that returned to "a community of simple monks in one class, only a few of whom were priests" (*CWA* 11). In *Reading Notebook #14* (undated, but evidently from the mid-1960s since it includes drafts of poems that would be incorporated into Merton's *Cables to the Ace*), Merton quotes from an unpublished conference given by Edward Schillebeeckx: "Monasticism is not situated on a functional level, either lay or priestly. It is solely a taking after God. And in the measure that monks lose sight of this & accept an apostolic ministry, in the measure that they seek to found a monastic life on the priesthood & to orient their spirituality in this way, then monks deviate from their state, deviate from monasticism. And so the Church is at the same time more & more deprived of a state of which she has great need—pure monasticism" (75).

[14] His statement here certainly does not correspond to his journal entries at the time of his ordination: see Thomas Merton, *Entering the Silence: Becoming a Monk and Writer. Journals, vol. 2: 1941–1952*, ed. Jonathan Montaldo (San Francisco:

to be an integral and valued part of his spirituality throughout the hermitage years and right up to the time of his death, but as the recognition of a confusion of roles, an institutionalizing of the charismatic, a clericalizing of what was originally and essentially a lay movement.[15] As he explained during this dialogue, "The monk is a

---

HarperCollins, 1996) 314–22; Thomas Merton, *The Sign of Jonas* (New York: Harcourt, Brace, 1953) 190–96, 198–99, and particularly the Introduction to Part Four, "*To the Altar of God*" (181–83), where he calls his ordination "*the one great secret for which I had been born*" (181). See also "The White Pebble" in Thomas Merton, *Selected Essays*, ed. Patrick F. O'Connell (Maryknoll, NY: Orbis, 2013) 3–14, and his poem "*Senescente Mundo*" in Thomas Merton, *The Tears of the Blind Lions* (New York: New Directions, 1949) 31–32; Thomas Merton, *The Collected Poems of Thomas Merton* (New York: New Directions, 1977) 221–22 (subsequent references will be cited as "*CP*" parenthetically in the text) (for a discussion, see Patrick F. O'Connell, "Old World, New Priest: Thomas Merton's '*Senescente Mundo*,'" *The Merton Journal* 26.2 [Advent 2019] 3–12). Note also that the very last entry in Merton's journal, on December 8, 1968, refers to his celebration of Mass for the Feast of the Immaculate Conception at St. Louis Church in Bangkok (Thomas Merton, *The Other Side of the Mountain: The End of the Journey. Journals, vol. 7: 1967–1968*, ed. Patrick Hart [San Francisco: HarperCollins, 1998] 329); Thomas Merton, *The Asian Journal*, ed. Naomi Burton Stone, Brother Patrick Hart, and James Laughlin (New York: New Directions, 1973) 254 (subsequent references will be cited as "*AJ*" parenthetically in the text).

[15] In *Meaning*, Bouyer writes: "If, in fact, at the present day, monks have become an important part of the clergy, such a circumstance, whatever proportions it may assume, remains accidental. All great monastic legislators, from St Benedict downwards, pass it over" (5); he later refers to the "gibe" found in the apophthegms of the Desert Fathers: "the two kinds of persons whom the monk must flee more than all others, it is said humorously, are bishops and women" (133; Merton himself refers to "Desert Fathers" who "fled from bishops" in his correspondence with Ronald Roloff, OSB [*SCh* 155]); on a more serious note, Bouyer cites the teaching of the great Eastern Fathers: "we have only to read St John Chrysostom's *De Sacerdote*, or, if you prefer, the correspondence and poems of St Gregory Nazianzen to discover how acute the conflict created by a priestly vocation superimposed upon a monastic vocation, appeared to them" (165). Chitty notes that "Both Antony and Pachomius avoided ordination" and cites Pachomius's custom of "call[ing] in a priest of one of the neighbouring churches, not wishing any of the brethren to seek ordination—for . . . 'the beginning of the thought of love of command is ordination'" (Chitty 31, 23); see also the anecdotes of Macarius, who "moved to another village to escape enrolment in the clergy," and of Peter of Iberia, who, "getting wind" of plans to ordain him, "jumped down from a roof . . . and escaped" (temporarily, as it turned out) (13, 87); Merton translates a slightly different version of the former story as the last of the sayings in *WD* (79–81); see also the story of Abbot Isaac's efforts to avoid ordination (thwarted by an ass!) (*WD* 65).

layperson in the desert, who is not incorporated into the hierarchy. The monk has nothing to do with the establishment."[16] In calling attention to the "lay" character of his life as a hermit, then, Merton was not expressing a simple rejection of monasticism but claiming

---

[16] *PAJ* 49. Merton's most extensive consideration of early monasticism and ordination comes in *Reading Notebook #57*, in his notes on the sixth chapter of Adalbert de Vogüé's *La Communauté et Abbé dans la Règle de saint Benôit* (Paris-Brussels: Desclée-de-Brouwer, 1961); Merton summarizes de Vogüé's findings that both the Rule of Benedict and the earlier *Regula Magistri* are "suspicious of priests" within the monastery, and he goes on to abstract eleven points drawn from the chapter, with extensive citation of primary sources, including: "Monks fly from priesthood as an *honor* . . . and as a distraction" (#5); "Refusals to cooperate in ordination or in exercise of priestly functions" (#6); "However—need of monastic priests for sacramental life of community" (#8); "Hence monks wanted a holy Abba to be also ordained priest—since he already exercised spiritual authority" (#9); "Still—in west the priest-abbot not common; certainly still doubtful that St Benedict consented to ordination" (#10). De Vogüé's overall position, very similar to that of Bouyer in *The Meaning of the Monastic Life*, is that monasticism is essentially a lay rather than a clerical vocation: "Priesthood and monasticism are two different things. The former is ordained for the government of the people of God, the latter consists of a break with the present world. . . . Monasticism is therefore in line with baptism. It is nothing else but a supreme effort to die with Christ and live in him, in other words to realize daily the sacramental action of baptism. It can therefore be said that monasticism is in line with the function of the laity. Not only is it not confined to clerics, but the tendency to solitude, which defines its nature, runs counter in principle to the pastoral vocation of the priest" (Adalbert de Vogüé, *Community and Abbot in the Rule of St Benedict*, trans. Charles Philippi and Ethel Rae Perkins, 2 vols., Cistercian Studies Series 5 [Kalamazoo, Ml: Cistercian Publications, 1988] 2.294–95). De Vogüé concludes his chapter by noting the relevance of this distinction between cleric and monk for contemporary monastic renewal: "the Rule provides a place for priesthood only in cases of real necessity. The priest-monk, far from constituting the ideal type of monk, is conceived rather as an anomaly, fraught with danger, but inevitable, of which efforts are made to mitigate the inconveniences by means of severe warnings. In our day, in a completely changed situation, these inconveniences no longer make themselves felt, but if the practice of general ordination to the priesthood has brought about their cessation, it has also created new difficulties, which the Benedictine Rule was not able to foresee. So it is true that monasticism, on the whole, cannot renounce its lay character without casting a slur on one of the essential features of its vocation" (*Community and Abbot* 2.303). Given Merton's extensive notes on this work, read in the early 1960s (*Reading Notebook #57* is undated, but the article cited immediately following the notes on de Vogüé was published in 1963), it is highly probable that it served as the principal source for Merton's comments on monasticism and priesthood, and indeed on the specifically lay character of monasticism in general.

the recovery of an important strand of authentic monastic and religious life.[17]

II

To affirm the "lay" dimension of monasticism is therefore to resist the temptation to equate one's identity with one's role, one's worth with one's status, the meaning of one's life with one's office. It means the rejection of all idealized projections and socially acceptable images of oneself, including even the image of monk. "The monk does not come into the desert to reinforce his own ego-image, but to be delivered from it" (*CWA* 285). Merton finds the truth of this insight exemplified in one of the stories of the Desert Fathers, in which a restless apprentice monk asks permission to go visit the sick, but is told by his spiritual father, his *abba*, to stay put in his cell. A clue to the meaning of the story, Merton notes, is the Greek word used for visiting the sick, *episkopein*, with its connotations of superiority and condescension: "'looking them over as if one were a bishop' we would be inclined to say" (*CWA* 254). It is a story about trying to find oneself, to affirm one's own worth, by adopting a conventionally approved role; the young man's motive for performing a work of charity, however admirable in itself, is to feel good about himself, but the wise elder refuses to allow his disciple to take refuge in this self-deception. Merton comments,

> Afflicted with boredom and hardly knowing what to do with himself, the disciple represents to himself a more fruitful and familiar way of life, in which he appears to himself to "be someone" and to have a fully recognizable and acceptable identity, a "place in the Church," but the Elder tells him that his place in the Church will never be found by following these ideas and

---

[17] For overviews of Merton's evolving understanding of monastic life, see Patrick F. O'Connell, "Hermit," "Monasticism," "Monk" in William H. Shannon, Christine M. Bochen, and Patrick F. O'Connell, *The Thomas Merton Encyclopedia* (Maryknoll, NY: Orbis, 2002) 195–97, 300–303, 306–309. Full-length studies include Lawrence S. Cunningham, *Thomas Merton & the Monastic Vision* (Grand Rapids, MI: Eerdmans, 1999), and Bonnie Thurston, *Shaped by the End You Live For: Thomas Merton's Monastic Spirituality* (Collegeville, MN: Liturgical Press, 2020).

> images of a plausible identity. Rather it is found by traveling a
> way that is new and disconcerting because it has never been
> imagined by us before, or at least we have never conceived it as
> useful or even credible for a true Christian—a way in which we
> seem to lose our identity and become nothing. (CWA 254)

The truth, of course, is that the self constructed according to social norms is not the self created in the image of God, and that false self must die in order for the authentic self, the mysterious, hidden identity known only to its Creator, to emerge. To call a monk a "lay" Christian is to recognize that at least one essential aspect of the monastic vocation is to be a standing warning that the very notion of an "official" Christian, a "professional" Christian, is in grave danger of confusing outward function with inner identity; it risks substituting appearance for reality. Both the cleric and the nonmonastic lay person need the monk as a salutary reminder that to be a Christian, a disciple, is not a matter of playing a role or of filling an office but of committing one's entire life to the person of Jesus.

This "lay" character also has a liberating aspect to it: the monk is not confined to a fixed role, a limited set of duties or obligations. The very nature of the monastic life, insofar as it is not "clerical," not provided with a definite niche in the ecclesial structure, testifies to the freedom of the Christian. Contrary to Martin Luther's critique, however accurate it may have been in the historical circumstances of his time,[18] monasticism is intended to be a sign of sheer grace, of salvation by faith, not works—by a person, not a system. According to Merton, "The monastic vocation is traditionally regarded as a charism of liberty in which the monk does not simply turn his back on the world, but on the contrary becomes free with the perfect freedom of the sons of God by virtue of the fact that, having followed Christ into the wilderness and shared in His temptations and sufferings, he can also follow Him wherever else He may go" (CWA 227; see also CWA 360–61). Such freedom is risky because it places the monk in the desert, "where the secure routines of man's city offer no support" (CPr 27), but it is precisely from these "secure routines," which stifle vitality and creativity and try to domesticate the Spirit

---

[18] See CWA 181–86 and 360–61 for a discussion of Luther and monasticism.

that blows where it wills, that one needs to be liberated: "The world needs men who are free from its demands, men who are not alienated by its servitudes in any way" (*CWA* 227). The monk is, or should be, such a person. In his final talk in Thailand, Merton goes so far as to define a monk as "essentially someone who takes up a critical attitude toward the world and its structures . . . somebody who says, in one way or another, that the claims of the world are fraudulent" (*AJ* 329).

Here, of course, the prophetic, countercultural dimension of the monastic life is evident. The monk "retains the eschatological privilege and duty of smashing idols—worldly, ecclesiastical, secular and even monastic" (*CWA* 189), because his detachment from all that is provisional and secondary allows him "to gaze steadily at the whole truth of Christ" (*CWA* 188) and so to reject the absolute claims that any institution or structure or authority makes about itself. The monk is one "who at once loves the world yet stands apart from it with a critical objectivity which refuses to become involved in its transient fashions and its more manifest absurdities" (*CWA* 227; see also *CWA* 8–9, 92–93). Hence Merton's description in Calcutta of the monk as "a marginal person . . . essentially outside of all establishments" (*AJ* 305), at the periphery of contemporary "mass society" with its tendency to depersonalize and dehumanize, yet thereby in a unique position not simply to withdraw from society but to offer it a challenging and life-affirming critique—the vision of a new humanism rooted in the dignity of the person as image of God.

If from one perspective—that of status, efficiency, productivity—the monk is marginal, from another he is at the very heart of the human enterprise. "The monk," Merton said in his final talk, "dwells in the center of society as one who has attained realization—he . . . has come to experience the ground of his own being in such a way that he knows the secret of liberation and can somehow communicate it to others" (*AJ* 333). In discovering his own true center, he is in communion with all other human beings through compassionate identification. The monk affirms authentic human values by incarnating them himself and by recognizing and defending them in others, especially when they are threatened or violated. "The monastic life today stands over against the world with a mission to affirm not only the message of salvation but also those most basic human values which the world most desperately needs to regain: personal integrity, inner peace, authenticity, inner depth, spiritual joy, the capacity to love, the capacity to enjoy God's creation and give thanks" (*CWA* 81). For Merton there is no conflict between these common human aspirations and a specifically Christian and monastic identity and vocation because the central Christian doctrines of creation, incarnation, and redemption are a repeated, ever-deepening revelation and affirmation of human dignity. "Monastic spirituality today," Merton believes, "must be a personalistic and Christian humanism that seeks and saves man's intimate truth, his personal identity, in order to consecrate it entirely to God" (*CWA* 82). It is more essential, in other words, to focus on how monks can contribute to the full humanization, which is also the divinization, of all people, than to stress what differentiates the monk from "the laity." While the monk participates in the project of human transformation in a unique way, the way of solitude and inner exploration, he is nevertheless participating in a project common to the entire *laos*, all the people of God. "What is essential in the monastic life," Merton declared on the last day of his life, "is not embedded in buildings, is not embedded in clothing, is not necessarily embedded even in a rule. It is . . . something deeper than a rule. It is concerned with this business of total inner transformation. All other things serve that end" (*AJ* 340).

III

It is in this context that Merton's concern for monastic renewal must be situated. The perennial temptation of monasticism is to substitute an alternate set of "secure routines" for those of the world, to make institutional structures rather than charismatic freedom the defining characteristic of monastic life. Comparing the contemporary monk with the Desert Fathers, Merton notes: "With us it is often rather a case of men leaving the society of the 'world' in order to fit themselves into another kind of society, that of the religious family which they enter. . . . The social 'norms' of a monastic family are also apt to be conventional, and to live by them does not involve a leap into the void—only a radical change of customs and standards" (*WD* 9–10). When monastic life becomes a form of security rather than a challenge to risk, to grow, to die and rise with Christ, it betrays its essential meaning.

An even more serious danger is that "The institution is identified with God, and becomes an end in itself" (*CWA* 19). This is, of course, a form of idolatry, in which the basic humanity of the individual is sacrificed to the requirements of the institution: "the monk is given to understand that there is no alternative for him but to regard this institutional life in all its detail, however arbitrary, however archaic, however meaningless to him, as the *only way* for him to be perfect in love and sincere in his quest for God" (*CWA* 19). The corollary of this approach is that the way of the nonmonastic world is often regarded as a corrupting system that must be rejected totally, as exemplified, for example, by "the rigid, authoritarian, self-righteous, ascetic" monk Ferrapont in Fyodor Dostoevsky's *The Brothers Karamazov*, "who delivers himself from the world by sheer effort, and then feels qualified to call down curses upon it."[19] By denying and rejecting the human element outside the monastery, one ends by suppressing and rejecting the humanity in oneself and in the monastic community.

While this temptation to reduce monasticism to its formal components is a perennial one, its consequences are particularly harmful in the contemporary period when the structure and routine are in large part relics of a past era with very little connection to the monks' former, "lay" lives. The problem is merely compounded when "updating" consists in adopting structures and practices of secular society that are basically depersonalizing: "if the monastery comes to resemble a big business and a plant surrounded by noise and clatter, the monks . . . will tend to be more and more alienated, taking refuge from routines in which they cannot take a serious human interest because they are the same impersonal and organized routines they left in the world" (*CWA* 81). Renewal cannot consist merely in the substitution of one set of structures for another: it must "concentrate on the *charism of the monastic vocation* rather than on the *structure of monastic institutions or the patterns of monastic observance*" (*CWA* 14). The recollection and recovery of the "lay" dimension of monastic

---

[19] *CPr* 30 (Merton calls Dostoevsky's monk "Therapont" here); it is Ferrapont's opposite, the Staretz Zossima, "the kind, compassionate man of prayer who identifies himself with the sinful world in order to call down God's blessing upon it," and whose "monastic spirit is charismatic rather than institutional," whom Merton sees as the model "in the present era of monastic renewal" (30–31).

history and identity function as a check on the tendency of structure to replace charism; it counteracts the temptation to substitute for a life of authentic human freedom a closed, self-sufficient "*societas perfecta*" which replaces and judges life in "the world."

IV

Merton's hermitage is a response to the dilemma of contemporary monasticism, which is of course his own dilemma as well. "Doubtless," he writes, "this can be seen as a perfecting of my monastic life and also as a final disillusionment with monastic life."[20] Ironically, it is a perfecting precisely by its recovery of some degree of the primitive "lay" freedom from the artificiality of structure and the tyranny of routine, which are of course the primary source of the disillusion.[21] His new life is an affirmation of his ordinariness: " 'Solitude' becomes for me less and less of a specialty, more and more just 'life' itself. I do not seek to 'be a solitary' or anything else, for 'being' anything is a distraction. It is enough to 'be' in an ordinary human mode with one's hunger and sleep, one's cold and warmth, rising and going to bed, putting on blankets and taking them off."[22] The simplicity here may be somewhat misleading. Merton's words echo, perhaps deliberately, D. T. Suzuki's concluding words in his dialogue with Merton about the Desert Fathers: "Q. What is Tao? (We may take Tao as meaning the ultimate truth or reality.) A. It is one's everyday mind. Q. What is one's everyday mind? A. When tired, you sleep; when hungry, you eat."[23] Merton's response puts the Zen master's paradox in a Christian context:

---

[20] *VC* 190; for a slightly different version of this passage, see *DWL* 256.

[21] In *CWA* Merton notes that Dom Jacques Winandy proposes a canonical separation of the eremitical life from the religious state, bringing it "closer to the lay state than to the status of religious or of monk" (295); while he himself is concerned, both theoretically and practically, "with the possibility of a renewal of eremitism within the religious state itself" (295), his recognition of the ambiguities of the hermit's position relative to the monastic community allows him both to define the hermit as "the monk par excellence" (296) and to call the "hermit life . . . expressly a lay life" (*HGL* 501; *AHW* 23).

[22] *VC* 192; for a slightly different version of this passage see *DWL* 257.

[23] Thomas Merton, *Zen and the Birds of Appetite* (New York: New Directions, 1968) 134 (subsequent references will be cited as "*ZBA*" parenthetically in the text).

> Christianity moves in an essentially historical dimension toward the "restoration of all things in Christ." Yet with Christ's conquest of death and the sending of the Holy Spirit that restoration has already been accomplished. What remains is for it to be made manifest. . . . To one who has seen it, the most obvious thing is to do what Dr. Suzuki suggests: to live one's ordinary life. In the words of the first Christians, to praise God and to take one's food "in simplicity of heart." The simplicity referred to here is the complete absence of all legalistic preoccupation about right and wrong ways of living. "When tired you sleep, when hungry you eat." (*ZBA* 138)

In this attentiveness to the ordinary, this mindfulness, revelation appears in the most unexpected places, as in the lovely final entry of *A Vow of Conversation*, the journal of Merton's entry into solitude, when Merton sees deer grazing near the hermitage:

> The thing that struck me most—when you look at them directly and in movement, you see what the primitive cave painters saw. Something you never see in a photograph. It is most awe-inspiring. The *muntu* or the "spirit" is shown in the running of the deer. The "deerness" that sums up everything and is sacred and marvelous. A contemplative intuition, yet this is perfectly ordinary, everyday seeing—what everybody ought to see all the time. The deer reveals to me something essential, not only in itself, but also in myself. Something beyond the trivialities of my everyday being, my individual existence. Something profound. The face of that which is both in the deer and in myself.[24]

In this experience is the proof that the Tao is indeed one's everyday mind, that the mystery of reality is hidden in the depths of the ordinary, that the contemplative vision is available to all, though few will notice. The gift of the hermitage for Merton himself, and his gift to others, is this overcoming of the dichotomy between the everyday and the transcendent.

> The voice of God is not clearly heard at every moment; and part of the "work of the cell" is *attention*, so that one may not miss any sound of that voice. What this means, therefore, is not only attention to inner grace but to external reality and to one's self

---

[24] *VC* 208; for a slightly different version of this passage, see *DWL* 291.

as a completely integrated part of that reality. Hence, this implies also a forgetfulness of oneself as totally apart from outer objects, standing back from outer objects; it demands an integration of one's own life in the stream of natural and human and cultural life of the moment.[25]

It demands a reappropriation of the fundamentally human capacity to encounter the sacred in the midst of the ordinary, which is authentically but not exclusively monastic. Far from isolating him from the rest of humanity, Merton's move to the hermitage had the effect of attuning him more sensitively and perceptively to the common needs and aspirations of every person, which he experienced in himself. The paradox of Merton's last years, which found him at once seeking and finding greater solitude and more in touch with the political, social, and cultural crises of the time, is resolved in his existential awareness of this integration of self and world as complementary, interpenetrating signs and instruments of the divine presence, concealed in plain sight.

V

Probably the most appealing, and most revealing, description of the "lay" character of Merton's solitary life is found in his essay *Day of a Stranger*, originally written, he tells us, "in answer to a request from a South American editor to describe a 'typical day' in my life."[26] The day chosen was in May 1965 when Merton was on the threshold

---

[25] *VC* 189; an earlier, less developed version of this passage is found in *DWL* 255.

[26] Quoted by Robert E. Daggy in his introduction to Thomas Merton, *Day of a Stranger* (Salt Lake City: Gibbs M. Smith, 1981) 7 (subsequent references will be cited as "*DS*" parenthetically in the text). It should be noted that the final version of this essay is considerably revised and expanded from the initial draft, available in *DWL* 239–42 (for a helpful discussion of the successive drafts, see the introduction to *DS* [17–21]). Much of the material quoted in the following discussion was added by Merton in the process of revision; exceptions will be cited in the notes. The South American editor was Ludovico Silva, who published the Spanish translation as "Día de un Extraño" in the July–September issue of the Venezuelan journal *Papeles* (41–45) (see Thomas Merton, *The Courage for Truth: Letters to Writers*, ed. Christine M. Bochen [New York: Farrar, Straus, Giroux, 1993] 226).

of his permanent removal to the hermitage, and the essay reveals the essential elements of the life of solitude as Merton had already begun to experience it. In describing his day Merton clearly intends that the distinctions between lay and religious, monastic and nonmonastic be relativized and transcended. His life is presented as a unique way of experiencing a common humanity.

At least five dimensions of this life that integrate him with the world shared with the rest of humanity are interwoven throughout the essay. Most immediately apparent is the question of his own identity, evident even in the title, where the word "stranger" might initially suggest someone whose way of life is strange or exotic, but which eventually takes on the connotations of one who doesn't "fit in," whose identity cannot be defined by a public role, a recognized place in society at large, or monastic society in particular—cannot, in fact, be defined at all. Merton takes pains to dispel the impression of strangeness in the first sense by emphasizing that in fundamental ways his life is no different from anybody else's. He pointedly and humorously demythologizes any mystique of the monk as superior to or set apart from ordinary people: "This is not a hermitage—it is a house. ('Who was that hermitage I seen you with last night? . . .') What I wear is pants. What I do is live. How I pray is breathe."[27] But this very ordinariness protects and nurtures the mystery of identity.[28] As he had not yet been relieved of the office of novice master, he still had a "public" self, but this does not constitute his deepest, truest identity: "I have duties, obligations, since here I am a monk. When I have accomplished them, I return to the woods where I am nobody."[29] Like "all the silent Tzu's and Fu's" that surround him in spirit, he is

---

[27] *DS* 41; see the similar language in Merton's March 9, 1967 letter to Ruether: "All you do is breathe and look around and wash dishes, type, etc. Or just listen to the birds" (*HGL* 502–3; *AHW* 34).

[28] See Merton's introduction to *WD*: "These monks insisted on remaining human and 'ordinary.' This may seem to be a paradox, but it is very important. If we reflect a moment, we will see that to fly into the desert in order to be extraordinary is only to carry the world with you as an implicit standard of comparison. . . . The simple men who lived their lives out to a good old age among the rocks and sands only did so because they had come into the desert to be themselves, their *ordinary* selves, and to forget a world that divided them from themselves. There can be no other valid reason for seeking solitude" (22–23).

[29] *DS* 57; for an earlier version of this passage, see *DWL* 241.

"without office and without obligation" (*DS* 63), whose identity cannot be defined by what he does, or how society classifies him: "I live in the woods as a reminder that I am free not to be a number" (*DS* 31). His deepest identity is hidden even from himself and does not become available through introspective self-examination: "In an age when there is much talk about 'being yourself' I reserve to myself the right to forget about being myself, since in any case there is little chance of my being anybody else. Rather it seems to me that when one is too intent on 'being himself' he runs the risk of impersonating a shadow" (*DS* 31). His identity remains a mystery, but the mystery is constituted not by his being a hermit, but because he is a human being. His life is a reminder to others that they too are free not to be numbers, that they too risk impersonating shadows, but are not inevitably doomed to do so. His life is a sign that no one's life is, in essence, or should be, in practice, reduced to the function they perform or the role they play.

This rejection of a superior, esoteric existence is reinforced by the attention paid to the ordinary rhythms and routines of everyday life, from which the hermit is not exempt. Merton deliberately, and slyly, uses the term "rituals," with its associations with religious rites, to describe the most "secular" of activities, not excluding even a visit to the outdoor privy:

> Rituals. Washing out the coffee pot in the rain bucket. Approaching the outhouse with circumspection on account of the king snake who likes to curl up on one of the beams inside. Addressing the possible king snake in the outhouse and informing him that he should not be in there. Asking the formal ritual question that is asked at this time every morning: "Are you in there, you bastard?" More rituals. Spray bedroom (cockroaches and mosquitoes). Close all the windows on south side (heat). Leave windows open on north and east sides (cool). Leave windows open on west side until maybe June when it gets very hot on all sides. Pull down shades. Get water bottle. Rosary. Watch. Library book to be returned. (*DS* 53)

A passage such as this is a reminder that grace builds on nature but does not replace it. Human life is inescapably incarnate, fleshly, and thus part of the value of even the most ordinary activities is to keep one rooted in concrete actuality, to guard against the fatal self-deception that the "religious" person lives on a different plane of reality from everyone else.[30] In performing his "rituals," Merton is attuned to the rhythms of the day—closing the south windows as the sun rises while leaving north and east windows open for cross-ventilation—and the rhythms of the season—leaving west windows open until the heat of June. There is a sense of correspondence with the natural patterns of time—the watch is picked up only when he is ready to make his daily trip down to the monastery. At the same time, the presence of cockroaches and mosquitoes (not to mention the king snake) makes clear that the hermitage is no idyllic, edenic, self-enclosed world; it is part of the normal, ambiguous environment in which all people find themselves, and so signifies an inevitable yet freely accepted solidarity with the human condition. Yet there is something different as well, at least from the standard middle-class experience and expectation. If the hermit participates in routines common to all, he is also a sign of contradiction to the busyness, the noise, the technological gadgetry taken for granted in contemporary society but in fact not necessary at all. "Washing out the coffee pot in the rain bucket" reminds those who rely on the dishwasher, or even on hot and cold running water, that full humanity does not depend on access to the latest conveniences. Both familiar and unfamiliar, the hermit's rituals are not a glorification of the primitive—Merton was quite grateful when modern plumbing and electricity arrived at the hermitage—but a subtle admonition not to absolutize the relative, not to confuse the natural with the artificial, the necessary with the optional.

This passage already suggests a third aspect of this "lay" existence, immersion in the natural world in all its concrete particularity. Merton locates himself in a setting that is not reducible to a set of mapmaker's coordinates: it is "in Kentucky" but that is not its essential defining characteristic: "Do I have a 'day'? Do I spend my 'day' in a 'place'? I know there are trees here. I know there are birds here. I know the

---

[30] In *CWA* Merton writes, "Transformation is not a repudiation of ordinary life but its definitive recovery in Christ" (100). See also this insight as found in Merton's famous "Fourth and Walnut" epiphany (Thomas Merton, *Conjectures of a Guilty Bystander* [Garden City, NY: Doubleday, 1966] 140–42; see also the original journal version of this passage from March 19, 1958, in Thomas Merton, *A Search for Solitude: Pursuing the Monk's True Life. Journals, vol. 3: 1952–1960*, ed. Lawrence S. Cunningham [San Francisco: HarperCollins, 1996] 181–82).

birds in fact very well, for there are precise pairs of birds (two each of fifteen or twenty species) living in the immediate area of my cabin. I share this particular place with them: we form an ecological balance. This harmony gives the idea of 'place' a new configuration."[31] There is a sense of respect here, a recognition that the trees and birds were in this place before he was and will continue to be there when he is no more; therefore, it is his responsibility not to impose his pattern on them but to become aware of and participate in their pattern, their harmony. This relationship is humorously expressed later in the essay in the delightful variation on St. Francis's sermon to the birds: "'Esteemed friends, birds of noble lineage, I have no message to you except this: be what you are: be *birds*. Thus you will be your own sermon to yourselves!' Reply: 'even this is one sermon too many!'" (*DS* 51). It is not the birds but the preacher who needs to hear and heed the instruction "be what you are," which could in fact be considered the sermon of the birds.

This appreciation of harmony does not exclude an awareness of dissonance in nature, a sense that it too participates in some way in the fallenness of creation. "As to the crows," Merton notes, "they form part of a different pattern. They are vociferous and self-justifying, like humans. They are not two, they are many. They fight each other and the other birds, in a constant state of war."[32] But if nature at times parallels the conflicts and confusion of the human world (and so serves as an object lesson undermining the pretensions and posturing of human arrogance), it also stands as a sign of contradiction to the getting and spending in which the great world looks to find its meaning. Birds and business are on different schedules: "The birds begin to wake. It will soon be dawn. In an hour or two the towns will wake, and men will enjoy everywhere the great luminous smiles of production and business" (*DS* 45). Like the birds, the hermit is attuned to other rhythms than those presented by the commercial world. He is sensitive not only to *chronos*, clock-time, but to *kairos*, the decisive moment of revelation and transfiguration: "It is necessary for me to see the first point of light which begins to be dawn. It is necessary to be present alone at the resurrection of Day, in the black silence when

---

[31] *DS* 33; for an earlier version of this passage, see *DWL* 239.
[32] *DS* 33; for an earlier version of this passage, see *DWL* 239.

the sun appears. In this completely neutral instant I receive from the Eastern woods, the tall oaks, the one word 'DAY,' which is never the same. It is never spoken in any human language."[33] This responsiveness to nature is not intended to substitute for or to exclude human contact. Rather, in Merton's view, the ecological balance of his physical environment provides a pattern for "a mental ecology too, a living balance of spirits in this corner of the woods. There is room here for many other songs than those of birds," voices of poets singing in many languages, voices of Eastern sages and Western church fathers, voices of Hebrew prophets and "feminine voices from Angela of Foligno to Flannery O'Connor, Teresa of Avila, Julian of Norwich, and, more personally and warmly still, Raïssa Maritain."[34] The natural world provides a context in which the wisdom of the human world can be properly heard and appreciated: "It is good to choose the voices that will be heard in these woods, but they also choose themselves, and send themselves here to be present in this silence" (*DS* 35, 37).

But the human world penetrates the hermit's existence not only through the insights of artists and visionaries. A fourth element of Merton's life in the hermitage that is shared with all humanity is the necessity to confront the dilemmas of social and political life. Merton frames his essay with references to airplanes. After a sardonic opening paragraph on the pseudo-mystical elevation of modern jets, in which passengers are suspended in a moving stillness "with timeless cocktails . . . contemplation that *gets you somewhere!*" (*DS* 29) he turns to "Other jets, with other contemplations" (*DS* 29), the grotesquely perverted mimicry of "the SAC plane, the metal bird with a scientific egg in its breast!"[35] The essay, and the day, end with the same image: "Meanwhile the metal cherub of the apocalypse passes over me in

---

[33] *DS* 51; for an earlier version of this passage, see *DWL* 241. Merton writes to Ruether, "One of the things I love about my life, and, therefore, one of the reasons why I would not change it for anything, is the fact that I live in the woods and according to a tempo of sun and moon and season in which it is naturally easy and possible to walk in God's light, so to speak, in and through his creation" (*HGL* 502; *AHW* 34).

[34] *DS* 35; for an earlier version of this passage, see *DWL* 239–40.

[35] *DS* 31; the original version of this passage does not use the bird/egg image: see *DWL* 239.

the clouds, treasuring its egg and its message" (*DS* 63). Merton permits himself and his reader no illusion that withdrawal into solitude means escape from the perils human society has created for itself: "like everyone else, I live in the shadow of the apocalyptic cherub" (*DS* 31). If there were ever a time when the monk had the luxury of ignoring the problems of the wider world, that time is forever gone. Monks, and even hermits, live in the same world as everyone else, and therefore have the same obligations and responsibilities to defend life and resist the forces of death. The hermit is able to address the struggle between light and darkness in society because he has experienced that same struggle in his own heart, and he is able to articulate a word of hope because he knows that the darkness has not finally overcome the light:

> In the formlessness of night and silence a word then pronounces itself: Mercy. It is surrounded by other words of lesser consequence: "destroy iniquity," "wash me," "purify," "I know my iniquity." *Peccavi*. Concepts without interest in the world of business, war, politics, culture, etc. Concepts also often without interest to ecclesiastics. Other words: Blood. Guile. Anger. The way that is not good. The way of blood, guile, anger, war. Out there the hills in the dark lie southward. The way over the hills is blood, guile, dark, anger, death. Selma, Birmingham, Mississippi. Nearer than these, the atomic city, from which each day a freight car of fissionable material is brought to be hid carefully beside the gold in the underground vault which is at the heart of this nation. "Their mouth is the opening of the grave; their tongues are set in motion by lies; their heart is void." Blood, lies, fire, hate, the opening of the grave, void. Mercy, great mercy. (*DS* 43, 45)

The final word is mercy, but its power is revealed not by refusing to hear the other words but by confronting them, knowing the full extent of their ugliness, and refusing to be overwhelmed by them because one has learned, through no merit of one's own, that there is a deeper, more lasting reality than hate and death.

Though the term is not used, this passage is of course a description of the divine office, as "psalms grow up silently by themselves without effort in this light which is favorable to them" (*DS* 43). Throughout *Day of a Stranger* the explicitly spiritual, religious, Christian dimension discloses itself unobtrusively, woven into the pattern of personal identity, of ordinary routines, of natural harmonies, or as here, of social and political confusions and threats. It is the final integrating factor that unites the hermit with his brothers and sisters, but only because it has itself been integrated with the rest of life. It is the "one central tonic note that is unheard and unuttered" but which makes possible the harmony of all creation, "the *consonantia* of heat, fragrant pine, quiet wind, bird song."[36] Viewed in isolation, Merton "the stranger" comments, "Spiritual life is guilt," but when the artificial separation between worldly and spiritual aspects of life is overcome, when religion is not restricted to formal rituals at specified times, all life is recognized as holy: "Up here in the woods is seen the New Testament: that is to say, the wind comes through the trees and you breathe it" (*DS* 41). The divine presence, the *pneuma* that blows where it wills, is as "natural," and as essential, as breathing.

At the heart of the call to solitude is the invitation to recognize and embrace the Love hidden in the depth of all that is real. "One might say I had decided to marry the silence of the forest. The sweet dark warmth of the whole world will have to be my wife. Out of the heart of that dark warmth comes the secret that is heard only in silence, but it is the root of all the secrets that are whispered by all the lovers in their beds all over the world."[37] The secret is that all particular loves, insofar as they are authentic, are participations in the one Love; that all particular surrenders are concrete ways of participating in the primal and primary surrender of self to absolute reality, the fullness of truth. It is the assurance of the unity that grounds all diversity, the One manifested in the many, the "hidden wholeness" of creation as the epiphany of the divine, what Merton calls *Sophia*, Holy Wisdom.[38] Merton's vocation to solitude is not exclusive but inclusive, not something to distinguish him from others but a sign of the easily

---

[36] *DS* 61; for an earlier version of this passage, see *DWL* 242; for an insightful discussion of this passage in the context of the entire essay, see Donald Grayston, "*Consonantia* in Thomas Merton: Harmony Personal, Social and Cosmic," *The Merton Annual* 28 (2015) 97–111.

[37] *DS* 49; for an earlier version of this passage, see *DWL* 240.

[38] See Merton's prose poem "*Hagia Sophia*" in Thomas Merton, *Emblems of a Season of Fury* (New York: New Directions, 1963) 61–69; *CP* 363–71; the phrase "hidden wholeness" is from the opening sentence of this work.

overlooked significance of each life and all life. "So perhaps I have an obligation to preserve the stillness, the silence, the poverty, the virginal point of pure nothingness which is at the center of all other loves." This is not an obligation imposed by any institution or required by any rule. It is an expression of charismatic freedom, love responding to Love, heart speaking to Heart. "I attempt to cultivate this plant without comment in the middle of the night and water it with psalms and prophecies in silence. It becomes the most rare of all the trees in the garden, at once the primordial paradise tree, the *axis mundi*, the cosmic axle, and the Cross. *Nulla silva talem profert*. There is only one such tree. It cannot be multiplied."[39] There are not, finally, many trees, but one Tree, many loves, but one Love, many lives, but one Life. At this still point, the distinctions between secular and sacred, lay and monastic, are transcended in a contemplative intuition that is also ordinary, everyday awareness of a common humanity,[40] sharing the same earth, revolving around the same center, redeemed by the same cross in order to live the same glorious freedom of the children of God.

---

[39] *DS* 49; for an earlier version of this passage, see *DWL* 240. The Latin passage is a verse from the hymn "Pange Lingua" of Venantius Fortunatus (sixth century) and means: "No forest brings forth such [a tree]."

[40] Merton writes to Ruether, "my own small concerns with monasticism may seem completely irrelevant. And I am not defending them. Because they are not just monastic concerns, they are human and universal. What makes it difficult to express this is the fact that, for instance, 'being a hermit' seems to mean trying to be a very peculiar and special kind of artificial man, whereas for me what it means is being nothing but man, or nothing but a mere man reduced to his simple condition as man, that is to say as a non-monk even, a non-layman, a non-categorized man, a plain simple man. . . . What would seem to others to be the final step into total alienation seems to me to be the beginning of the resolution of all alienation and the preparation for a real return without masks and without defenses into the world, as mere man" (*HGL* 508; *AHW* 46).

8

From Communication to Communion:
Merton on Language and Silence

On October 23, 1968, a little more than a week after he had arrived in Asia on what would be the final stage of his life's journey, Thomas Merton was in Calcutta at an interreligious conference sponsored by the Temple of Understanding, an organization founded eight years earlier "to foster education, communication and understanding among the world religions."[1] He had prepared a presentation on "Monastic Experience and East-West Dialogue" in which he emphasized the crucial importance of fostering relationships among adherents of the major religious traditions as an alternative both to cross-cultural misunderstanding and conflict and to a kind of soulless global "culture" dedicated to efficiency, pragmatism, and profits. He stated: "I am convinced that communication in depth, across the lines that have hitherto divided religious and monastic traditions, is now not only possible and desirable, but most important for the destinies of Twentieth-Century Man" (*AJ* 313). But he emphasized that to be truly and lastingly meaningful, such interaction needed to move beyond an academic and theoretical focus to the "existential level of experience and of spiritual maturity" (*AJ* 312). He wrote:

---

[1] Thomas Merton, *The Asian Journal*, ed. Naomi Burton Stone, Brother Patrick Hart, and James Laughlin (New York: New Directions, 1973) 47, n. 21 (subsequent references will be cited as "*AJ*" parenthetically in the text).

> True communication on the deepest level is more than a simple sharing of ideas, of conceptual knowledge, or formulated truth. The kind of communication that is necessary on this deep level must also be "communion" beyond the level of words, a communion in authentic experience. . . . This demands among other things a "freedom from automatisms and routines," and candid liberation from external social dictates, from conventions, limitations, and mechanisms which restrict understanding and inhibit experience of the new, the unexpected. (*AJ* 315)

One engaging in such encounters, he goes on to say,

> must be wide open to life and to new experience because he has fully utilized his own tradition and gone beyond it. This will permit him to meet a discipline of another, apparently remote and alien tradition, and find a common ground of verbal understanding with him . . . on which they both meet beyond their own words and their own understanding in the silence of an ultimate experience which might conceivably not have occurred if they had not met and spoken. . . . This I would call "communion." I think it is something that the deepest ground of our being cries out for, and it is something for which a lifetime of striving would not be enough. (*AJ* 315–16)

He concluded that "the importance of serious communication, and indeed of 'communion,' among contemplatives of different traditions, disciplines, and religions" was that it "can contribute much to the development of man at this crucial point of his history," and suggested that the role of the monk, of whatever tradition, was to preserve through discipline and practice the contemplative dimension of human experience not simply for the sake of personal enlightenment but in order "to keep the way open for modern technological man to recover the integrity of his own inner depths" (*AJ* 317).

While situating this vision of the significance of the contemplative dimension of authentic communication in the context of interreligious dialogue, Merton was drawing on and recapitulating his unsystematic but pervasive reflections on the respective roles and contributions of language and silence to human fulfillment and self-transcendence, a subject that had engaged and fascinated him throughout his nearly three decades as monk and author. These words of invitation and challenge, written nearly at the end of his relatively short life, can thus serve as an appropriate point of entry for considering significant aspects of Merton's ongoing investigation of the necessary but necessarily limited contributions of language to the discovery and exercise of full human selfhood.

Speaking Freely

It is noteworthy that Merton places language at the center of humanity's primordial relationship with the Creator. Drawing on the insights of the Greek patristic writers, he describes the intimacy of Adam with God before the Fall as being characterized by the term *parrhesia*, which literally means "saying everything," and which Merton suggests is best rendered as "freedom of speech."[2] In its most common connotation, Merton points out, "The word represents . . . the rights and privileges of a citizen in a Greek city state. This 'free speech' is at once the duty and the honor of speaking one's own mind fully and frankly in the civil assemblies by which the state is governed" (*NM* 72). Thus it describes the full freedom of self-expression and spontaneous, unself-conscious intimacy that the human person was created to enjoy with God.

> The image of "parrhesia" which suggests to us Adam conversing familiarly with a God Who came down to walk in the afternoon in the garden of Paradise is strangely effective in bringing home to us the spiritual implications of Adam's oneness with himself, with God, and with the world around him. The "free speech" the Fathers speak of is a symbolic expression of that perfect adaptation to reality, which came from the fact that man was exactly what he was intended to be by God: that is to say, he was perfectly himself. (*NM* 74)

It includes not only humanity's relation with the Creator but with the rest of creation as well. Adam's act of naming the creatures is an integral dimension of his *parrhesia*. God allows Adam the freedom of choosing the name of each creature, and so of participating, in a way,

---

[2] Thomas Merton, *The New Man* (New York: Farrar, Straus & Cudahy, 1961) 72 (subsequent references will be cited as "*NM*" parenthetically in the text).

in the creative act itself. "It is as if the Lord waited upon Adam to confer this accidental perfection upon His created world—as if there were one final touch that was left entirely to man's freedom" (*NM* 83). This act of naming becomes then a kind of paradigm for all human creativity, which includes but is not limited to communication with other persons.

> After having drawn forth the living beings out of nothingness, God elicits from the depths of Adam's own liberty words, names and signs. These, in their turn, will flower into many kinds of creative intellectual activity. They will become, first of all, poems which will express man's inexpressible intuitions of hidden reality of created things. They will become philosophy and science, by which man will objectify and universalize his private vision of the world into thought-systems that can be shared by everyone. Finally, words will become *sacred* signs. They will acquire the power to set apart certain elements of creation and make them holy. (*NM* 84–85)

But as the act of naming takes place before there are other persons with whom to share these names, the implication is that the deepest function of language is not simply to convey information but to make contact with reality at its ontological core.

> The primary function of the word is a contemplative rather than a communicative statement of what exists. Even if we never talk to anyone, or think in terms of conversations with others, the mental word, dressed in its proper sound stands in the depths of our intelligence to bear witness to reality and to worship God. In this sense the word is a kind of seal upon our intellectual communion with Him, before it becomes a means of communication with other men. (*NM* 88)

Here of course we find the same juxtaposition of "communication" and "communion" that will reappear in Merton's Calcutta address. Though here the focus is on the priority of communion with God before communication with other people, Merton points out as well that *parrhesia* also encompasses "Adam's existential communion with the reality around him in and through the Reality of God which he constantly experienced within himself" (*NM* 76), above all the communion with other persons which transcends what can be expressed in language that is simply objective and conceptual. After the creation of Eve, Adam immediately responds to the gift of the woman not simply by engaging in interpersonal conversation but by composing and reciting what Merton calls "a gnomic poem,"[3] addressed "at once to himself and to the whole universe" (*NM* 90)—the awed recognition of his intrinsic connection with this other being, of the woman as bone of his bone and flesh of his flesh, and as the reason for leaving the security of the family to become united to her.

Language in a Fallen World

This of course is a description of how language ideally should function, how it would have functioned in a perfect world, in an unfallen world. But as Merton wryly notes, "The Genesis story tells of Adam's 'freedom of speech' with God not so much by directly describing it as by saying what replaced it when it was taken away. The *Parrhesia* of Adam in Eden is known by inference, by implication. We see it by the contrast of his state after the fall with what is implied to have gone before" (*NM* 72). Adam "remained in contact with God, with himself, and with the reality around him as long as he permitted no lie to come between himself and the light" (*NM* 76). But sin is precisely the acceptance of a lie, the spurious claim of an illusory freedom, an assertion of autonomy by which one denies one's dependence upon the Creator and aspires to be one's own source of being and of meaning, a self-deceiving and self-defeating estrangement from one's transcendent ground and from one's own authentic identity. Communication is distorted by self-concealment and self-justification, and communion is replaced by alienation.

---

[3] In his novitiate conferences on Genesis, Merton makes a similar comment about Eve's "poetic memorial of the birth of her first child" (Cain): "I have begotten a man through God"—"a phrase which sums everything up . . . . The custom of these gnomic poetic utterances . . . common in Genesis" is to "'fix' definitively the meaning of an event (cf. Japanese poems)" (Thomas Merton, *Notes on Genesis and Exodus: Novitiate Conferences on Scripture and Liturgy* 2, ed. Patrick F. O'Connell [Eugene, OR: Cascade, 2021] 18 [subsequent references will be cited as "*NGE*" parenthetically in the text]).

> Adam's fall was therefore the willful acceptance of unreality, the consent to receive and even prefer a lie to the truth about himself and about his relationship to God. . . . The experience of falsity destroyed in him the instinctive taste for spiritual truth. Illusion entered in to spoil the existential flow of communication between his soul and God. (*NM* 77)

This is the debased state of language in a postlapsarian world, archetypically represented by the biblical story of Babel,[4] which Merton dramatizes in his verse play *The Tower of Babel: A Morality*,[5] his only venture into that literary genre. In the play, the deceptive appearance of unanimity in the earthly city is in fact a kind of *simulacrum*, an insubstantial representation, of what the human heart most deeply desires and obscurely recognizes that it has cast away. Accepted as a divine gift rather than claimed as an autonomous human accomplishment, language has the power to effect not only communication but communion, a source of strength and freedom for those who "knew the same truth and lived by it, working together" (*SI* 64; *CP* 262), as the builders of the tower claimed to be doing in words that concealed, even from themselves, their mixed motives of fear and desire, self-glorification and self-doubt, eventually leading to the chaos and disorder of the fallen tower. Built on a lie, the lie of its own autonomy, the earthly city has no solid foundation and therefore cannot stand. By refusing to embrace their own humanity, to accept their own contingency not as a curse but as a blessing—evidence of

---

[4] See also Merton's brief commentary on the Babel passage (Gen. 11:1-8) in *NGE* 34–36, where Merton finds "something very American" in the "false optimism" of the tower-builders, "united by pride and self-interest" and "based on a very fragile unity . . . as long as there is prosperity."

[5] Thomas Merton, *The Strange Islands* (New York: New Directions, 1957) 43–78 (subsequent references will be cited as "*SI*" parenthetically in the text); Thomas Merton, *The Collected Poems of Thomas Merton* (New York: New Directions, 1977) 247–73 (subsequent references will be cited as "*CP*" parenthetically in the text). For an overview, see Patrick F. O'Connell, "*Tower of Babel, The*" in William H. Shannon, Christine M. Bochen, and Patrick F. O'Connell, *The Thomas Merton Encyclopedia* (Maryknoll, NY: Orbis, 2002) 490–91 (subsequent references will be cited as "*Encyclopedia*" parenthetically in the text). For a detailed discussion of the various stages of composition of this work, see Patrick F. O'Connell, "A Four Storey *Tower*: The Building of Thomas Merton's *Babel*," *The Merton Annual* 37 (2024) 138–214.

their own dependence upon and therefore intimate connection to their divine source and their divine goal—the builders of Babylon lost precisely what they thought they were gaining: "Wanting to be gods, they were made less than themselves. / They might have become gods / If they had deigned to remain men." By their futile efforts to be like God without God, "its builders cursed themselves" (*SI* 74; *CP* 270), rejecting the likeness that was already theirs as created in the divine image, refusing the divinization, the communion in divine love, for which they were made. Yet the final word is the "*verbum crucis*" (*SI* 77; *CP* 273), the word of the cross, not one of rejection but of renewed invitation, a word of life spoken at the point of death—an intimation that humanity is not inevitably doomed to subsist in illusion, that the word of truth is ultimately more powerful than the lie.

But though the world has been redeemed by the enfleshment of the Word of God who confronts and overcomes the forces of deception and despair and restores to humanity the possibility to live in conformity with the truth by fidelity to one's own authentic identity, though the reign of God has been definitively established by Christ's triumph over death, it remains largely hidden in a world that is still pervaded by the distorted use of language. Thus throughout his work Merton repeatedly casts light upon the misuse of language to conceal the truth in order to control others and to deny their intrinsic dignity and goodness as made in the divine image, for the sake of maintaining or enhancing the power or privilege or prestige of the few, ultimately rooted in a fear to confront one's own radical contingency. Despite their own self-assured conviction that they are living in an enlightened era, free from the superstitions of their ancestors, Merton finds his contemporaries beset by "idolatry, substituting falsehood for the truth of God. A false conscience is a false god, a god which says nothing because it is dumb and which does nothing because it has no power. It is a mask through which we utter oracles to ourselves, telling ourselves false prophecies, giving ourselves whatever answer we want to hear."[6] It is a world dominated by deceptive political propaganda, seductive advertising, banal and complacent

---

[6] Thomas Merton, *Thoughts in Solitude* (New York: Farrar, Straus & Cudahy, 1958) 77 (subsequent references will be cited as "*TS*" parenthetically in the text).

conventional wisdom that fails to penetrate beneath the most superficial of human wants and needs.

> Clearly the "powers" and "elements" which in Paul's day dominated men's minds through pagan religion or through religious legalism, today dominate us in the confusion and the ambiguity of the Babel of tongues that we call mass-society. . . . It is in this confusion of images and myths, superstitions and ideologies that the "powers of the air" govern our thinking—even our thinking about religion![7]

Merton finds the present state of discourse mirroring the description of sin as self-contradiction presented in the New Testament:

> Reading the Vulgate I run across the Latin word *simulacrum* which has implications of a mask-like deceptiveness, of intellectual cheating, of an ideological shell-game. The word *simulacrum*, it seems to me, presents itself as a very suggestive one to describe an advertisement, or an over-inflated political presence, or that face on the TV screen. The word shimmers, grins, cajoles. It is a fine word for something monumentally phony. . . . Does it not occur to us that if, in fact, we live in a society in which is par excellence that of the *simulacrum*, we are the champion idolaters of all history? (*FV* 152)

This idolatry is exposed in its most blatant and most destructive form in the perversion of language to dehumanize and obliterate other human beings both psychologically and physically. In his late essay "War and the Crisis of Language," Merton relentlessly exposes the ways in which language becomes an instrument of violence and so is subjected to violence itself as its true function is subverted and negated:

> Language itself has fallen victim to total war, genocide and systematic tyranny in our time. In destroying human beings, and human values, on a mass scale, the Gestapo also subjected the

---

[7] Thomas Merton, *Faith and Violence: Christian Teaching and Christian Practice* (Notre Dame, IN: University of Notre Dame Press, 1968) 150 (subsequent references will be cited as "*FV*" parenthetically in the text).

German language to violence and crude perversion. . . . Officialese has a talent for discussing reality while denying it and calling truth itself into question. Yet the truth remains. This doubletalk is by its very nature invested with a curious metaphysical leer. The language of Auschwitz is one of the vulnerable spots through which we get a clear view of the demonic.[8]

Merton memorably conveys this degradation of language in his poem "Chant to Be Used in Processions around a Site with Furnaces" (*ESF* 43–47; *CP* 345–49), a dramatic monologue by a concentration camp commandant, taken almost entirely from actual documents, in which euphemisms and bureaucratic abstractions ultimately fail to conceal the horror of what is actually happening, what Merton elsewhere calls "the Unspeakable."[9] Likewise his poem on Hiroshima, *Original Child Bomb*,[10] conveys by ironic understatement the enormity of the destructive event masked by the official use of terminology associated with birth ("the womb of Enola Gay"), the innocence of a child (the bomb as "Little Boy," "Original Child"), and religious doctrines (the code names "Trinity" and "Papacy").[11]

While less directly implicated in massive violence, the language of political propaganda and of advertising is seen by Merton as marked by the same reductive and dehumanizing impulses. He notes, following Jacques Ellul, that propaganda is most effective when it includes a veneer of factual truth that increases its plausibility and lulls its recipients into a complacent trust in their own powers of discernment and good judgment, when in fact the data presented is being manipulated to further a predetermined end that does not

---

[8] Thomas Merton, *The Nonviolent Alternative*, ed. Gordon C. Zahn (New York: Farrar, Straus, Giroux, 1980) 155 (subsequent references will be cited as "*NA*" parenthetically in the text). See also Merton's remarks on the lethal consequences of the perversion of language to dehumanize others in the holocaust in his "Letter to Pablo Antonio Cuadra concerning Giants" (Thomas Merton, *Emblems of a Season of Fury* [New York: New Directions, 1963] 73–74 [subsequent references will be cited as "*ESF*" parenthetically in the text]; *CP* 375).

[9] Thomas Merton, *Raids on the Unspeakable* (New York: New Directions, 1966) 4 (subsequent references will be cited as "*RU*" parenthetically in the text).

[10] Thomas Merton, *Original Child Bomb: Points for Meditation to Be Scratched on the Walls of a Cave* (New York: New Directions, 1961); *CP* 291–302.

[11] For an overview, see Patrick F. O'Connell, "*Original Child Bomb*" (*Encyclopedia* 342–45).

logically follow from the objective evidence provided: "The real violence exerted by propaganda is this: by means of apparent truth and apparent reason, it induces us to surrender our freedom and self-possession. It predetermines us to certain conclusions, and does so in such a way that we imagine that we are fully free in reasoning them by our own judgment and our own thought."[12] Likewise the subliminal compulsion of advertising permits and encourages the prospective consumer to suppose he or she is making rational decisions while actually succumbing to the subtle or not-so-subtle intimation that some product or other is essential, or at least will contribute substantially, to some aspect of personal self-realization, when in fact "the advertising imagery which associates sexual fulfillment with all the most trivial forms of satisfaction—in order to separate the buyer from his dollar—creates a mental and moral climate that is unfavorable to genuine love."[13] The impulse to accept this mendacity as truth is reinforced by the pervasive temptation to substitute the supposed conclusions of society in general for the lonely and sometimes harrowing process of reaching a mature personal decision:

> This is one of the few real pleasures left to modern man: this illusion that he is thinking for himself when, in fact, someone else is doing his thinking for him. . . . One is left, therefore, not only with the sense that one has thought things out for himself, but that he has also reached the correct answer without difficulty—the answer which is shown to be correct because it is the answer of everybody. (*CGB* 216–17)

In *New Seeds of Contemplation*, Merton describes the results of this abdication of responsibility for making one's own decisions in terms of his fundamental insight on the levels of human interaction:

> Where men live huddled together without true communication, there seems to be greater sharing, and a more genuine communion. But this is not communion, only immersion in the gen-

---

[12] Thomas Merton, *Conjectures of a Guilty Bystander* (Garden City, NY: Doubleday, 1966) 216 (subsequent references will be cited as "*CGB*" parenthetically in the text).

[13] Thomas Merton, *Love and Living*, ed. Naomi Burton Stone and Brother Patrick Hart (New York: Farrar, Straus, Giroux, 1979) 36 (subsequent references will be cited as "*L&L*" parenthetically in the text).

eral meaninglessness of countless slogans and clichés repeated over and over again so that in the end one listens without hearing and responds without thinking. The constant din of empty words and machine noises, the endless booming of loudspeakers end by making true communication and true communion almost impossible.[14]

While he presented this abuse of language in mythic and archetypal terms in *The Tower of Babel* in the mid-1950s, in his book-length anti-poem *Cables to the Ace*,[15] published the year of his death, Merton employs the strategy of exposing the incoherence of contemporary discourse by an ironic, parodic feedback of the essentially meaningless jargon that passes for information and communication in modern, or perhaps early postmodern, mass society. The poet immerses his readers in the cacophony of seemingly pointless verbiage in order to convince them, or rather allow them to convince themselves, that language has been violently wrenched from its true function to reflect and interpret reality; it has too often become a substitute for reality, all appearance and no substance, in order to facilitate social control and political oppression. Rather than a medium for developing relationships and expressing personal commitment, language has been reduced to a self-referential, closed system of passive impersonality. By pushing the abuse of language to the point of absurdity, by exposing through parody the meaningless babble of contemporary discourse, the poet has cleared the way for a movement into the silence and emptiness of contemplation. The poem has demonstrated that the failures of language, once recognized, can prove to be as adequate a starting point for contemplative realization as any other. If symbolism, as we shall see, is a kind of *via positiva* that points beyond itself to transcendent experience, "anti-poetry" can function as a *via negativa* which impels one to silence by inducing revulsion from its meaningless cacophony. Yet in this silence, the true word can once again

---

[14] Thomas Merton, *New Seeds of Contemplation* (New York: New Directions, 1961) 54–55 (subsequent references will be cited as "*NSC*" parenthetically in the text).

[15] Thomas Merton, *Cables to the Ace or Familiar Liturgies of Misunderstanding* (New York: New Directions, 1968); *CP* 393–454. For an overview, see Patrick F. O'Connell, "*Cables to the Ace*" (*Encyclopedia* 36–38).

be heard and spoken, and one can discover anew one's own true name.

Thus for Merton the process of redemption includes the redemption of language, the restoration of the word to its authentic function. In religious terms, this entails a new dimension of *parrhesia*, the freedom to acknowledge one's own dishonesty and self-deception and to rely on the transformative power of God to restore a true appreciation of and relationship with reality. This, Merton goes to say,

> is the only *parrhesia* which we shall ever experience. The "free speech" with which God and man now familiarly converse together is and can only be the conversation that begins with, or implies, pardon. The *parrhesia* which can be ours is a greater gift than Adam's. It comes to us in the terrible yet healing mercy by which God gives us the courage to approach Him exactly as we are. (*NM* 95–96)

Authentic Communication

Merton sees three interrelated stages in this redemptive reappropriation of language. The first and most fundamental is simply a humble recommitment to speaking the truth—that is, to trustworthy communication—which entails a recognition that such dedication is necessarily fragile and fallible and so excludes all self-righteous pretentions to a superior degree of honesty that allows one complacently or arrogantly to evaluate others' sincerity.

> Unless we are made "new men," created according to God "in justice and the holiness of truth," we cannot avoid some of the lying and double-dealing which have become instinctive in our natures. . . . Sincerity must be bought at a price: the humility to recognize our innumerable errors, and fidelity in tirelessly setting them right.[16]

Genuine dialogue and community are possible only among those who have committed themselves, consciously or not, to speaking the truth in love, "who have first of all accepted their own fragile lot, who have

---

[16] Thomas Merton, *No Man Is an Island* (New York: Harcourt, Brace, 1955) 192.

chosen to exist contingently, and thereby have accepted the solitude of the person who must think and decide for himself without the warm support of collective fictions."[17] An intrinsic dimension of the church, in its vocation to proclaim and incarnate the Word of God, is to serve as a sign of contradiction to the inauthentic conception of community and to affirm and nurture genuine human dialogue and to promote mutual understanding and respect: "The Church has an obligation *not* to join in the incantation of political slogans and in the concoction of pseudo-events, but to *cut clear through the deviousness and ambiguity of both slogans and events with her simplicity and her love*" (*FV* 161). This is the vision of church that Merton finds in the renewed openness to the world that characterized Pope John XXIII:

> One of the admirable things about Pope John is his simple fidelity to the *Socratic* principle which is essential to our Western cultural tradition. . . . The Socratic principle, as Pope John definitely sees, means not only the willingness to discuss, but the readiness to meet one's adversary *as an equal and as a brother*. The moment one does this, he ceases to be an adversary. Some seem to fear that in such encounters, meeting the adversary on his own ground, we leave the protection of the Church and Catholic truth. They forget that if we meet the non-Christian *as a brother* we meet him on ground that is *Christian*. If we fear to meet him on what is really our own ground, is this not perhaps because we ourselves are not sufficiently Christian? (*CGB* 197–98)

The monastery, precisely because it is not caught up in the incessant stream of words, slogans, images, and information that flood the consciousness of people immersed in the mass media, is paradoxically in a position to make a unique contribution to the Christian community's obligation to participate in the ongoing conversation with all seekers after truth:

> the monastery should be capable of being a place of dialogue, nontechnical and nonexpert, no doubt, but a place where men of our time would feel they could encounter and somehow

---

[17] Thomas Merton, *Mystics and Zen Masters* (New York: Farrar, Straus and Giroux, 1967) 267 (subsequent references will be cited as "*MZM*" parenthetically in the text).

"touch" a deep and existential experience of the Mystery of Christ as lived and revealed in a community of men who really measure up to the challenges and promises of a contemplative vocation.[18]

Merton finds models for this modest but tenacious determination not to violate the integrity of language in ancient and modern sages and prophets, both within and beyond the borders of institutional Christianity: in Clement of Alexandria, who recognized seeds of the Logos in the Greek philosophers and believed that "the function of education is to awaken souls to the 'spark of goodness deposited in them by the Creator,' and by that awakening to lead them to enlightenment";[19] in St. Thomas Aquinas, who wrote: "We must love them both, those whose opinions we share and those whose opinions we reject. For both have labored in the search for truth and both have helped us in the finding of it" (*CGB* 115); in the Taoist sage Chuang Tzu, who teaches that "There is a time to listen, in the active life as everywhere else, and the better part of action is waiting, not knowing what next, and not having a glib answer" (*CGB* 156); in the ancient Greek philosopher Herakleitos, who was "like 'the Lord at Delphi who neither utters nor hides his meaning but shows it by a sign.' His words would be neither expositions of doctrine or explanations of mystery, but simply pointers, plunging toward the heart of reality."[20]

Among his contemporaries two preeminent models from outside the circle of Christian faith exemplified a dedication to truth that served both as inspiration for and critique of his own tradition's willingness to risk its security and status to remain faithful to the Word, whether convenient or inconvenient. French author Albert Camus articulated as few others of his generation the difficulties faced by contemporary people who desire to escape the dominant misuse of the instruments of mass communication:

---

[18] Thomas Merton, *Contemplation in a World of Action* (Garden City, NY: Doubleday, 1971) 204.
[19] Thomas Merton, *Clement of Alexandria: Selections from* The Protreptikos (New York: New Directions, 1962) 10.
[20] Thomas Merton, *The Behavior of Titans* (New York: New Directions, 1961) 86.

> Camus, deeply concerned as he is with the loneliness and estrangement of man, is also preoccupied even more deeply still with the problem of communication. . . . The great difficulty facing the man who really wants to communicate with his brother is not the lack of words or of media, but the fact that words and media are now so commonly and so systematically used in order to cheat and to lie.[21]

But he did not simply describe the problem but committed himself to a creative response, a refusal to say what he did not mean, and a refusal to remain silent in the face of oppression and its attendant misinformation:

> The whole truth of Albert Camus is centered upon the idea of *telling the truth*. . . . The novels, stories, and essays of Camus explore this question from many angles, and everywhere they reach the conclusion: we live in a world of lies, which is therefore a world of violence and murder. We need to rebuild a world of peace. We cannot do this unless we can recover the language and think of peace. . . . To all of us, Camus is saying: "Not lying is more than just not dissimulating one's acts and intentions. *It is carrying them out and speaking them out in truth.*" (LE 274)

Even more powerful for Merton than the witness of Camus is that of Gandhi, whose commitment to nonviolent resistance and transformation of self and society is rooted in his central concept of *satyagraha*, which literally means the force or power of truth.

> The vow of *satyagraha* is the vow to die rather than say what one does not mean. The profound significance of *satyagraha* becomes apparent when one reflects that "truth" here implies much more than simply conforming one's words to one's inner thought. It is not by words only that we speak. Our aims, our plans of action, our outlook, our attitudes, our habitual response to the problems and challenges of life, "speak" of our inner being and reveal our fidelity or infidelity to ourselves.[22]

---

[21] Thomas Merton, *The Literary Essays of Thomas Merton*, ed. Brother Patrick Hart (New York: New Directions, 1981) 276 (subsequent references will be cited as "*LE*" parenthetically in the text).

[22] Thomas Merton, *Seeds of Destruction* (New York: Farrar, Straus and Giroux, 1964) 230.

Merton emphasizes that this commitment not simply to speaking but to living the truth is perceived by Gandhi as fidelity to one's deepest and most authentic identity, the conviction that "truth is the law of our being" (*CGB* 72). Consequently the "question of language" is an integral dimension of nonviolence conceived not merely as a tactic but as a way of life most reflective of one's true humanity:

> Nonviolence, as Gandhi conceived it, is in fact a kind of language. The real dynamic of nonviolence can be considered as a purification of language, a restoration of true communication on a human level, when language has been emptied of meaning by misuse and corruption. Nonviolence is meant to communicate love not in word but in act. Above all, nonviolence is meant to convey and to defend truth which has been obscured and defiled by political doubletalk. . . . Nonviolence is not for power but for truth. It is not pragmatic but prophetic. It is not aimed at immediate political results, but at the manifestation of fundamental and crucially important truth. Nonviolence is not primarily the language of efficacy, but the language of *kairos*. (*NA* 74–75)

For Merton, then, the duty of the contemporary Christian is first of all to be as dedicated to speaking and living the truth as these contemporary non-Christians: "communication becomes possible, and with it community, once it is admitted that our words are capable of being true or false and that the decision is largely up to us. . . . We are thus called to take care of our language, and use it clearly. The great task of man is not to serve the lie" (*LE* 272). For a Christian this commitment is rooted in the central belief in the incarnation, the embodied, personal presence of the Logos, the Word of God, in space and time: "Christ, Whom we can see and remember and imagine, is the way to an unimaginable Father. The Beginning. The *Principium*. The End. From Whom the Word Himself IS, for Whom the Word IS. By Whom we are in the Word. For Whom we are" (*NM* 173). And this divine presence is to be recognized and affirmed and celebrated in every encounter with every other human being, all of whom are believed to be created in the image of the Word.

> Christ is found not in loud and pompous declarations but in humble and fraternal dialogue. He is found less in a truth that

is imposed than in a truth that is shared. . . . It is true that the visible Church alone has the official mission to sanctify and teach all nations, but no man knows that the stranger he meets coming out of the forest in a new country is not already an invisible member of Christ and perhaps one who has some providential or prophetic message to utter. . . . God speaks, and God is to be heard, not only on Sinai, not only in my own heart, but in the *voice of the stranger*. (*ESF* 81–82; *CP* 383–84)

Here is the spiritual and theological foundation for a dialogue and communication that excludes no one, which includes a willingness to speak for those whose voice is silenced by fear or indigence or ignorance or oppression and when the occasion calls for it, as Merton notes in his whimsical but quite serious reference to the story of the emperor's new clothes, "to do what the child did, and keep on saying the king is naked, at the cost of being condemned criminals" (*RU* 62).

Symbolism

Beyond the level of communication, of dialogue and witness, Merton identifies a second level, in which the word functions not merely as the medium for conveying information but also as a marker that points toward a dimension of intuitive insight beyond its own denotation. In a 1966 essay appropriately entitled "Symbolism: Communication or Communion?" Merton distinguishes between the indicative sign, the function of which "is communication, and first of all, the communication of factual or practical knowledge" (*L&L* 57), and the true symbol, which "does not merely point to some hidden object" but "contains in itself a structure which in some way makes us aware of the inner meaning of life and of reality itself" and has the capability to bring one "to the center of the circle, not to another point on the circumference . . . to the very heart of all being, not to an incident in the flow of becoming" (*L&L* 54–55). The symbol does not replace the use of language to communicate information but complements this function by serving as a portal to experiencing the underlying unity of being deeper than the distinction between subject and object. It is the vehicle not of knowledge (*scientia*) but of wisdom (*sapientia*), the intuitive, participatory dimension of insight into reality.

> The symbol awakens awareness, or restores it. Therefore, it aims not at communication but at communion. Communion is the awareness of participation in an ontological or religious reality: in the mystery of being, of human love, of redemptive mystery, of contemplative truth. The purpose of the symbol, if it can be said to have a "purpose," is not to increase the quantity of our knowledge and information but to deepen and enrich the *quality* of life itself by bringing man into communion with the mysterious sources of vitality and meaning, of creativity, love, and truth, to which he cannot have direct access by means of science and technique. (*L&L* 68)

A constitutive part of the degradation of language in the contemporary world is the diminishment or loss of the ability to recognize and respond to the symbolic dimension of language, the reduction of the symbol to the level of the corporate logo or the political image that, instead of unifying, becomes a sign of exclusivity, differentiating the select group from its rivals and inferiors. "The pseudo-symbols of the mass movement become signs of the pseudo-mystique in which the mass man loses his individual self in the false, indeed the demonic void, the general pseudo-self of the Mass Society. . . . The symbols of Mass Society are ciphers on the face of a moral and spiritual void" (*L&L* 58). This symbolic consciousness rejects a narrowly utilitarian and pragmatic relationship to the rest of the natural world; it implicitly refutes any ideology that justifies treating another person as a means rather than an end.

It is the vocation of the poet and the creative writer, as well as of the contemplative, to reaffirm the validity and the value of the symbol in a culture that exalts the preeminence of the sign. "The business of the poet is to reach the intimate, that is ontological, sources of life which cannot be clearly apprehended in themselves by any concept, but which, once intuited, can be made accessible to all in symbolic and imaginative celebration" (*LE* 30). This is not, or should not be, an esoteric enterprise available only to a coterie of linguistic adepts. The artist is simply one who is aware of the deeper significance of ordinary objects and ordinary experience, and has the ability to make others who are willing to pay attention participate in this awareness. "It is the businessman, the propagandist, the politician, not the poet, who devoutly believes in 'the magic of words,'" Merton writes to a gathering of young Latin American poets.

> For the poet there is precisely no magic. There is only life in all its unpredictability and all its freedom. All magic is a ruthless venture in manipulation, a vicious circle, a self-fulfilling prophecy. Word-magic is an impurity of language and of spirit in which words, deliberately reduced to unintelligibility, appeal mindlessly to the vulnerable will. Let us deride and parody this magic with other variants of the unintelligible, if we want to. But it is better to prophesy than to deride. To prophesy is not to predict, but to seize upon reality in its moment of highest expectation and tension toward the new. This tension is discovered not in hypnotic elation but in the light of everyday existence. Poetry is innocent of prediction because it is itself the fulfillment of all the momentous predictions hidden in everyday life. Poetry is the flowering of ordinary possibilities. It is the fruit of ordinary and natural choice. This is its innocence and dignity. (*RU* 159)

This is the vision that Merton discovered in some of his favorite poets, in Dante's triumphant final evocation of "The love that moves the sun and other stars";[23] in Blake's perception of "the world in a grain of sand";[24] in Rilke's "inseeing" that transcends "self-consciousness, separateness, and spectatorship" by empathetic identification with that which is seen (*MZM* 245); in Eliot's synthesis of time and eternity

---

[23] Dante Alighieri, *Paradiso*, canto 33; for Merton's initial encounter with Dante at Cambridge, see Thomas Merton, *The Seven Storey Mountain* (New York: Harcourt, Brace, 1948) 122–23; for his reading of Dante while teaching at St. Bonaventure College, see Thomas Merton, *Run to the Mountain: The Story of a Vocation. Journals, vol. 1: 1939–1941*, ed. Patrick Hart (San Francisco: HarperCollins, 1995) 303–4; during the spring and early summer of 1943, he eventually accumulated 114 pages of handwritten notes on the successive cantos, evidently in preparation for a course on Dante which he was planning to teach: see "Manuscript notes on *The Divine Comedy* of Dante," leaves 227–340 of the "Fitzgerald File" of Merton materials in the archives of the Friedsam Memorial Library, St. Bonaventure University, St. Bonaventure, NY.

[24] William Blake, "Auguries of Innocence" in *The Complete Poetry and Prose of William Blake*, ed. David Erdman (Garden City, NY: Doubleday Anchor, 1997) 40. Merton included this poem in his never-published collection of religious verse: see Patrick F. O'Connell, "Thomas Merton's Projected Anthology of Religious Poetry," *The Merton Seasonal* 25.3 (Fall 2000) 20–28. This opening line is used as the general title for the audio series of most of Merton's novitiate conferences on poetry: Thomas Merton, *Seeing the World in a Grain of Sand: Thomas Merton on Poetry* [17 lectures on 7 CDs] (Rockville, MD: NowYouKnowMedia, 2013).

at the "still point of the turning world";[25] in Dickinson's "debauchee of dew" leaning against the sun like a drunkard against a lamppost;[26] in Edwin Muir's exercise of "the Edenic office of the poet who follows Adam and reverifies the names given to creatures by his first father" (*LE* 29). It is the wisdom he finds as well in novelists such as Flannery O'Connor, who in *The Violent Bear It Away* finds a depth of insight in the primitive backwoods prophet Tarwater that is missing in the sophisticated positivism of the schoolteacher Rayber (*MZM* 259–62); in the simple faith in the Blood of the Lamb of the black cook Dilsey in William Faulkner's *The Sound and the Fury* (see *LE* 504–14) or the "wisdom of the Indian in the wilderness" in Faulkner's "The Bear," "a kind of knowledge by identification, an intersubjective knowledge, a communion in cosmic awareness and in nature" (*LE* 108); or in Boris Pasternak's insight in *Dr. Zhivago* that

> Language is not merely the material or the instrument which the poet uses. This is the sin of the Soviet ideologist for whom language is simply a mine of terms and formulas which can be pragmatically exploited. When in the moment of inspiration the poet's creative intelligence is married with the inborn wisdom of human language (the Word of God and Human Nature—Divinity and Sophia) then in the very flow of new and individual intuitions, the poet utters the voice of that wonderful and mysterious world of God-manhood—it is the transfigured, spiritualized and divinized cosmos that speaks through him, and through him utters its praise of the Creator.[27]

It is the perception glimpsed in Merton's own poems, such as "Grace's House" (*ESF* 28–29; *CP* 330–31), in which a child's drawing becomes a symbol of the paradise consciousness of childhood in-

---

[25] T. S. Eliot, "Burnt Norton" in *The Complete Poems and Plays: 1909–1950* (New York: Harcourt, Brace and World, 1962) 119. Merton's three conferences from April and May 1965 on Eliot's poetry, including *Four Quartets* (of which "Burnt Norton" is the first) were issued as *T. S. Eliot and Prayer* (Kansas City, MO: Credence Cassettes, 1995) and *Prayer and the Yoke of Christ* (Kansas City, MO: Credence Cassettes, 2004).

[26] Emily Dickinson, *Complete Poems*, ed. Thomas H. Johnson (Boston: Little Brown, 1960) 149. Merton discussed this poem in a January 29, 1965 novitiate conference, found in *Seeing the World in a Grain of Sand* #9: "Expressions of Spiritual Experience."

[27] Thomas Merton, *Disputed Questions* (New York: Farrar, Straus & Cudahy, 1960) 20–21 (subsequent references will be cited as "*DQ*" parenthetically in the text).

nocence and unselfconscious holistic vision,[28] or "Night-Flowering Cactus" (*ESF* 49–50; *CP* 351–52), in which the plant that blooms only on a single night each year becomes a symbol of the Word issuing from silence,[29] or "Song for Nobody" (*ESF* 35–36; *CP* 337–38), in which the simple beauty of a flower is recognized as being beyond all usefulness and therefore an implicit analogue for contemplative awareness.[30]

But of course a symbolic consciousness is by no means restricted to poets and other artists, as the communion between author and audience clearly demonstrates. While not everyone may have the talent and skills to articulate this dimension of human awareness, everyone has the capability to experience it, however difficult that may be in an unsympathetic cultural environment. Moreover, Merton maintains, the symbol serves not only aesthetic but spiritual and religious purposes.

> Symbol . . . reveals the One as present within our own subjective and interior entity. It reveals that the subjectivity of the subject is, in fact, now, deeply rooted in the infinite God, the Father, the Word, the Spirit, or in Hindu terms Atman, *sat–cit–ananda*. The symbol . . . proclaims that, in one way or another, according to the diversity of religions, the believer can and does even now return to Him from Whom he first came. It does not simply promise a new and effective communication by which the believer can make himself heard by the Deity and can even exercise a certain persuasive force upon Him. It does much more: it opens the believer's inner eye, the eye of the heart, to the realization that he must come to be centered in God because that, in fact, is where his center is. (*L&L* 74–75)

In Christian spiritual teachings, specifically, there is "a tradition of symbolic theology in which positive symbols and analogies of theological teaching are accepted for what they are: true but imperfect approximations which lead us gradually toward that which cannot be properly expressed in human language" (*FV* 269).

---

[28] For further discussion, see Patrick F. O'Connell, "'The Surest Home Is Pointless': A Pathless Path through Merton's Poetic Corpus," *CrossCurrents* 58.4 (2008) 526–34.

[29] For further discussion, see Patrick F. O'Connell, "Nurture by Nature: Emblems of Stillness in a Season of Fury," *The Merton Annual* 21 (2008) 134–42.

[30] For further discussion, see "Nurture by Nature" 122–28.

From Language to Silence

Thus symbolic awareness is an intermediate stage on the way to full contemplative communion that is found in the abyss of a silence beyond words. This is the apophatic way, literally the way that cannot be spoken, the unitive participation in the fullness of being that is beyond words, beyond images, beyond concepts, beyond expression.

> It can be suggested by words, by symbols, but in the very moment of trying to indicate what it knows the contemplative mind takes back what it has said, and denies what it has affirmed. For in contemplation we know by "unknowing." Or, better, we know *beyond* all knowing or "unknowing." Poetry, music and art have something in common with the contemplative experience. But contemplation is beyond aesthetic intuition, beyond art, beyond poetry. Indeed, it is also beyond philosophy, beyond speculative theology. It resumes, transcends and fulfills them all, and yet at the same time it seems, in a certain way, to supersede and to deny them all. (NSC 1–2)

Such awareness is not a rejection of language or of discursive thought, but a recognition that words and images and concepts, the finite products of finite minds, can only provide a proper orientation toward that which is infinite and eternal and absolute, can at best offer only analogies for ultimate truth.

> To know God by "unknowing" is not mere agnosticism. To agree that God is not really to be imagined "out there" is not the same as denying all objective knowledge of his transcendence. To admit, with St. John of the Cross, that we encounter God in the "inmost center" (or "ground") of our own being is not to deny His personality but to affirm it more forcefully than ever, for He is also, precisely, the cause of our own personality and it is in response to His love that our freedom truly develops to personal maturity. A twelfth-century Cistercian, Isaac of Stella, describes this apophatic experience of God as the "falling away of the intelligence not *from* God but *in* God." (FV 270–71)

Part of Merton's attraction to Eastern spiritual traditions was his recognition of a parallel appreciation of the significance of silence and the limitations of language in attaining and describing transcendent experience. He liked to cite the opening verses of the *Tao Te Ching*, in which "Lao Tzu distinguished between the Eternal Tao 'that can not be named,' which is the nameless and unknowable source of all being, and the Tao 'that can be named,' which is the 'Mother of all things.'"[31] His successor Chuang Tzu goes even further, maintaining that "only when one was in contact with the mysterious Tao which is beyond all existent things, which cannot be conveyed either by words or by silence, and which is apprehended only in a state which is neither speech nor silence . . . could one really understand how to live" (*WCT* 21). That is, he rejects a dualistic perspective in which words and silence are posed as alternatives and silence is misconstrued as a kind of technique for attaining and possessing the eternal Tao as an object. *The Ox Mountain Parable* of the Confucian sage Meng Tzu teaches that "Without the night spirit, the dawn breath, silence, passivity, rest, man's nature cannot be itself" (*CGB* 123), is cut off from the deep springs of creativity and renewal. Zen, which synthesizes the wisdom of Mahayana Buddhism and the great Taoist masters, deliberately undermines the pretensions of language to

> tempt us all too easily to see things only in a way that fits our logical preconceptions and our verbal formulas. Instead of seeing *things* and *facts* as they are we see them as reflections and verifications of the sentences we have previously made up in our minds. . . . Zen uses language against itself to blast out these preconceptions and to destroy the specious "reality" in our minds so that we can *see directly*. . . . Since the Zen intuition seeks to awaken a direct metaphysical consciousness beyond the empirical, reflecting, knowing, willing and talking ego, this awareness must be immediately present to itself and not mediated by either conceptual or reflexive or imaginative knowledge.[32]

At the great Buddhist shrine at Polonnaruwa, a week before his death, it is "the silence of the extraordinary faces. The great smiles. Huge and yet subtle. Filled with every possibility, questioning nothing,

---

[31] Thomas Merton, *The Way of Chuang Tzu* (New York: New Directions, 1965) 20–21 (subsequent references will be cited as "*WCT*" parenthetically in the text).

[32] Thomas Merton, *Zen and the Birds of Appetite* (New York: New Directions, 1968) 48–49.

knowing everything, rejecting nothing" that so impresses Merton, a peace and silence that a doctrinaire mind could find threatening, but that conveys to Merton the central Mahayana insight of the union of *sunyata* and *karuna*: "everything is emptiness and everything is compassion" (*AJ* 233, 235).

Of course silence is not considered by Merton to be restricted only to the later stages of the spiritual journey. Penetrating beneath the superficial identity of the social persona, it is essential to authentic self-knowledge: "In the long run, the discipline of creative silence demands a certain kind of faith. For when we come face to face with ourselves in the lonely ground of our own being, we confront many questions about the value of our existence, the reality of our commitments, the authenticity of our everyday lives" (*L&L* 39). Likewise it enables persons to recognize the inner depths of one another and thus enhances mutual respect and love: "Real silence is not isolation. People who live in silence can and do communicate. Silence can carry many different messages; it can be a powerful form of communication."[33] It is, or should be, an integral part of the rhythm of any healthy and creative human life, a complement that enhances the value of language rather than undermining it. "A man cannot understand the true value of silence unless he has a real respect for the validity of language: for the reality which is expressible in language is found, face to face and without medium, in silence. Nor would we find this reality in itself, that is to say in its own silence, unless we were first brought there by language" (*TS* 114). Silence provides the necessary context for meaningful speech, and meaningful speech points beyond itself to a deepened and enriched silence:

> For language to have meaning, there must be intervals of silence somewhere, to divide word from word and utterance from utterance. He who retires into silence does not necessarily hate language. Perhaps it is love and respect for language which impose silence upon him. For the mercy of God is not heard in words unless it is heard, both before and after the words are spoken, in silence. (*DQ* 195)

---

[33] Thomas Merton, *The Springs of Contemplation: A Retreat at the Abbey of Gethsemani*, ed. Jane Marie Richardson (New York: Farrar, Straus, Giroux, 1992) 7.

In refusing to trivialize language by using it to fill a salutary emptiness with meaningless verbiage as a way of avoiding or escaping a confrontation with one's own contingency and mortality, silence prepares for the final word that expresses the meaning of one's whole life:

> Silence is ordered to the ultimate summing up in words of all we have lived for. . . . If our life is poured out in useless words, we will never hear anything, will never become anything, and in the end, because we have said everything before we had anything to say we shall be left speechless at the moment of our greatest decision. But silence is ordered to that final utterance. It is not an end in itself. Our whole life is a meditation of our last decision—the only decision that matters. And we meditate in silence. (*TS* 91–92)

This perspective on the relationship between word and silence in the context of facing one's own death leads back to Calcutta in October 1968, only six weeks before his life would end shortly after speaking at another conference in Thailand on December 10. For some reason Merton decided not to deliver his Calcutta talk as it had been written—perhaps because he considered it too "wordy." He simply tells his audience that he doesn't regard it as "a terribly good paper" (*AJ* 306) but that it is available in printed form for them to read if they so desire. Instead he presents his main ideas in a more informal style, more sharing than lecturing. He concludes with the following words, which are perhaps better known than any other of the many words that have been quoted thus far, and can perhaps be considered as at least one part of his final testament, his expression in speech of what he had learned in silence:

> I stand among you as one who offers a small message of hope, that first, there are always people who dare to seek on the margin of society, who are not dependent on social acceptance, not dependent on social routine, and prefer a kind of free-floating existence under a state of risk. And among these people, if they are faithful to their own calling, to their own vocation, and to their own message from God, communication on the deepest level is

possible. And the deepest level of communication is not communication, but communion. It is wordless. It is beyond words, and it is beyond speech, and it is beyond concept. Not that we discover a new unity. We discover an older unity. My dear brothers, we are already one. But we imagine that we are not. And what we have to recover is our original unity. What we have to be is what we are. (*AJ* 307–8)

Final Integration:
Culture, Multiculturalism, Transcultural Consciousness

Among the many writers, some scholarly, some popular, some eccentric (to put it charitably) who decades ago had already begun looking ahead to what might be in store for us in the present century—the new millennium—one of the more interesting and influential was the distinguished Harvard political scientist Samuel P. Huntington, who had written an important book entitled *The Clash of Civilizations and the Remaking of World Order*,[1] in which he predicted the social, cultural, and political arrangements in a post-communist, post-ideological world. The good news of his analysis was that he had foreseen a renewed emphasis on and commitment to religion in the years ahead; the bad news was that he predicted this resurgence of religion would be a divisive rather than a unifying force. In this case, we can at least begin to judge the book by its cover, which featured three identical photos of a globe—the "Unisphere," symbol of the 1964 New York World's Fair, ironically enough—against a darkening sky, on which are superimposed a cross, the star and crescent of Islam, and the Taoist yin/yang circle. In Huntington's view, these symbolized the major groupings of civilizations that, as his title suggests, were fated to clash in the coming century, a prescient if not prophetic

---

[1] Samuel P. Huntington, *The Clash of Civilizations and the Remaking of World Order* (New York: Simon & Schuster, 1996).

foreshadowing of the ominous national and international events of the first quarter of the twenty-first century, from the terrorist attacks of September 11, 2001; through the rise of so-called Christian nationalism evident in the invasion of the United States Capitol on January 6, 2021, in an attempt to overturn the results of the 2020 election; to the return of Donald Trump to the White House with an unyielding "America First" agenda four years later; and to the present state of widespread hostility, division, and conflict throughout the world, including Vladimir Putin's invasion of Ukraine, given virtually uncritical support by the Russian Orthodox hierarchy; the seemingly interminable conflict in the Middle East, marked both by Islamic fundamentalists bent on obliterating the state of Israel and by ultra-Orthodox Jewish settlers in the West Bank equally determined to restore the boundaries of biblical Israel; and the global migrant crisis, which frequently has included a strong element of interreligious hostility that is both a cause of flight and an effect of efforts to find asylum elsewhere.

On one level, Huntington's book was a valuable warning against an arrogant and short-sighted presumption, in the aftermath of the decline of Marxism, of the inevitable triumph of "Western values," which are too easily reduced to the vision of a globe girdled in the air by a belt of Rupert Murdoch's or Elon Musk's satellites, and on the ground by a network of Walmarts and McDonald's. He was already aware that for millions of people this global "free market" is the equivalent of cultural extinction and would be fiercely resisted. To attempt to build a "new world order" on a homogenized, universalized consumer society is to invite either supine cultural and economic conformity or widespread rebellion and resultant chaos. But his alternative, to accept separate cultural spheres of influence, based principally on religious allegiance, and to abjure any interference, or even significant involvement, beyond one's own sphere, seemed to invite an atmosphere of mutual suspicion and heightened intolerance. It suggested that for the foreseeable future a vision of global unity, of the human family, must be subordinated to a recognition of the plurality of separate and, to a considerable extent, mutually exclusive civilizations. But such a view, at least by default, is in danger of encouraging the most reactionary and chauvinistic elements in any society, those who magnify differences and ignore or even conceal commonalities. The book proposed a retreat into a sort of neo-isolationism, not of nation-states but of multinational "civilizations," in order to minimize both the occasions and the consequences of clashes between those who hold incompatible worldviews. As a solution, this is far from ideal, as Huntington himself realized, but he considered it preferable to the most likely alternative, in which the various blocs attempt to impose, or infiltrate, their cultural and economic agendas onto others, with resentment and violent resistance as the inevitable consequence.

Reading Huntington's diagnosis and proposed solution, one might find oneself asking the question of Ebenezer Scrooge to the Ghost of Christmas Future: "Are these the shadows of the things that Will be, or are they shadows of things that May be, only?"[2] Is a world of divisions, of cultural and religious exclusiveness and antagonism, inevitable, or is there hope for a different scenario, a world that will combine respect for diversity with a recognition and fostering of underlying unity? In a brief afterthought, headed "The Commonalities of Civilization," that concludes his book (318–21), Huntington did sketch an alternative vision, or emphasis, that would identify and encourage ideals and values shared by the different cultural blocs. But a mere four pages devoted to common values after more than three hundred pages focusing on points of division would seem to be too little and too late to be very persuasive. The major thesis of the book remained the need to recognize and live with conflicting agendas, basically an adaptation of the strategy of the "cold war" to the new era of a multipolar world.

In this atmosphere of potential and actual polarization, the figure of Thomas Merton stands as a sign of contradiction and a sign of reconciliation. If Huntington is right and religious affiliations become a major determinant of the fault lines between civilizations, Merton's personal interest in and involvement with other religious traditions can be recognized not just as a private, or a spiritual, or a monastic concern, but as having significant social and political implications, offering a model of cross-cultural interaction very different from the alienation, fragmentation, and friction that Huntington foresaw. As

---

[2] Charles Dickens, *A Christmas Carol* (1843), in *The Christmas Books*, 2 vols. (Baltimore: Penguin, 1971) 1.124.

Pope Francis suggested in his 2015 address to the joint session of Congress, Merton models an alternative future, and his example calls Christians and others to work to make that future a reality. It may well be that for the world in the new millennium to flourish, two of the most passionate and intense commitments of Merton's later life, to peacemaking and nonviolence and to interreligious dialogue, must be integrated and made a priority by persons and communities of faith throughout the world. Voices of mutual respect and shared wisdom must not by drowned out by shouts of intolerance and insensitivity. Dialogue must not be destroyed by diatribe. Religious people of all traditions have both an opportunity and an obligation to shape the emerging consciousness of the new millennium by recognizing and nurturing bonds of spiritual kinship that transcend differences of race and culture and creed. This is what Thomas Merton did in his own life and advocated in his writings. He emphasized repeatedly that it is "absolutely essential" for contemporary secular society to recover "a dimension of *wisdom* oriented to contemplation as well as to wise action," and that to develop this sapiential awareness, "it is no longer sufficient merely to go back over the Christian and European cultural traditions. The horizons of the world are no longer confined to Europe and America. We have to gain new perspectives, and on this our spiritual and even our physical survival may depend."[3] For Merton, any authentic "remaking of world order" requires not merely minimizing "the clash of civilizations" but maximizing experience of and commitment to cultural interdependence.

Merton's mature works certainly exemplify a receptivity to other cultures. His late poem *The Geography of Lograire*,[4] for example, with its evocation of Melanesian cargo cultists and Bantu philosophers,

---

[3] Thomas Merton, *Mystics and Zen Masters* (New York: Farrar, Straus and Giroux, 1967) 80 (subsequent references will be cited as "*MZM*" parenthetically in the text); Thomas Merton, *Selected Essays*, ed. Patrick F. O'Connell (Maryknoll, NY: Orbis, 2013) 111 (subsequent references will be cited as "*SE*" parenthetically in the text).

[4] Thomas Merton, *The Geography of Lograire* (New York: New Directions, 1969); Thomas Merton, *The Collected Poems of Thomas Merton* (New York: New Directions, 1977) 455–609 (subsequent references will be cited as "*CP*" parenthetically in the text). For an overview, see Patrick F. O'Connell, "Geography of Lograire, The" in William H. Shannon, Christine M. Bochen, and Patrick F. O'Connell, *The Thomas Merton Encyclopedia* (Maryknoll, NY: Orbis, 2002) 169–74.

of Muslim world travelers and Native American ghost dancers, of nineteenth-century Arctic explorers and seventeenth-century English ranters, might be considered a manifesto of cultural diversity; but the form of the poem, what has been called its mandala design, invoking the four points of the compass, suggests not just diversity but an underlying unity, a shared human condition, a common human dilemma, a solidarity in the universal human quest for meaning and for transcendence. Merton's inclusive perspective can provide a point of convergence and reconciliation which has an appeal for all parties, a vision which is authentically catholic, universal, without submerging the particular in the general. Its emphasis on dialogue, shared insights, and mutual respect highlights Merton's awareness of an emerging global culture that must prize unity-in-difference if it is to avoid both a totalitarian uniformity and a destructive fragmentation. Six distinct but interrelated aspects can be considered as contributing to developing what Merton describes as a "transcultural consciousness."

Developing Transcultural Consciousness

Logically as well as chronologically, the starting point for Merton's transcultural perspective is a thorough grounding in his own Western tradition. Though at times he fantasized about enrolling as a Negro,[5] or a Navajo,[6] in reaction to the stupidity and viciousness of members of his own race, he never repudiated or underestimated the authentic values of Western civilization. On the contrary, he declared himself to be "deeply in sympathy with, and I think imbued with, the traditional religious culture of the West";[7] and this sympathy extended beyond the religious to the broader cultural milieu of Europe: reflecting on lines from Vergil's *Georgics*, first encountered in prep school

---

[5] See his October 5, 1963 letter to Robert Lax in Thomas Merton and Robert Lax, *When Prophecy Still Had a Voice: The Letters of Thomas Merton & Robert Lax*, ed. Arthur W. Biddle (Lexington: University Press of Kentucky, 2001) 251.

[6] See his January 5, 1968 letter to John Howard Griffin in Thomas Merton, *The Road to Joy: Letters to New and Old Friends*, ed. Robert E. Daggy (New York: Farrar, Straus, Giroux, 1989) 139–40.

[7] Thomas Merton, *Conjectures of a Guilty Bystander* (Garden City, NY: Doubleday, 1966) 293 (subsequent references will be cited as "*CGB*" parenthetically in the text).

days, he writes, "To have learned such lines as these and many others is to have entered into a kind of communion with the inner strength of the civilization to which I belong, and whatever may be the roar of Acheron (which these days seems much more definitive than the voice of Classicism) this inner strength is, in itself, indestructible" (*CGB* 237).[8] Some of the most lyrical pages in *Conjectures of a Guilty Bystander* are those in which he reflects on the roots of his own intellectual and spiritual inheritance, as when he speaks of Paris as the cultural capital of Western Christendom, and remarks, "the sign of Paris is on me, indelibly!" (*CGB* 163), both because it was there that his parents first met as art students and because of the varied streams of tradition—Dionysian, Victorine, Franciscan, Thomistic—which converged there and influenced his own formation. This love and gratitude for his own cultural legacy is even more deeply expressed a few pages later when he speaks of the "resonances" he feels with many predecessors and contemporaries, the "good choir" of "Maritain, Van der Meer de Walcheren, Bloy, Green, Chagall, Satie . . . variety and unity" and then "another, earlier music most deep with me: Blake, Tauler, Eckhart, Ruysbroeck. They sang me into the Church, these voices. And Dante's voice" (*CGB* 170).[9] It is of these and the tradition they represent that he writes, "I know that I must keep alive in myself what I have once known and grown into: and if anyone else wants a part of it, I can try to pass it on" (*CGB* 169).[10] For Merton this heritage is not exclusively intellectual but broadly and deeply experiential, so that the landscapes of southern France and the sounds and silences of the English countryside, scenes of his cosmopolitan upbringing, can be described as "angels," as messengers of revelation. He notes, "All this is not purely supernatural, doubtless: and yet it is precisely in this quasi-sacramental way, by means of this cultural matter with a mysterious Christian form, that

---

[8] See also the earlier version of this passage in Thomas Merton, *Turning Toward the World: The Pivotal Years. Journals, vol. 4: 1960–1963*, ed. Victor A. Kramer (San Francisco: HarperCollins, 1996) 251–52 [9/29/1962] (subsequent references will be cited as "*TTW*" parenthetically in the text).

[9] See also the earlier version of this passage in Merton's journal entry for August 7, 1961 (*TTW* 149).

[10] See also the earlier version of this and the following quotation in Merton's journal entry for August 6, 1961 (*TTW* 147–49).

God works in our lives, since we are creatures of history, and tradition is vitally important to us" (*CGB* 167). It is essential to realize, then, that Merton does not come to an encounter with other cultures empty-handed; his own tradition is vitally present in him and available to be communicated to others. Secure in his own cultural identity, he was not threatened by different ideas or customs, and so was able to respond to them creatively rather than to react defensively.

But if Merton is no rootless, alienated wanderer, in search of a replacement for a culture he had rejected, or felt had rejected him, neither is he an apologist for Western hubris, a cultural imperialist bent on proving the superiority of his own position and determined to impose it on others. A second reason for becoming thoroughly conversant with one's own culture, and the second aspect of Merton's transcultural consciousness, is to recognize the shortcomings and distortions of one's tradition, its past sins, its current problems, its future threats. This self-critical attitude is itself one of the strengths of Western culture, in Merton's opinion, though one increasingly endangered by a conformist, materialist, and totalitarian mindset. He writes:

> Our ability to see ourselves objectively and to criticize our own actions, even our own failings, is the source of a very real strength. But to those who fear truth, who have begun to forget the genuine Western heritage and to become immersed in crude materialism without spirit, this critical tendency presents the greatest danger. Indeed it must seem perilous to those who cultivate a simultaneous complacent certitude of might and right in order to destroy without hesitation the ideological enemy. (*CGB* 62)

The tendency to take oneself too seriously, to believe one's own propaganda, what Merton calls "the dogmatic *humorlessness* of the self-designated realists" (*CGB* 62), is the antithesis of this self-critical attitude and a betrayal of the authentic stream of Western consciousness. "I for one," Merton comments, "mean to preserve all the Europe that is in me as long as I live, and above all I will keep laughing until they close my mouth with fallout" (*CGB* 62). Thus Merton's prophetic critique of the crimes and the follies of his own country and his own culture is an expression of fidelity and commitment to the best and most genuine impulses of that culture. It is, of course, no less critical for that. His analyses of the depersonalization that he discovers at the heart of the problems of war, of racism, of colonial exploitation, of quantified, technological, soulless mass society, are all the more powerful for his belief that these evils are antithetical to the authentic genius of the West, albeit they reflect strands of thought and behavior present from the earliest days of European civilization. Merton realizes that this self-betrayal poses serious obstacles to intercultural dialogue, since the failure to recognize and reverence the intrinsic dignity of the human person has been projected outward as contempt for and conquest of the other. For Merton "the greatest sin of the European–Russian–American complex which we call the West is not only greed and cruelty, not only moral dishonesty and infidelity to truth, but above all its *unmitigated arrogance toward* the *rest of the human race*. Western civilization is now in full decline into barbarism (a barbarism that springs *from within itself*) because it has been guilty of a twofold disloyalty, to God and to Man,"[11] for to despise, degrade, and destroy those made in the image of God is to deny the Creator as well. Thus Merton displays a profound yet healthily realistic ambivalence toward his own tradition. He recognizes that any Westerner encountering other cultures brings a double heritage, representing both the admirable and the shameful aspects of white, European civilization. To neglect or deny either of these dimensions is to doom any encounter to frustration, since it will be based not on honesty but on either self-hatred or an unwarranted, self-satisfied complacency. By acknowledging the full impact of Western culture on its own people and the rest of the world, Merton positions himself for a mutually beneficial contact with non-Western cultures.

The third dimension of this transcultural identity, then, is the modest, humble, honest effort to comprehend other civilizations on their own terms. It is particularly important, in Merton's view, not to make any premature attempt at assimilation, to reject the temptation to incorporate congenial elements of another culture into one's own worldview and to discard the rest. Such an approach would simply be colonialism in another guise. There must be a willingness to recognize and respect the integrity of another culture, to respond to it,

---

[11] Thomas Merton, *Emblems of a Season of Fury* (New York: New Directions, 1963) 78 (subsequent references will be cited as "*ESF*" parenthetically in the text); *CP* 380.

as best one can, as a whole. The attempt to refute or to co-opt the worldview of another culture, rather than to enter into sincere dialogue with it, is to make misunderstanding, tension, and perhaps even hostility, inevitable. "One cannot arrive at an understanding of any 'wisdom,' whether natural or supernatural, by arguing either for or against it. Wisdom is not penetrated by logical analysis." What is needed, rather, to appreciate the core values of another tradition, is the sympathetic effort to perceive the world from the standpoint of the other, to enter as far as possible into that framework: "The values hidden in Oriental thought actually reveal themselves only on the plane of spiritual experience, or perhaps, if you like, aesthetic experience" (*SE* 112).

Merton proposes a model of "dialogue as compassion, substitution, identification, taking upon himself the effects of what 'our own' have done, knowingly or otherwise, to 'them'" (*CGB* 132). The same principles which mark Merton's conception of nonviolence are essential to intercultural dialogue: a respect for the humanity and dignity of the other, a recognition that one does not have a monopoly on the truth, a willingness to learn from the other, a commitment to truth rather than to defending one's own position, a "person-oriented" approach which "does not seek so much to *control* as to *respond*, and to awaken response," which promotes "an openness of free exchange in which reason and love have freedom of action."[12] On its deepest level, this receptivity is an openness to the divine present within the other: "God speaks, and God is to be heard, not only on Sinai, not only in my own heart, but in the *voice of the stranger*. We must, then, see the truth in the stranger, and the truth we see must be a newly living truth, not just a projection of a dead conventional idea of our own—a projection of our own self upon the stranger" (*ESF* 82; *CP* 384). To do this is to take a risk, to put in jeopardy the comfortable, secure conception of truth one already has, but it is also to make possible a widened, broadened, deepened awareness of truth which is pure gift, grace, revelation. Unlike the conqueror, imposing alien ideas and customs on another, unlike the tourist, oblivious to the inner meaning of quaint foreign behavior, the transcultural person

---

[12] Thomas Merton, *Faith and Violence: Christian Teaching and Christian Practice* (Notre Dame, IN: University of Notre Dame Press, 1968) 28 (subsequent references will be cited as "*FV*" parenthetically in the text).

realizes that others "have a life, a spirit, a thought, a culture of their own which has its own peculiar individual character," and that "the stranger has something very valuable, something irreplaceable to give him: something that can never be bought with money, never estimated by publicists, never exploited by political agitators: the spiritual understanding of a friend who belongs to a different culture" (*ESF* 85; *CP* 387).

Having made the commitment to patient listening, to allowing the other culture to reveal itself on its own terms, the transcultural pilgrim is then able to relate new insights to his or her own tradition, to allow the voice of the other to speak to his or her own condition. The fourth dimension of transcultural identity moves from comprehension to convergence and synthesis as one sees the strengths and weaknesses of one's own culture from a new standpoint, through the eyes of the other. Thus for Merton one of the benefits of the encounter with Eastern thought is the reawakening of awareness of the sapiential, contemplative dimension of Western culture which has frequently been overshadowed by the more pragmatic, goal-oriented, activist mentality which has predominated at least from the time of the Renaissance. The other culture may become a mirror in which to perceive our own neglected values as well as a challenge to reexamine problematic elements, as the pure consciousness of Zen provides an alternative to "the Cartesian and scientific consciousness of modern man, whose basic axiom is that the 'cogitating consciousness' ('clothed with the ideas of objects') is the foundation of all truth and certitude" (*MZM* 241). The great exemplar of this cross-cultural enlightenment for Merton is Gandhi, who discovered the riches of his own tradition by coming into contact with the thought of the West: "he recognized that the West had something good about it that was good not because it was Western but because it was also Eastern: that is to say, it was universal. It was through his acquaintance with writers like Tolstoy and Thoreau, and then his reading of the New Testament, that Gandhi rediscovered his own tradition and his Hindu *dharma* (religion, duty)."[13] Of course he returned the favor by alerting Westerners to elements in their own tradition, specifically the nonviolent dimension

---

[13] Thomas Merton, ed., *Gandhi on Non-Violence: Selected Texts from Non-Violence in Peace and War* (New York: New Directions, 1965) 4 (subsequent references will be cited as "*GNV*" parenthetically in the text).

of the teaching of Christ, which had become obscured by centuries of cultural overlay which had little to do with the gospel. "One of the great lessons of Gandhi's life remains this: through the spiritual traditions of the West, he, and India, discovered his Indian heritage and with it his own 'right mind.' And in his fidelity to his own heritage and its spiritual sanity, he was able to show men of the West and of the whole world a way to recover their own 'right mind' in their own tradition" (*GNV* 4).

That the questions raised and the insights offered by another worldview are profoundly relevant to the development of one's own tradition was a truth known by the early generations of Christians, for whom Platonism provided "a language and sensibility that were equipped to penetrate in a specially significant way the depths of the revealed mystery of Christ" (*SE* 112). It characterized the flowering of medieval Christian society, which was enriched by "turning to the non-Christian world—to Aristotle and to Islam" (*CGB* 205). Merton sees the great intellectual synthesis of the medieval era, the theology of Aquinas, which he characterizes as "a theology of intellectual reconciliation, which . . . justifies itself by uniting opposites and looking beyond the stereotypical solutions of problems" (*CGB* 187), as arising precisely out of this fruitful interaction of different traditions: "The theology of St. Thomas was fully rooted in the Christian culture of his time, but also in the culture that was resulting from the encounter between Christianity and Islam, which did so much to create the modern Western world" (*CGB* 185). This same cross-pollination, Merton maintains, is needed today if the West, if the world, is to surmount its crises:

> The cultural heritage of Asia has as much right to be studied in our colleges as the cultural heritage of Greece and Rome. If the West continues to underestimate and to neglect the spiritual heritage of the East, it may hasten the tragedy that threatens man and his civilization. If the West can recognize that contact with Eastern thought can renew our appreciation for our own cultural heritage, a product of the fusion of Judeo-Christian religion with Greco-Roman culture, then it will be easier to defend that heritage, not only in Asia but in the West as well. (*MZM* 45–46)

These dimensions already discussed could be considered crosscultural or intercultural, but a fully transcultural perspective entails two more aspects that Merton also describes and exemplifies. Besides considering another culture on its own terms and discovering how to integrate it with one's own tradition, there is a further step in which the artifacts of another culture become part of one's own heritage. One recognizes a kinship that transcends cultural differences and grounds itself in what all human beings share, precisely their humanity! Thus in the preface to *Mystics and Zen Masters*, Merton announces that the aim of someone like himself is "not merely to look at these other traditions coldly and objectively from the outside, but, in some measure at least, to try to share in the values and the expression which they embody. In other words, he is not content to write about them without making them, as far as possible, 'his own'" (*MZM* ix). It is this breadth of vision and sympathy that Merton sees embodied in Gandhi: "The Indian mind that was awakening in Gandhi was inclusive not exclusive. It was at once Indian and universal. . . . It was a spirit which was, he believed, strong enough to heal every division" (*GNV* 5). While acknowledging that it is perhaps impossible to achieve fully this transcultural appropriation, Merton is nevertheless convinced that in the emergent global society, it is crucially important to go beyond a narrow, parochial conception of culture: "We hopefully look forward not to an age of eclecticism and syncretism, certainly, but to an age of understanding and adaptation that will be able to synthesize and make use of all which is good and noble in all the traditions of the past. . . . we must hope for a new world culture that takes account of all civilized philosophies" (*MZM* 65). Certainly Merton's own affinity for Chuang Tzu, for instance, exemplifies this transcultural bond. When he speaks, in *Day of a Stranger*, of the "mental ecology" of his hermitage, the "living balance of spirits in this corner of the woods," he includes along with Western writers "the reassuring companionship of many silent Tzu's and Fu's," and singles out for special notice "Chuang Tzu whose climate is perhaps most the climate of this silent corner of woods. A climate in which there is no need for explanation."[14] He is likewise attracted to Zen precisely because he finds it to be "consciousness unstructured by particular form or particular system, a trans-cultural, trans-religious, trans-

---

[14] Thomas Merton, *Day of a Stranger* (Salt Lake City: Gibbs M. Smith, 1981) 35.

formed consciousness."[15] It is this capacity to transcend the limitations of one's own worldview, to become "in a certain sense identified with everybody,"[16] which Merton, drawing on the Persian-American psychoanalyst Reza Arasteh, calls "final integration":

> The man who has attained final integration is no longer limited by the culture in which he has grown up. . . . He accepts not only his own community, his own society, his own friends, his own culture, but all mankind. . . . He is fully 'Catholic' in the best sense of the word. He has a unified vision and experience of the one truth shining out in all its various manifestations, some clearer than others, some more definite and certain than others. He does not set these partial views up in opposition to each other, but unifies them in a dialectic or an insight of complementarity. (*CWA* 212)

Here then is authentic transcultural consciousness, which shatters the narrow parameters in which the discussion of cultural diversity is too often constricted, an atmosphere in which petty rivalries and mutual incomprehension are evidence not of final integration but of a disintegration which is hopefully only a passing phase on the way to unity. For Merton believes that this vision can no longer be the preserve of a few but is now "becoming a need and aspiration of mankind as a whole" (*CWA* 216), a necessity if humanity is to surmount the existential crisis in which it finds itself.

Yet as critically important as this mutual interpenetration of various traditions certainly is, Merton reminds us that absolute loyalty is due neither to a single culture nor to a synthesis of all cultures. The ultimate stage of transcultural consciousness transcends the very category of culture itself: "The path to final integration for the individual, and for the community lies, in any case, beyond the dictates and programs of any culture ('Christian culture' included)" (*CWA* 216), because all culture, all human achievement, is provisional, partial, a limited approximation of the divine design for humanity, the

---

[15] Thomas Merton, *Zen and the Birds of Appetite* (New York: New Directions, 1968) 4 (subsequent references will be cited as "*ZBA*" parenthetically in the text).

[16] Thomas Merton, *Contemplation in a World of Action* (Garden City, NY: Doubleday, 1971) 211 (subsequent references will be cited as "*CWA*" parenthetically in the text).

fullness of truth, the reign of God. "For a Christian," Merton writes, "a transcultural integration is eschatological. The rebirth of man and of society on a transcultural level is a rebirth into the transformed and redeemed time, the time of the Kingdom, the time of the Spirit, the time of 'the end.' It means a disintegration of the social and cultural self, the product of purely human history, and the reintegration of that self in Christ, in salvation history, in the mystery of redemption, in the Pentecostal 'new creation'" (*CWA* 216). It is of this final level of awareness that Merton spoke during his 1968 journey to the East, at the Spiritual Summit Conference in Calcutta, a level of awareness by which one goes beyond communication to communion, beyond the integration available through human effort to the unity offered by divine gift, a communion "beyond words, . . . beyond speech, beyond concept," and we might add, beyond culture. It is on the final level of transcultural consciousness, at once primordial and eschatological, that one discovers the original unity of all humanity, that "we are already one," and is empowered to recover that unity, "to be . . . what we are."[17]

Resources for Final Integration

This vision of global unity Merton articulates is a compelling one, but the challenges of actualizing it in a world of ever more fragmented ethnic and cultural enclaves is daunting. What resources do Merton's life and words provide to meet these challenges? They can be helpfully grouped under three headings: solitude, solidarity, social transformation.

Solitude is an essential foundation for the encounter of differing religious traditions in at least three important ways. First of all, solitude entails detachment, an "unhooking" from all socially constructed determinants of identity, a relativizing of the claims of race, class, nation. Solitude exposes the inadequacies of "the superficial, false social self, the image made up of the prejudices, the whimsey, the posturing, the pharisaic self-concern and the pseudo dedication which are the heritage of the individual in a limited and imperfect

---

[17] Thomas Merton, *The Asian Journal*, ed. Naomi Burton Stone, Brother Patrick Hart, and James Laughlin (New York: New Directions, 1973) 308 (subsequent references will be cited as "*AJ*" parenthetically in the text).

group."¹⁸ It likewise rejects as "the most tenacious and damaging of illusions" the egotistic self-assertion of those who try to reshape society in their own image, "who seek, in a word, the triumphant affirmation of their own will, their own power, considered as the end for which they exist,"¹⁹ and are thereby just as bound by a socially defined identity, and doomed as well to eventual frustration. The liberation offered by solitude from the demands and restrictions of group identity, defined in opposition to other groups, is itself an insight shared across cultures. Merton cites the eighth-century Hindu philosopher Sankara's recognition of the need to "disregard those attributes which have been superimposed" on the true self from the outside and quotes his command, "Cease to identify yourself with race, clan, name, form and walk of life" (*AJ* 95).

The cleansing fires of solitude must purify even religious identity, insofar as that is perceived and experienced primarily as a sociological category, a source of group cohesion, a criterion of acceptability, and a principle of exclusivity and exclusion: solitude gives rise to "a humility which refuses arrogantly to set up the Church as an 'eternal' institution in the world" (*CGB* 42). At the same time, solitude makes possible a more profound realization of the inner meaning of one's own spiritual tradition. Solitude for the Christian is an existential encounter with the One whom Merton calls "this Solitary God"; it shares the divine solitude by participating in the central mysteries of redemption, "through the Passion and Resurrection of Christ—through the solitude of Gethsemani and of Calvary, and the mystery of Easter, and the solitude of the Ascension: all of which precede the great Communion of Pentecost" (*DQ* 204–5). This deepening of one's own religious convictions, the second component of solitude, is not a hindrance to genuine relationships with those of other faiths but the necessary basis for any meaningful interchange that is not to be reduced to a facile and superficial "least common denominator" spirituality or to a turbid and muddled syncretism,

---

[18] Thomas Merton, *Disputed Questions* (New York: Farrar, Straus & Cudahy, 1960) 206 (subsequent references will be cited as "*DQ*" parenthetically in the text).

[19] Thomas Merton, *"Honorable Reader": Reflections on My Work*, ed. Robert E. Daggy (New York: Crossroad, 1989) 87–88 (subsequent references will be cited as "'*HR*'" parenthetically in the text).

which Merton emphatically repudiated as "a mishmash of semireligious verbiage and pieties, a devotionalism that admits everything and therefore takes nothing with full seriousness" (*AJ* 316).

Merton is drawn to explore other religious traditions not in spite of but because of his faith in Christ and his gospel, which reveals a God of infinite love. Solitude offers an experiential awareness of universality, for there one encounters as one's own center the Center of all reality: "in this inmost 'I' my own solitude meets the solitude of every other man and the solitude of God. Hence it is beyond division, beyond limitation, beyond selfish affirmation" (*DQ* 207). The depth of solitude is thus complemented by its breadth, enabling one to recognize affinities with other traditions: "the more I am able to affirm others, to say 'yes' to them in myself, by discovering them in myself and myself in them, the more real I am. I am fully real if my own heart says yes to *everyone*. . . . If I affirm myself as a Catholic merely by denying all that is Muslim, Jewish, Protestant, Hindu, Buddhist, etc., in the end I will find that there is not much left for me to affirm as a Catholic: and certainly no breath of the Spirit with which to affirm it" (*CGB* 129).

In statements such as this we recognize that solitude has passed over into solidarity. Here too we can focus on three key elements. The first of these is respect, "a respect for persons based on respect for *being* instead of doing" (*CGB* 283). Solidarity is not merely a goal to be sought but a fact to be recognized, rooted in the shared identity of every person as, in Christian terms, created in the image and likeness of God. The fundamental respect for others that is the basis for solidarity is built on an affirmation of the dignity intrinsic to any human being, whatever his or her beliefs. It prescinds from the question of whether others are deserving of our respect, from what Merton considers the "basic temptation" (*CGB* 156) to make acceptance of others contingent on their conforming to our expectations. Such arrogance can lead only to suspicion, mistrust, and hostility, as the history of Western encounters with other cultures has repeatedly proven. Genuine respect is able "to get along without constantly applying the yardstick of 'worthiness' . . . to laugh, after all, at all preposterous ideas of 'worthiness'" (*CGB* 157). It rejects contemporary Western society's obsessive focus on achievements and productivity as criteria for acceptability, according to which "men are valued not for what they are but for what they *do* or what they *have*." Respect depends rather on the essentially contemplative insight, common to all cultures where wisdom is still cherished, that "without a sense of *being* and a respect for being, there can be no real appreciation for the person" (*CGB* 282).

Thus solidarity develops through an existential realization of what is ontologically true. Such growth is both the initiative for and the consequence of dialogue, the second element of solidarity. Interreligious and intercultural exchange is of course at the heart of Merton's contemplative alternative to the clash of civilizations, or to a soulless global "culture" dedicated to efficiency, pragmatism, and profits, a possibility he considered just as likely. "We are witnessing the growth of a truly universal consciousness in the modern world. This universal consciousness may be a consciousness of transcendent freedom and vision, or it may simply be a vast blur of mechanized triviality and ethical cliché" (*AJ* 317). Those committed to spiritual values and discipline have a responsibility to form this universal consciousness through dialogue. While he had no grandiose expectations of "visible results of earth-shaking importance," Merton stated that he was nevertheless "convinced that communication in depth . . . is now not only possible and desirable, but most important for the destinies of Twentieth-Century Man" (*AJ* 313). He considered the final decades of the second millennium after Christ to be a time of "crisis, a moment of crucial choice," when the potential loss of humanity's "spiritual heritage" (*AJ* 317) could result in a world fragmented into hostile segments or regimented into sterile conformity. Dialogue both assumes and confirms that what unites is more significant and ultimately more powerful than what divides. While acknowledging the very real and substantial differences among religions on the level of concepts and doctrines, Merton maintained that the "great similarities and analogies in the realm of religious experience. . . . a very real quality of existential likeness" (*AJ* 312), could provide mutual support and mutual insight across confessional boundaries and thereby shape a global awareness oriented to wisdom rather than to technique and control.

Dialogue not only creates insights; it creates relationships that transcend communication to reach the deeper dimension of communion, an experience of "original unity" that "is beyond words . . .

beyond speech . . . beyond concept" (*AJ* 308). This existential identification with another—even with someone of a different culture, faith, or tradition—is the most profound level of solidarity. It can be observed in Merton's correspondence with his Muslim friend Abdul Aziz,[20] or in his account of his visit with the aged Zen master D. T. Suzuki.[21] It is perhaps articulated most memorably in his statement on behalf of Thich Nhat Hanh, the Vietnamese Buddhist monk exiled from his war-torn country:

> I have said Nhat Hanh is my brother, and it is true. . . . I have far more in common with Nhat Hanh that I have with many Americans, and I do not hesitate to say it. It is vitally important that such bonds be admitted. They are the bonds of a new solidarity and a new brotherhood which is beginning to be evident on all the five continents and which cuts across all political, religious and cultural lines to unite young men and women in every country in something that is more concrete than an ideal and more alive than a program. (*FV* 108)[22]

Such solidarity as this, like the grain of wheat that falls to the ground and dies (John 12:24), is the true seed of social transformation, based not on a political program, though politics are certainly not to be excluded as a means, but on spiritual insight: transformation of

---

[20] Thomas Merton, *The Hidden Ground of Love: Letters on Religious Experience and Social Concerns*, ed. William H. Shannon (New York: Farrar, Straus, Giroux, 1985) 43–67 (subsequent references will be cited as "*HGL*" parenthetically in the text).

[21] Thomas Merton, *Dancing in the Water of Life: Seeking Peace in the Hermitage. Journals, vol. 5: 1963–1965*, ed. Robert E. Daggy (San Francisco: HarperCollins, 1997) 115–17.

[22] That such a commitment to human solidarity is able to embrace even a professed enemy is movingly demonstrated by Merton's fellow Cistercian Dom Christian de Chergé, Prior of Our Lady of Atlas Monastery in Algeria, one of the monks killed by Muslim insurgents in May 1996 (beatified with his fellow Algerian martyrs on December 8, 2018); in a message left to be opened in the event of his death, he thanks God for all his friends, finally including even "you too, my last minute friend, who will not know what you are doing, Yes, for you too I say this THANK YOU AND THIS 'A-DIEU'—to commend you to this God in whose face I see yours" (*National Catholic Reporter* 33.28 [May 16, 1997] 17). Here is the full revelation of cross-cultural identification, able to recognize even in the face of one's assassin the face of God.

society through transformation of consciousness. But the process of growth and the bearing of fruit cannot be calculated according to a human timetable. There is no guarantee that even widespread interreligious and transcultural contact will secure global justice and peace, nor even that outreach to "separated brothers" will be reciprocated. It is quite possible that Huntington's prognosis of crosscultural tensions and clashes may prove to be accurate, and that the present century may continue to be as marred by conflict as the century that preceded it. But even, or especially, given such a future, fidelity to a different vision and a different practice is essential. Such a faith-based commitment to social transformation of a multicultural world entails a three-fold witness. First is the witness of resistance, a refusal to accept the divisions and antagonisms dictated by shapers of policy and makers of public opinion. In Merton's view, such a stance is not only social and political but fundamentally religious, "a sign of contradiction" to the secular world's tendency "to recreate a god in its own image, a god who justifies its own slogans"; it is allegiance to the God of all humanity, whose "mysterious transcendency places Him infinitely beyond the reach of catchwords, advertisements and politics" (*DQ* 204). Merton points, once again, to Gandhi as the great twentieth-century exemplar of this witness of resistance, by his "unmasking of political falsehood, awakening all men to the demands of the time and to the need for renewal and unity on a world scale" (*GNV* 10). In a period when "totalitarian and nationalist consciousnesses," with their "paranoid fury, exploding into alienation, division, and destruction," were spreading in the West and even in the East, "the spirit which Gandhi discovered in himself was reaching out to unity, love, and peace. It was a spirit which was, he believed, strong enough to heal every division" (*GNV* 5).

For Merton, as for Gandhi, the need to say "no" to artificial divisions and the hatreds they spawn is matched by the need to say "yes" to all that creates and strengthens bonds of acceptance and understanding. The witness of resistance is complemented by the witness of reconciliation, which is grounded in the willingness to forgive and to seek forgiveness. According to Gandhi, this process of reconciliation is central to the "logic" of nonviolence, which "recognizes that sin is an everyday occurrence which is in the very nature of action's constant establishment of new relationships within a web of relations, and it needs forgiving, dismissing, in order to make it possible for life to go on" (*GNV* 14). The witness of reconciliation refuses to allow the future to be determined by the past, held hostage by the desire for, or the fear of, retribution. Even at the height of the Vietnam War, Merton could express in his preface to the Vietnamese translation of *No Man Is an Island* his hope that the cycle of violence could be broken: "There must be a new force, the power of love, the power of understanding and human compassion, the strength of selflessness and cooperation, and the creative dynamism of *the will to live and to build, and the will to forgive. The will for reconciliation*" ("HR" 125).

Yet this hope for social transformation does not depend on the gratification of short-term success. Even Gandhi failed to prevent the division of India and Pakistan and was killed by one of his co-religionists for daring to pray with Muslims and other non-Hindus. It is a hope with an eschatological character to it, a hope that believes with Martin Luther King, Jr., that "the arc of the moral universe is long, but it bends toward justice."[23] The secret center of any authentically spiritual effort to transform the world is the mysterious witness of restoration, a conviction that present divisions are less real, less true, less permanent than that "original unity" (*AJ* 308) which is God's will for the human family, and a commitment to model, to enflesh that unity and thereby transmit it to the next generation in confidence of its ultimate full realization. This is the witness, at once specifically Hindu and universally applicable, that Merton found in Gandhi: "simply to follow conscience without regard for the consequences to himself in the belief that this was demanded of him by God and that the results would be the work of God. Perhaps indeed for a long time these results would remain hidden as God's secret. But in the end the truth would manifest itself."[24] The same trust and the same testimony are at the heart of the Christian belief in the reign of God, at once future and present, which "demands to be typified and prepared

---

[23] See Martin Luther King, Jr., "Address at the Conclusion of the Selma to Montgomery March (March 25, 1965)" in *A Call to Conscience: The Landmark Speeches of Dr. Martin Luther King, Jr.*, ed. Clayborne Carson and Kris Shepard (New York: Warner Books, 2001) 111–32; also available at: https://kinginstitute.stanford.edu/our-god-marching.

[24] Thomas Merton, *Seeds of Destruction* (New York: Farrar, Straus and Giroux, 1964) 225.

by such forms of heroic social witness that make Christian mercy plain and evident in the world." By heeding the proclamation of Jesus that the reign of God is indeed at hand (Mark 1:15), the true witness can experience and make available to others, even in the midst of clashing civilizations, "the eschatological climate of the new creation."[25]

Having reflected on the key components of interreligious understanding, we are now able to recognize, I believe, the essential quality that unites them. That quality is compassion, the profound identification with the sufferings and struggles and needs and hopes of one another on the journey toward self-fulfillment through self-surrender and self-transcendence. This is not an additional element or stage but the source and the dynamism and the goal of the entire process, the secret spring from which solitude and solidarity and social transformation emerge, the hidden current that flows through them all, the mysterious end to which they are directed. For Merton, solitude is inseparable from compassion; he writes to the Japanese, "He who is truly alone truly finds in himself the heart of compassion with which to love not only this man or that, but all men" ("*HR*" 118). Solidarity is inseparable from compassion; he writes to the Vietnamese, "Compassion teaches me that when my brother dies, I too die. Compassion teaches me that my brother and I are one" ("*HR*" 123). Social transformation is inseparable from compassion; he writes to the Koreans, "The Christian, in deep compassion, must seek to help his fellow man to escape from the terrible effects of greed and hatred. He must therefore be concerned with social justice and with peace on earth" ("*HR*" 99–100).

Compassion is the common stream from which all religious traditions drink in their "deep, unutterable thirst for the rivers of Paradise."[26] It is the quality by which we realize that the God of Islam, who "is invoked as the 'Compassionate and the Merciful'" (*HGL* 48), is the same God as the Lord of Israel, whose "compassion . . . is for every living thing" (Sir 18:13), and who is also the "compassionate

---

[25] Thomas Merton, *Love and Living*, ed. Naomi Burton Stone and Brother Patrick Hart (New York: Farrar, Straus, Giroux, 1979) 219.

[26] Thomas Merton, *The Inner Experience: Notes on Contemplation*, ed. William H. Shannon (San Francisco: HarperCollins, 2003) 30.

and merciful" God of Jesus Christ (Jas 5:11). In their shared awareness of compassion, imaged as "love of the mother for the child" (*MZM* 77; cf. 79), the cosmic vision of Taoism touches the personalism of the Confucian ideal. It was compassion, a recognition of the suffering common to all in sickness, old age, and death, that drove Siddhartha Gautama from the security and pleasures of his palace to search for liberation, and it was compassion that compelled the enlightened Buddha to share his experience of the "Middle Way" to salvation. He is the supreme manifestation of that "mindfulness" which is committed to "the protection of all beings against suffering by nonviolence and compassion" (*ZBA* 93), exemplified in the Buddhist tradition by the figure of the bodhisattva, who dedicates himself to the liberation of all sentient beings, and by "compassionate love . . . identifies all the sufferers in the round of birth and death with the Buddha, whose enlightenment they potentially share" (*ZBA* 38). And of course it is compassion that brings Jesus of Nazareth to the banks of the Jordan, where he identifies himself fully with poor, broken, sinful, suffering humanity awaiting the baptism of John, and then leads him into the desert, the same desert that Merton called "the wilderness of compassion . . . the only desert that shall truly flourish like the lily. . . . It is in the desert of compassion that the thirsty land turns into springs of water, that the poor possess all things."[27] It is compassion that inspires Jesus to preach and to teach and to heal those who come to him: "he had compassion for them, because they were like sheep without a shepherd" (Mark 6:34). Finally, it was compassion that brought Jesus to the cross, to take upon himself the suffering and sin and oppression of all humanity, to share our death and invite us, by dying to ourselves, to share his victory over suffering and death as well.

Thomas Merton recognized compassion as the meaning of his own solitary vocation: "I disappear from the world as an object of interest in order to be everywhere in it by hiddenness and compassion" ("HR" 65). It was the motivation for a renewed concern for the world and its problems: "I have learned, I believe, to look back into that world

---

[27] Thomas Merton, *The Sign of Jonas* (New York: Harcourt, Brace, 1953) 334; Thomas Merton, *Entering the Silence: Becoming a Monk and Writer. Journals, vol. 2: 1941–1952*, ed. Jonathan Montaldo (San Francisco: HarperCollins, 1996) 463.

with greater compassion, seeing those in it not as alien to myself, not as peculiar and deluded strangers, but as identified with myself" ("*HR*" 63). And compassion was the goal of his final journey, the last stage of his life's quest. In the opening entry of his *Asian Journal*, he writes, "May I not come back without having . . . found also the great compassion, mahakaruna" (*AJ* 4),[28] a prayer that was answered at the culmination of his pilgrimage, before the statues of the Buddhas at Polonnaruwa: "The rock, all matter, all life, is charged with dharmakaya . . . everything is emptiness and everything is compassion" (*AJ* 235; *OSM* 323). While this epiphany reveals, in Buddhist terms, "the unity of sunyata and karuna" (*AJ* 143; *OSM* 278), it is a perfect expression as well of the central Christian belief that *kenosis*, the self-emptying of God in Christ, is the ultimate expression of divine compassion and the perfect model for human compassion. It is Merton's witness to the truth that civilizations do not inevitably clash, a foretaste of that ultimate, eschatological "remaking of world order" on the basis, to quote the closing words of his final talk, of "that full and transcendent liberty which is beyond mere cultural differences and mere externals—and mere this or that" (*AJ* 343). In this unintended last testament, Merton points beyond the partial and contingent to the emptiness and fullness of final integration in the new creation, as glimpsed in the revelatory *kairos* of the present moment. This is the holistic vision that he strove (imperfectly of course) to incarnate, to enflesh in his own practice, and that by word and example he encouraged, and continues to encourage, his readers to recognize as well, and to make visible and tangible in the particular circumstances of their own lives, their own times.

---

[28] Also found in Thomas Merton, *The Other Side of the Mountain: The End of the Journey. Journals, vol. 7: 1967–1968*, ed. Patrick Hart (San Francisco: HarperCollins, 1998) 205 (subsequent references will be cited as "*OSM*" parenthetically in the text).

Bibliography

Apel, William. *Signs of Peace: The Interfaith Letters of Thomas Merton*. Maryknoll, NY: Orbis, 2006.

Bernard of Clairvaux, St. *On Loving God, Treatises 2*. Translated by Robert Walton, OSB. *The Works of Bernard of Clairvaux* 5, Cistercian Fathers 13. Washington, DC: Cistercian, 1974.

Bernard of Clairvaux, St. *On the Song of Songs 1*. Translated by Kilian Walsh, OCSO. *The Works of Bernard of Clairvaux*, Cistercian Fathers 1. Kalamazoo, MI: Cistercian, 1976.

Bernard of Clairvaux, St. *On the Song of Songs 2*. Translated by Kilian Walsh, OCSO. *The Works of Bernard of Clairvaux*, Cistercian Fathers 7. Kalamazoo, MI: Cistercian, 1976.

Blake, William. *The Complete Poetry and Prose of William Blake*, ed. David Erdman. Garden City, NY: Doubleday Anchor, 1997.

Bochen, Christine M. "Review Symposium on George Kilcourse's *Ace of Freedoms: Thomas Merton's Christ*: Three Perspectives." *Horizons* 21 (1994) 340.

Bonaventure, St. *Itinerarium Mentis in Deum*: Works of Saint Bonaventure II. Translated by Philotheus Boehner, OFM. St. Bonaventure, NY: Franciscan Institute, 1956.

Bouyer, Louis, *A History of Christian Spirituality* I: *The Spirituality of the New Testament and the Fathers*. Translated by Mary P. Ryan. London: Burns & Oates, 1963.

Bouyer, Louis. *The Meaning of the Monastic Life*. Translated by Kathleen Pond. New York: P. J. Kenedy, 1955.

Burton, Patricia A. with Albert Romkema. *More Than Silence: A Bibliography of Thomas Merton*. Lanham, MD: Scarecrow Press, 2008.

Burton-Christie, Douglas. "Rediscovering Love's World: Thomas Merton's Love Poems and the Language of Ecstasy." *CrossCurrents* 39.1 (Spring 1989) 64–82.

Carr, Anne E. *A Search for Wisdom and Spirit: Thomas Merton's Theology of the Self*. Notre Dame, IN: University of Notre Dame Press, 1988.

Carson, Rachel. *Silent Spring*. Boston: Houghton Mifflin, 1962.

Chitty, Derwas J. *The Desert a City: An Introduction to the Study of Egyptian and Palestinian Monasticism under the Christian Empire*. Oxford: Blackwell, 1966.

Chitty, Derwas J., trans. *The Letters of St. Antony the Great*. Fairacres, Oxford: SLG Press, 1975.

Cosacchi, Daniel. *Great American Prophets: Pope Francis's Models of Christian Life*. New York: Paulist Press, 2022.

Cunningham, Lawrence S. *Thomas Merton & the Monastic Vision*. Grand Rapids, MI: Eerdmans, 1999.

Daggy, Robert E. "A Note on Thomas Merton's 'Old Uncle Tom.'" *Kentucky Poetry Review* 28.1 (Spring 1992) 93–94.

Dante Alighieri. *Paradiso*. Translated by Dorothy L. Sayers and Barbara Reynolds. Baltimore: Penguin, 1962.

Dear, John. *Thomas Merton, Peacemaker: Meditations on Merton, Peacemaking, and the Spiritual Life*. Maryknoll, NY: Orbis, 2015.

Deignan, Kathleen, CND. "'Love for the Paradise Mystery': Thomas Merton, Contemplative Ecologist." *CrossCurrents* 58.4 (December 2008) 545–69.

Dickens, Charles. *A Christmas Carol* (1843). In *The Christmas Books*, 2 vols. (1.38–134). Baltimore: Penguin, 1971.

Dickinson, Emily. *Complete Poems*, ed. Thomas H. Johnson. Boston: Little Brown, 1960.

Eliot, T. S. *The Complete Poems and Plays: 1909–1950*. New York: Harcourt, Brace and World, 1962.

Finley, James. *Merton's Palace of Nowhere: A Search for God through Awareness of the True Self*. Notre Dame, IN: Ave Maria Press, 1978.

Forest, Jim. *Living with Wisdom: A Life of Thomas Merton*. Rev. ed. Maryknoll, NY: Orbis, 2008.

Forest, Jim. *The Root of War Is Fear: Thomas Merton's Advice to Peacemakers*. Maryknoll, NY: Orbis, 2016.

Francis, Pope. "Address of the Holy Father to a Joint Session of the United States Congress – September 24, 2015," *The Merton Annual* 28 (2015) 16–23.

Grayston, Donald. "*Consonantia* in Thomas Merton: Harmony Personal, Social and Cosmic," *The Merton Annual* 28 (2015) 97–111.

Griffin, John Howard. *Follow the Ecstasy: Thomas Merton, The Hermitage Years, 1965–1968*. Fort Worth, TX: Latitudes Press, 1983.

Henry, Gray and Jonathan Montaldo, eds. *We Are Already One: Thomas Merton's Message of Hope, Reflections to Honor His Centenary (1915–2015).* Louisville, KY: Fons Vitae, 2014.

Hillis, Gregory K. *Man of Dialogue: Thomas Merton's Catholic Vision.* Collegeville, MN: Liturgical Press, 2021.

Hopkins, Gerard Manley. *Poems and Prose,* selected and edited by W. H. Gardner. Baltimore: Penguin, 1953.

Horan, Daniel P. *Engaging Thomas Merton: Spirituality, Justice, and Racism.* Maryknoll, NY: Orbis, 2023.

Horan, Daniel P. *The Franciscan Heart of Thomas Merton: A New Look at the Spiritual Inspiration of His Life, Thought, and Writing.* Notre Dame, IN: Ave Maria Press, 2014.

Huntington, Samuel P. *The Clash of Civilizations and the Remaking of World Order.* New York: Simon & Schuster, 1996.

Imperato, Robert. *Merton and Walsh on the Person.* West Palm Beach, FL: Liturgical Publications, 1987.

Kilcourse, George. *Ace of Freedoms: Thomas Merton's Christ.* Notre Dame, IN: University of Notre Dame Press, 1993.

King, Martin Luther, Jr. "Address at the Conclusion of the Selma to Montgomery March (March 25, 1965)." In *A Call to Conscience: The Landmark Speeches of Dr. Martin Luther King, Jr.*, ed. Clayborne Carson and Kris Shepard (111–32). New York: Warner Books, 2001.

Lahey, G. F., SJ. *Gerard Manley Hopkins.* London: Humphrey Milford/Oxford University Press, 1930.

Leclercq, Jean, OSB. "Saint Bernard and the Monastic Theology of the Twelfth Century" in *Saint Bernard, Theologian,* 2 vols. (1.1–18). Berryville, VA: Our Lady of the Holy Cross Abbey, 1961.

McBrien, Richard P. *Catholicism.* Revised and updated ed. San Francisco: HarperCollins, 1994.

Merton, Thomas. *The Ascent to Truth.* New York: Harcourt, Brace, 1951.

Merton, Thomas. *The Asian Journal,* ed. Naomi Burton Stone, Brother Patrick Hart, and James Laughlin. New York: New Directions, 1973.

Merton, Thomas. *The Behavior of Titans.* New York: New Directions, 1961.

Merton, Thomas. *Cables to the Ace or Familiar Liturgies of Misunderstanding.* New York: New Directions, 1968.

Merton, Thomas. *Clement of Alexandria: Selections from* The Protreptikos. New York: New Directions, 1962.

Merton, Thomas. *Cold War Letters*, ed. Christine M. Bochen and William H. Shannon. Maryknoll, NY: Orbis, 2006.

Merton, Thomas. *The Collected Poems of Thomas Merton*. New York: New Directions, 1977.

Merton, Thomas. *Conjectures of a Guilty Bystander*. Garden City, NY: Doubleday, 1966.

Merton, Thomas. *Contemplation in a World of Action*. Garden City, NY: Doubleday, 1971.

Merton, Thomas. *Contemplative Prayer*. New York: Herder and Herder, 1969.

Merton, Thomas. *The Courage for Truth: Letters to Writers*, ed. Christine M. Bochen. New York: Farrar, Straus, Giroux, 1993.

Merton, Thomas. *Dancing in the Water of Life: Seeking Peace in the Hermitage. Journals, vol. 5: 1963–1965*, ed. Robert E. Daggy. San Francisco: HarperCollins, 1997.

Merton, Thomas. *Day of a Stranger*. Salt Lake City: Gibbs M. Smith, 1981.

Merton, Thomas. *Disputed Questions*. New York: Farrar, Straus & Cudahy, 1960.

Merton, Thomas. *Eighteen Poems*. New York: New Directions, 1985.

Merton, Thomas. *Emblems of a Season of Fury*. New York: New Directions, 1963.

Merton, Thomas. *Entering the Silence: Becoming a Monk and Writer. Journals, vol. 2: 1941–1952*, ed. Jonathan Montaldo. San Francisco: HarperCollins, 1996.

Merton, Thomas. *Faith and Violence: Christian Teaching and Christian Practice*. Notre Dame, IN: University of Notre Dame Press, 1968.

Merton, Thomas. *Figures for an Apocalypse*. New York: New Directions, 1947.

Merton, Thomas, ed. *Gandhi on Non-Violence: Selected Texts from Non-Violence in Peace and War*. New York: New Directions, 1965.

Merton, Thomas. *The Geography of Lograire*. New York: New Directions, 1969.

Merton, Thomas. *He Is Risen*. Niles, IL: Argus, 1975.

Merton, Thomas. *The Hidden Ground of Love: Letters on Religious Experience and Social Concerns*, ed. William H. Shannon. New York: Farrar, Straus, Giroux, 1985.

Merton, Thomas. *"Honorable Reader": Reflections on My Work*, ed. Robert E. Daggy. New York: Crossroad, 1989.

Merton, Thomas. *In the Dark before Dawn: New Selected Poems*, ed. Lynn R. Szabo. New York: New Directions, 2005.

Merton, Thomas. *The Inner Experience: Notes on Contemplation*, ed. William H. Shannon. San Francisco: HarperCollins, 2003.

Merton, Thomas. *An Introduction to Christian Mysticism: Initiation into the Monastic Tradition 3*, ed. Patrick F. O'Connell. Kalamazoo, MI: Cistercian Publications, 2008.

Merton, Thomas. *Learning to Love: Exploring Solitude and Freedom. Journals, vol. 6: 1966–1967*, ed. Christine M. Bochen. San Francisco: HarperCollins, 1997.

Merton, Thomas. *Life and Holiness*. New York: Herder and Herder, 1963.

Merton, Thomas. *The Life of the Vows: Initiation into the Monastic Tradition* 6, ed. Patrick F. O'Connell. Monastic Wisdom 30. Collegeville, MN: Cistercian Publications, 2012.

Merton, Thomas. *The Literary Essays of Thomas Merton*, ed. Brother Patrick Hart. New York: New Directions, 1981.

Merton, Thomas. *The Living Bread*. New York: Farrar, Straus & Cudahy, 1956.

Merton, Thomas. *Love and Living*, ed. Naomi Burton Stone and Brother Patrick Hart. New York: Farrar, Straus, Giroux, 1979.

Merton, Thomas. *The Monastic Journey*, ed. Brother Patrick Hart. Kansas City: Sheed, Andrews and McMeel, 1977.

Merton, Thomas. *Monastic Observances: Initiation into the Monastic Tradition* 5, ed. Patrick F. O'Connell. Collegeville, MN: Cistercian Publications, 2010.

Merton, Thomas. *Mystics and Zen Masters*. New York: Farrar, Straus and Giroux, 1967.

Merton, Thomas. *The New Man*. New York: Farrar, Straus & Cudahy, 1961.

Merton, Thomas. *New Seeds of Contemplation*. New York: New Directions, 1961.

Merton, Thomas. *No Man Is an Island*. New York: Harcourt, Brace, 1955.

Merton, Thomas. *The Nonviolent Alternative*, ed. Gordon C. Zahn. New York: Farrar, Straus, Giroux, 1980.

Merton, Thomas. *Notes on Genesis and Exodus: Novitiate Conferences on Scripture and Liturgy* 2, ed. Patrick F. O'Connell. Eugene, OR: Cascade, 2021.

Merton, Thomas. *Original Child Bomb: Points for Meditation to Be Scratched on the Walls of a Cave*. New York: New Directions, 1961.

Merton, Thomas. *The Other Side of the Mountain: The End of the Journey. Journals, vol. 7: 1967–1968*, ed. Patrick Hart. San Francisco: HarperCollins, 1998.

Merton, Thomas. *Prayer and the Yoke of Christ*. Kansas City, MO: Credence Cassettes, 2004.

Merton, Thomas. "The Present 'Crisis' in Monasticism," *The Merton Annual* 37 (2024) 11–28.

Merton, Thomas. *Preview of the Asian Journey*, ed. Walter H. Capps. New York: Crossroad, 1989.

Merton, Thomas. *Raids on the Unspeakable*. New York: New Directions, 1966.

Merton, Thomas. *Reading Notebook #14* (unpublished).

Merton, Thomas. *Reading Notebook #16* (unpublished).

Merton, Thomas. *Reading Notebook #17* (unpublished).

Merton, Thomas. *Reading Notebook #24* (unpublished).

Merton, Thomas. *Reading Notebook #57* (unpublished).

Merton, Thomas. Foreword to "Reflections on Love: Eight Sacred Poems" (n.p., 1966).

Merton, Thomas. *The Road to Joy: Letters to New and Old Friends*, ed. Robert E. Daggy. New York: Farrar, Straus, Giroux, 1989.

Merton, Thomas. *Run to the Mountain: The Story of a Vocation. Journals, vol. 1: 1939–1941*, ed. Patrick Hart, OCSO. San Francisco: HarperCollins, 1995.

Merton, Thomas. *The School of Charity: Letters on Religious Renewal and Spiritual Direction*, ed. Brother Patrick Hart. New York: Farrar, Straus, Giroux, 1990.

Merton, Thomas. *A Search for Solitude: Pursuing the Monk's True Life. Journals, vol. 3: 1952–1960*, ed. Lawrence S. Cunningham. San Francisco: HarperCollins, 1996.

Merton, Thomas. *Seasons of Celebration*. New York: Farrar, Straus and Giroux, 1965.

Merton, Thomas. *Seeds of Contemplation*. New York: New Directions, 1949.

Merton, Thomas. *Seeds of Destruction*. New York: Farrar, Straus and Giroux, 1964.

Merton, Thomas. *Seeing the World in a Grain of Sand: Thomas Merton on Poetry* [17 lectures on 7 CDs]. Rockville, MD: NowYouKnowMedia, 2013.

Merton, Thomas. *Selected Essays*, ed. Patrick F. O'Connell. Maryknoll, NY: Orbis, 2013.

Merton, Thomas. *The Seven Storey Mountain*. New York: Harcourt, Brace, 1948.

Merton, Thomas. *The Sign of Jonas*. New York: Harcourt, Brace, 1953.

Merton, Thomas. *Silence in Heaven: A Book of the Monastic Life*. New York: Crowell, 1956.

Merton, Thomas. *The Silent Life*. New York: Farrar, Straus & Cudahy, 1957.

Merton, Thomas. *The Spirit of Simplicity*. Trappist, KY: Abbey of Gethsemani, 1948.

Merton, Thomas. *The Springs of Contemplation: A Retreat at the Abbey of Gethsemani*, ed. Jane Marie Richardson. New York: Farrar, Straus, Giroux, 1992.

Merton, Thomas. *The Strange Islands*. New York: New Directions, 1957.

Merton, Thomas. *T. S. Eliot and Prayer*. Kansas City, MO: Credence Cassettes, 1995.

Merton, Thomas. *The Tears of the Blind Lions*. New York: New Directions, 1949.

Merton, Thomas. *Thirty Poems*. Norfolk, CT: New Directions, 1944.

Merton, Thomas. *Thomas Merton in California: The Redwoods Conferences & Letters*, ed. David M. Odorisio. Collegeville, MN: Liturgical Press, 2024.

Merton, Thomas. *Thoughts in Solitude*. New York: Farrar, Straus & Cudahy, 1958.

Merton, Thomas. *Turning Toward the World: The Pivotal Years. Journals, vol. 4: 1960–1963*, ed. Victor A. Kramer. San Francisco: HarperCollins, 1996.

Merton, Thomas. *A Vow of Conversation: Journals 1964–1965*, ed. Naomi Burton Stone. New York: Farrar, Straus, Giroux, 1988.

Merton, Thomas. *The Waters of Siloe*. New York: Harcourt, Brace, 1949.

Merton, Thomas. *The Way of Chuang Tzu*. New York: New Directions, 1965.

Merton, Thomas. *When the Trees Say Nothing: Writings on Nature*, ed. Kathleen Deignan. Notre Dame, IN: Sorin Books, 2003.

Merton, Thomas. *The Wisdom of the Desert: Sayings from the Desert Fathers of the Fourth Century*. New York: New Directions, 1960.

Merton, Thomas. *Witness to Freedom: Letters in Times of Crisis*, ed. William H. Shannon. New York: Farrar, Straus, Giroux, 1994.

Merton, Thomas. *Zen and the Birds of Appetite*. New York: New Directions, 1968.

Merton, Thomas and James Laughlin. *Selected Letters*, ed. David D. Cooper. New York: Norton, 1997.

Merton, Thomas and Robert Lax. *When Prophecy Still Had a Voice: The Letters of Thomas Merton & Robert Lax*, ed. Arthur W. Biddle. Lexington: University Press of Kentucky, 2001.

Merton, Thomas and Rosemary Radford Ruether. *At Home in the World: The Letters of Thomas Merton & Rosemary Radford Ruether*, ed. Mary Tardiff. Maryknoll, NY: Orbis, 1995.

Mott, Michael. *The Seven Mountains of Thomas Merton*. Boston: Houghton Mifflin, 1984.

Nash, Roderick. *Wilderness and the American Mind*. New Haven: Yale University Press, 1967.

O'Connell, Michael J. "The Consolations of Thomas Merton: On Re-reading a Spiritual Classic in a Particularly Fraught Time." nothinggold.substack.com. (February 1, 2025).

O'Connell, Patrick F. "Eight Freedom Songs: Thomas Merton's Cycle of Liberation," *The Merton Annual* 4 (1994) 87–128.

O'Connell, Patrick F. "A Four Storey *Tower*: The Building of Thomas Merton's Babel," *The Merton Annual* 37 (2024) 138–214.

O'Connell, Patrick F. "A Long Shelf Life: Growing Up and Growing Old(er) with Thomas Merton," Gray Henry and Jonathan Montaldo, eds., *We Are Already One: Thomas Merton's Message of Hope, Reflections to Honor His Centenary (1915–2015)* (Louisville, KY: Fons Vitae, 2014) 235–40.

O'Connell, Patrick F. "Nurture by Nature: Emblems of Stillness in a Season of Fury," *The Merton Annual* 21 (2008) 117–49.

O'Connell, Patrick F. "Old World, New Priest: Thomas Merton's '*Senescente Mundo*,'" *The Merton Journal* 26.2 (Advent 2019) 3–12.

O'Connell, Patrick F. "Sacrament and Sacramentality in Thomas Merton's *Thirty Poems*" in Patrick F. O'Connell, ed., *The Vision of Thomas Merton* (Notre Dame, IN: Ave Maria Press, 2003) 155–84.

O'Connell, Patrick F. "'The Surest Home Is Pointless': A Pathless Path through Merton's Poetic Corpus," *CrossCurrents* 58.4 (2008) 522–44.

O'Connell, Patrick F. "Thomas Merton and the 'Edenic Office of the Poet': Three Poems from *The Tears of the Blind Lions*," *The Merton Annual* 32 (2019) 183–204.

O'Connell, Patrick F. "Thomas Merton's Projected Anthology of Religious Poetry," *The Merton Seasonal* 25.3 (Fall 2000) 20–28.

O'Connell, Patrick F. "'A Way of Life Impregnated with Truth': Did Thomas Merton Undervalue Confucianism?" in Patrick F. O'Connell, ed., *Merton & Confucianism: Rites, Righteousness and Integral Humanity*. Louisville, KY: Fons Vitae, 2021 (267–90).

Odorisio, David M. "'We Bump. We Burst into Secrets': Thomas Merton's Sufi Spirituality in California—Making Our 'Yes' to Life." *The Merton Seasonal* 50.3 (Fall 2025) 11–21.

Oyer, Gordon. *Signs of Hope: Thomas Merton's Letters on Peace, Race, and Ecology*. Maryknoll, NY: Orbis, 2021.

Padovano, Anthony T. *The Human Journey: Thomas Merton, Symbol of a Century*. Garden City, NY: Doubleday, 1982; reissued as *The Spiritual Journey of Thomas Merton*. Cincinnati, OH: Franciscan Media, 2014.

Pick, John. *Gerard Manley Hopkins, Priest and Poet*. 2nd ed. New York: Oxford University Press, 1966.

Pramuk, Christopher. *At Play in Creation: Merton's Awakening to the Feminine Divine*. Collegeville, MN: Liturgical Press, 2015.

Pramuk, Christopher. *Sophia: The Hidden Christ of Thomas Merton*. Collegeville, MN: Liturgical Press, 2009.

Pycior, Julie Leininger. *Dorothy Day, Thomas Merton, and the Greatest Commandment: Radical Love in Times of Crisis*. New York: Paulist Press, 2020.

Rubenson, Samuel. *The Letters of St. Antony: Monasticism and the Making of a Saint*. Minneapolis: Fortress, 1995.

Ruether, Rosemary Radford. "Monks and Marxists: A Look at the Catholic Left." *Christianity and Crisis* 33:7 (April 30, 1973) 75–79; rpt. *The Merton Annual* 35 (2022) 71–84.

Shannon, William H. *Silent Lamp: The Thomas Merton Story*. New York: Crossroad, 1992.

Shannon, William H. *Thomas Merton's Dark Path: The Inner Experience of a Contemplative*. New York: Farrar, Straus, Giroux, 1982.

Shannon, William H. *Thomas Merton's Paradise Journey: Writings on Contemplation*. Cincinnati: St. Anthony Messenger Press, 2000.

Shannon, William H., Christine M. Bochen, and Patrick F. O'Connell, *The Thomas Merton Encyclopedia*. Maryknoll, NY: Orbis, 2002.

Shaw, Jeffrey M. *Illusions of Freedom: Thomas Merton and Jacques Ellul on Technology and the Human Condition*. Eugene, OR: Pickwick, 2014.

Short, William, OFM. "Pied Beauty: Gerard Manley Hopkins and the Scotistic View of Nature." *The Cord* 45.3 (1995) 27–36.

Sweeney, Jon M., ed. *Awake and Alive: Thomas Merton According to His Novices*. Maryknoll, NY: Orbis, 2022.

Sweeney, Jon M., ed. *What I Am Living For: Lessons from the Life and Writings of Thomas Merton*. Notre Dame, IN: Ave Maria Press, 2018.

Thompson, Phillip M. *Returning to Reality: Thomas Merton's Wisdom for a Technological World*. Eugene, OR: Cascade, 2012.

Thurston, Bonnie. "Human Love and the Love of God in *Eighteen Poems*" in Paul M. Pearson, Danny Sullivan, and Ian Thompson, eds., *Thomas Merton: Poet, Monk, Prophet*. Abergavenny, Wales: Three Peaks Press, 1998 (68–79).

Thurston, Bonnie. *Shaped by the End You Live For: Thomas Merton's Monastic Spirituality*. Collegeville, MN: Liturgical Press, 2020.

Vinski, Edward J. *Thomas Merton: The Monk of Civil Rights*. Newcastle upon Tyne: Cambridge Scholars Publishing, 2023.

Vogüé, Adalbert de. *La Communauté et Abbé dans la Règle de saint Benôit*. Paris-Brussels: Desclée-de-Brouwer, 1961; *Community and Abbot in the Rule of St Benedict*. Translated by Charles Philippi and Ethel Rae Perkins. 2 vols. Cistercian Studies 5. Kalamazoo, MI: Cistercian Publications, 1988.

Waldron, Robert. *Thomas Merton—The Exquisite Risk of Love: The Chronicle of a Monastic Romance*. London: Darton, Longman, Todd, 2012.

Ware, Kallistos. *The Orthodox Way*. Rev. ed. Crestview, NY: St. Vladimir's Seminary Press, 1995.

Weis, Monica. *The Environmental Vision of Thomas Merton*. Lexington: University Press of Kentucky, 2011.

Acknowledgments

Excerpts from DISPUTED QUESTIONS by Thomas Merton. Copyright © 1960 by The Abbey of Our Lady of Gethsemani. Copyright renewed 1988 by Alan Hanson. Reprinted by permission of Farrar, Straus and Giroux. All Rights Reserved.

Excerpt from LOVE AND LIVING by Thomas Merton. Copyright © 1979 by The Merton Legacy Trust. Reprinted by permission of Farrar, Straus and Giroux. All Rights Reserved.

Excerpts from MYSTICS AND ZEN MASTERS by Thomas Merton. Copyright © 1967 by the Abbey of Gethsemani. Copyright renewed 1995 by Robert Giroux, James Laughlin, and Tommy O'Callaghan as trustees of the Merton Legacy Trust. Reprinted by permission of Farrar, Straus and Giroux. All Rights Reserved.

Excerpts from THE NEW MAN by Thomas Merton. Copyright © 1961 by Thomas Merton. Copyright renewed 1989 by The Trustees of the Merton Legacy Trust. Reprinted by permission of Farrar, Straus and Giroux. All Rights Reserved.

Excerpts from SEASONS OF CELEBRATION by Thomas Merton. Copyright © 1965 by The Abbey of Gethsemani. Copyright renewed 1993 by Robert Giroux, James Laughlin, and Tommy O'Callaghan. Reprinted by permission of Farrar, Straus and Giroux. All Rights Reserved.

Excerpts from THE SPRINGS OF CONTEMPLATION by Thomas Merton. Copyright © 1992 by The Merton Legacy Trust. Reprinted by permission of Farrar, Straus and Giroux. All Rights Reserved.

By Thomas Merton, from THE ASIAN JOURNAL OF THOMAS MERTON, copyright © 1975 by The Trustees of the Merton Legacy Trust. Reprinted by permission of New Directions Publishing Corp.

By Thomas Merton, from THE COLLECTED POEMS OF THOMAS MERTON, copyright © 1977 by The Trustees of the Merton Legacy Trust. Reprinted by permission of New Directions Publishing Corp.

By Thomas Merton, from DAY OF A STRANGER, copyright © 1967 by the Merton Legacy Trust. Reprinted by permission of New Directions Publishing Corp.

By Thomas Merton, from THE LITERARY ESSAYS OF THOMAS MERTON, copyright © 1960, 1966, 1967, 1968, 1973, 1975, 1978, 1981 by The Trustees of the Merton Legacy Trust, Copyright © 1959, 1961, 1963, 1964, 1965, 1981 by The Abbey of Gethsemani, Inc., Copyright © 1953 by Our Lady of Gethsemani Monastery. Reprinted by permission of New Directions Publishing Corp.

By Thomas Merton, from NEW SEEDS OF CONTEMPLATION, copyright © 1961 by The Abbey of Gethsemani, Inc. Reprinted by permission of New Directions Publishing Corp.

By Thomas Merton, from ZEN AND THE BIRDS OF APPETITE, copyright © 1968 by The Abbey of Gethsemani, Inc. Reprinted by permission of New Directions Publishing Corp.

Excerpts from CONJECTURES OF A GUILTY BYSTANDER by Thomas Merton, copyright © 1965, 1966 by The Abbey of Gethsemani. Used by permission of Doubleday, an imprint of the Knopf Doubleday Publishing Group, a division of Penguin Random House LLC. All rights reserved.

Contemplation in a World of Action by Thomas Merton. © 1971 University of Notre Dame Press. Reprinted with permission of the University of Notre Dame Press.

Faith and Violence: Christian Teaching and Christian Practice by Thomas Merton. © 1968 University of Notre Dame Press. Reprinted with permission of the University of Notre Dame Press.

Index

abbot: 135–36
abominations, of idolatry: 82; of superstition: 82
abstractions, bureaucratic: 165; demonic: 85
absurdity: 20
acceptability, criterion of: 197
acceptance, social: 181
accomplishment(s): 19, 162
accountability: 80
Acheron: 188
achievements, as criteria: 198
act, creative: 160
action: 6, 66, 79, 96, 130; Christian: 52, 117, 126; for justice: 117; for peace: 112, 117; freedom of: 191; labor of: 77; prophetic: 112; responsible: 17; wise: 186
activist, frenzy of: 68
activity, apostolic: 125; creative: 160; human: 35; intellectual: 160; purifying: 96
actuality, concrete: 150
Adam: 13, 19, 49, 77, 91–96, 100, 106, 159–61, 168; as giver of names: 159–60, 176; awakening of: 109; body of: 115; contingency of: 91; fall of: 104, 162; first: 92, 94; identity of: 91; liberty of: 160; vocation of: 91, 95–96; work of: 96
adversary: 169
advertisement: 82, 164
advertising: 165; compulsion of: 166; seductive: 163
affirmation of life: 86

afflicted: 51
affluence, organized: 85
age, atomic: 115; messianic: 128; new: 113–14, 119
agenda(s), cultural: 185; economic: 185; revolutionary: 119
aggiornamento: 7
aggressiveness: 60
agnosticism: 178
air, powers of: 164
airplanes: 153
Algeria: 200
alienation: xiii, 2, 14, 19, 39, 67–68, 87, 127, 156, 161, 185, 201; from creation: 90; from reality: 91; resolution of: 156; self-divided: 53
ambiguity: 86
ambivalence, healthy: 190; realistic: 190
America: 186; as earthly paradise: 97; as heir of Holy Roman Empire: 119
analysis, discursive: 10; logical: 10, 191
ananda: 177
anawim: 113
anchorite: 136
angel(s): 95, 100; landscapes as: 188
Angela of Foligno, St.: 153
anger: 154
anguish: 11, 58, 112
animals: 25, 74
annunciation, prophetic: 67, 85
antagonism, cultural: 185; religious: 185
Anthony, St.: 134, 136, 139

219

anti-poetry: 167
Apel, William: 6
apostolate: 118
appreciation, mutual: 104
approach, masculine: 76; person-oriented: 191; pragmatic: 76; utilitarian: 76
Arasteh, Reza: 195
Aristotle: 193
arrogance: 83, 198; complacent: 16; human: 36, 152; toward others: 190
art: 35, 79, 178; of God: 25, 27
artist(s): 87; awareness of: 174
Ascension, solitude of: 197
Ascent to Truth: 32, 48, 75
ascents: 135
asceticism: 58; exaggerated: 32–33; monastic: 60
Asia, cultural heritage of: 193
Asian Journal: 139, 143–44, 157–58, 180–82, 196–200, 202, 205
assassin, as last-minute friend: 200
assent, notional: 56; real: 56
assimilation, premature: 190–91
astronaut: 59
At Home in the World: 131–32, 137–38, 146, 149, 153, 156
Atman: 177
attention: 147
attitude, instrumental: 36; pragmatic: 23–24; self-critical: 189; utilitarian: 23–24
attraction, sign of: 96
Augustine, St.: 22, 77
Auschwitz: 17; language of: 165
authenticity: 144; charismatic: 103
authorities, political: 81; religious: 81
authority: xii; charismatic: 136; spiritual: 140
automatisms, freedom from: 158
autonomy: 19, 162; assertion of: 161; claims of: 86; delusive: 121; illusion of: 45, 91, 105; individual: 121; spiritual: 80; spurious: 90

awakening, from dreams: 109; in Eden: 109; of Adam: 109; of humanity: 108–9; to reality: 109
awareness: 88; contemplative: 31, 35, 39, 112; cosmic: 38, 75; ecological: 24; global: 199; ontological: 73; sapiential: 186; symbolic: 178; transformed: 46
awe, moment of: 89
axis mundi: 104, 156
axle, cosmic: 104, 156
Aziz, Abdul: 200

Babel: 162–63; of tongues: 164
Babylon, builders of: 163
balance, ecological: 28, 152–53; of spirits: 153
Bangkok: 139
baptism: 47, 57–58, 60, 71, 82, 121, 140; meaning of: 121–22
Barth, Karl: 76, 127
bass: 27
beauty: 22, 27–28; of creation: 37; of Gethsemani: 99–100; of grace: 36; of sonship: 36; of understanding: 36; of universe: 38, 74; of wisdom: 36
Behavior of Titans: 27, 66, 170
being(s), created: 33; divine: 92; ground of: 75; inanimate: 25, 74; love as ground of: 17; particular: 25; receptivity of: 90; respect for: 199; selfless: 92; sense of: 199; stillness of: 90
beliefs, change of: 56
Benedict, St.: 139–40; Rule of: 140
Bernard of Clairvaux, St.: 10, 22, 42, 56, 70–71
Berrigan, Daniel: 132
Biddle, Arthur W.: 187
bird(s): 28, 89, 152; metal: 153; precise pairs of: 151–52; sermon to: 29, 152
Birmingham: 154
birth, language of: 165

bishops: 139
Blake, William: 175, 188
blindness, culpable: 115
blood: 154
Bloy, Leon: 188
Bochen, Christine, M.: xii, 2–3, 24, 41–42, 44, 74, 108, 141, 148, 186
bodhisattva: 204
Boehner, Philotheus: 29–30
Bonaventure, St.: 15, 29
Bonhoeffer, Dietrich: 118, 133
boredom: 141
Bouyer, Louis: 134–36, 139–40
Brautmistik: 42
bride of Christ: 97
brokenness: 67
brotherhood, charism of: 103; Cistercian: 137
brutality, of police oppression: 85; of war: 85
Buddha: 204; enlightenment of: 204; Fire Sermon of: 61
Buddhism: 61, 73, 78; as Middle Way: 204; Mahayana: 179–80
Buddhists: 65, 198
Bultmann, Rudolf: 119
Burton, Patricia A.: 3
Burton-Christie, Douglas: 108
bush, burning: 101
business: 152; of poetry: 174; world of: 154
businessman: 174
busyness: 88, 151; of doing: 90

Cables to the Ace: 138, 167–68
cacophony, meaningless: 167
Cain: 161
Calcutta: 143, 157, 160, 181, 196
Calvary, solitude of: 197
Camus, Albert: 170–71
Canaanites, gods of: 80
capitalism, western: 119
Capps, Walter H.: 24, 138
captives, liberation to: 81
cargo cult, Melanesian: 186

Carmel, Mt.: 10
Carr, Anne: 19, 43
Carson, Clayborne: 202
Carson, Rachel: 23, 38–39, 97–98
Carthusians: 101
Catholic(s): 65, 198
Catholic Worker: 132
catholicity: xii, 65; true: 74
cell, monastic: 141; work of: 147
Chagall, Marc: 188
challenges: 87
change: 7
chaos: 184
charism: 136, 145; communal: 103; monastic: 102–3, 125; of brotherhood: 103; prophetic: 85
charity: 80, 100, 127; perfection of: 101; works of: 58
Chergé, Christian de: 200
cherub, apocalyptic: 153–54
chih: 72
child, innocence of: 165; of God: 135
Chitty, Derwas J.: 134
Christ, Jesus: 13; advent of: 112; agony of: 53; arrest of: 114; as anointed king: 112; as brother: 6; as fellow pilgrim: 6; as firstborn of creation: 35; as Image of Father: 44; as Incarnate Word: 82; as Just One: 116; as King of Peace: 115; as Logos: 105; as Messiah: 112, 116; as new Adam: 92, 94, 100, 114, 130; as Prince of Peace: 116, 129; as Redeemer: 88, 129; as Savior: 122; as Son: 44, 112, 130; as Splendor of Father: 44; as supreme prophet: 82; as Word: 53, 112, 177; Ascension of: 122; baptism of: 204; birth of: 112–13; Body and Blood of: 122; Body of: 49, 86, 121, 123; Bride of: 97; choice of: 17–18; coming of: 113; compassion of: 45, 52, 63, 128, 204; conformation to: 70–71; cross of: 44, 50, 53, 57, 60, 204;

crucified: 51; crucifixion of: 43, 114; crucifixion with: 20, 42–43; death of: 20, 43, 47–51, 53–56, 58, 60–61, 85, 112, 114, 121–22, 127, 136; disciple(s) of: 111–12, 114–15; divinization in: 47; dying with: 42–43, 45–48, 54, 57–58, 61–62, 69, 92, 140, 144; execution of: 114; faith in: 129; fidelity of: 129; figure of: 55; freedom of: 92; glorified: 35, 114, 121; glory of: 127; grace of: 105; heart of: 63; holiness of: 122; identification with: 45, 47, 53, 63; identity in: 121; identity of: 82; incarnation of: 30, 37, 98, 107, 112–13; incorporation in: 49, 81; kingdom of: 116, 121–22; life in: 43, 50, 61, 130, 140; life of: 50, 85, 114, 122, 127; Lordship of: 128; love for: 42; love of: 51, 55, 63, 117, 122, 128; member of: 173; mercy of: 128; message of: 117; mind of: 55; ministry of: 113; mission of: 82, 129; mystery of: 60, 121–22, 170, 193; mystical: 48, 92, 118, 130; mystical body of: 49; natural: 48; obedience of: 54, 92; participation in: 43, 45, 54, 57, 60–61, 82, 122, 136; passion of: 81, 94, 98, 101, 128, 137, 197; peace of: 128; person of: 14, 61, 66, 81, 136, 142; poor as: 113–14; power of: 45, 50, 77; preaching of: 112; presence of: 61, 127; putting on: 121; reign of: 118, 127; restoration in: 147; resurrected: 20; resurrection of: 20, 35, 43–45, 47–50, 54–58, 60–61, 85, 93, 98, 112, 114, 121–22, 127–28, 136, 197; risen: 9, 36, 47–49, 50, 54, 57, 93–94, 114–15, 121, 128; rising with: 43, 45–48, 50, 54, 57–58, 61–62, 69, 144; self in: 20–21; self-emptying of: 46; Spirit of: 8–9, 55, 71, 128; sufferings of: 142; teaching of: 129, 193; temptations of: 142; torture of: 114; triumph of: 114; union with: 20, 46, 48, 56, 93; uniqueness of: 66; victory of: 49–50, 93, 114–15, 117, 204; vindication of: 114; vocation of: 84; way of: 128; whole: 49; will of: 50, 60; words of: 111; work of: 35–36, 52, 66, 81, 122

Christendom: 118; Eastern: xi; Western: xi, 188

Christian(s), compassion of: 52; divided: xi; freedom of: 142; genuine: 90; humility of: 117; love of: 117; official: 142; openness of: 117; professional: 142; self-sacrifice of: 117; simplicity of: 117; task of: 117

Christianity: 78, 118; contemporary: 112; future of: 40; religionless: 133; secular: 133

Christmas, message of: 113

Christocentrism: 41–43

christology: 41

chronos: 152

Chuang Tzu: 105, 170, 179, 194

church: 8, 49, 66, 117; and kingdom: 117–19; as Body of Christ: 49, 86; as eternal institution: 197; as sociological entity: 118; boundaries of: 123–24; challenge to: 66; dynamism of: 130; Eastern: xi, 32; fidelity to: 87; goal of: 120; historical failure of: 119; identity of: 86–87, 128; love of: 86; lukewarm: 10; mission of: 50, 87, 112; mystery of: 135; of past: 15; origin of: 120; simplicity of: 86; task of: 9, 86; twenty-first-century: 66; visible: 173; vocation of: 9, 49, 86–87, 169; Western: xi; witness of: 111

Cincinnati: 108

circumincession: 93

cit: 177

citizen, ancient Greek: 159
city, atomic: 154; earthly: 162
civilization(s), clash of: 186, 199; European: 190; mutually exclusive: 184; other: 190; separate: 184; Western: 187, 190; white: 190
claims, fraudulent: 143; of class: 196; of nation: 196; of race: 196; of world: 143
clan, detachment from: 197
clarity, resplendent: 34
class, claims of: 196; idolatries of: 84
classicism, voice of: 188
Clement of Alexandria: 75, 170
Clement of Alexandria: 170
clergy, monastic: 139
clerics, secular: 137
cliché(s), ethical: 199; meaningless: 167
climate, change: 5; eschatological: 203
cockroaches: 150–51
coercion: 118; justification of: 119
cohesion, group: 197
cold: 146
Cold War Letters: 74–75
Collected Poems: 5, 27, 29–31, 37, 59, 67, 76, 88, 106–8, 139, 155, 162–63, 165, 167, 173, 176–77, 186, 190–92
colonialism: 190
colt, particular: 27
comfort: 113; idolatries of: 84; temptations of: 80; worship of: 82
commitment: 128, 189; personal: 56, 167; renewed: 127
communication: 157, 160–61, 172–74, 177, 196; as communion: 181–82; authentic: 168–73; beyond concept: 182; beyond speech: 182; beyond words: 182; foundation for: 173; in depth: 199; interpersonal: 160; jargon as: 167; mass: 170; problem of: 171; restoration of: 172; true: 158, 166–67, 172; trustworthy: 168; with God: 162

communion: 14, 48–49, 158, 160–61; beyond communication: 196; beyond concept: 196, 200; beyond culture: 196; beyond speech: 196, 200; beyond words: 196, 199; communication as: 181–82; contemplative: 178; existential: 70, 92, 96, 160; genuine: 166; human: 84; in cosmic awareness: 38, 75, 176; in divine life: 35; in divine love: 163; in nature: 38, 75, 176; in wisdom: 75; intellectual: 160; of Adam: 169; of author and audience: 177; of Pentecost: 197; spiritual: 62; symbol and: 174; transconfessional: 75; transcultural: 75; true: 167; with God: 92, 160; with humanity: 93; wordless: 182
community: 172; authentic: 43; biotic: 23; Christian: 86, 117, 120, 123, 127, 129; genuine: 48, 168; Gethsemani: 132; gift of: 86; human: 56; monastic: 101–3, 125; of faith: 128; of redeemed: 49, 128; paradisic: 102; perfect: 99; prophetic: 86; reformation of: 93; responsibility of: 86; vocation of: 120
compassion: ix, 180, 203–5; as integrating factor: 203–4; dialogue as: 191; divine: 50, 205; heart of: 203; human: 205; mutual: 45; of Christ: 45, 52, 128; of Christians: 52; of humanity: 45; power of: 202; wilderness of: 204
complacency: 118, 120; self-satisfied: 190; temptations of: 80
complementarity, insight of: 195
compromises: 125
compulsion(s), alien: 12; human: 47; of advertising: 166; of society: 60
concept(s): 199; abstract: 72
concern(s), monastic: 185; private: 185; spiritual: 185; vain: 103

condemnation: 83
condition, human: 45, 78, 187
conduct, reformation of: 71
confidence: 121
conflict: 113, 157
conformation, to Christ: 71
conformity: 84; cultural: 184; economic: 184; sterile: 199
Confucianism: 72
confusion(s): 61, 88, 129; abyss of: 20; idolatrous: 120; inner: 79; of ideologies: 164; of images: 164; of myths: 164; of superstitions: 164; political: 155; social: 155
Conjectures of a Guilty Bystander: vii, xi, 4, 7–8, 11–13, 16–18, 59, 65, 68, 74, 76, 86–90, 97, 103–4, 109, 116, 118–19, 121, 127–28, 151, 166, 169–70, 172, 179, 187–89, 191, 193, 197–99
conqueror: 191
conquest of other: 190
conscience, ecological: 5, 23; false: 163
consciousness, Cartesian: 192; Christian: 39; cogitating: 192; ecological: 24, 38–39, 97; metaphysical: 179; millennial: 24; nationalist: 201; paradise: 97, 104, 106, 176; paschal: 44; prophetic: 87; pure: 192; religious: 39; sapiential: 38, 67, 74; scientific: 192; sophianic: 67; symbolic: 174, 177; totalitarian: 201; transcultural: viii, 187–96; transformation of: 201; transformed: 194–95; trans-religious: 194; union of: 70; universal: 199; Western: 189
consolation(s): 87; God as: 102
consonantia: 155
Constantine: 119; conversion of: 118
consumer, prospective: 166
consumption: 36
contemplation: 6, 15, 44, 62, 66, 71, 77, 79, 90, 95–96, 100, 117, 124, 130, 186; as aristocratic: 69; as intellec-
tual: 69; as liberation: 95; Christian: 55, 69; definition of: 42; divine: 101; emptiness of: 167; goal of: 56; imageless: 32, 34, 55; monastic: 103; mystical: 69; natural: 15, 32–36; non-Christian: 71; of God: 33; of Trinity: 32; pseudo-: 36; purity of: 95; repose of: 71; silence of: 167; spirit of: 125; wordless: 55
Contemplation in a World of Action: xiii, 8, 15, 17–18, 22, 46, 54–55, 58–61, 69, 103, 115, 118, 121, 125–26, 133–38, 141–46, 151, 169–70, 195–96
contemplative: 67, 105; authentic: 90–91; true: 97
Contemplative Prayer: 46, 52, 58, 60, 124–25, 136, 142, 145
contempt for other: 190
contingency: 19, 91, 181; as blessing: 162; as curse: 162; of Adam: 91; radical: 163
continuity: 7
contradiction: 61; sign(s) of: 10, 61, 79, 81, 84, 96, 113, 117, 151–52, 169, 201
control: 113, 199; godlike: 16; institutional: 135; scientific: 39; social: 167; technical: 39
convention(s), dead: 7; liberations from: 158; slave of: 20
convergence: 187; cultural: 192
conversion(s): 8, 56, 58, 128; call to: 124; Christian: 13; ongoing: 123; to equity: 80; to justice: 80
Cooper, David D.: 30
cooperation, strength of: 202
Corpus Christi Church: 26
Cosacchi, Daniel: 1
cosmos: 66, 128; contemplation of: 32; divinized: 67, 176; separation from: 16; spiritualized: 67, 176; transfigured: 67, 130, 176
countryside, English: 188

courage: 53
Courage for Truth: 2, 148
covenant: 80
creation: 15–16, 21, 66, 84, 91–92, 104, 159; alienation from: 90; appreciation of: 75; as epiphany: 15, 24, 37; as manifestation of wisdom: 74; as revelation: 67; as utilitarian resource: 98; beauty of: 37; care for: 36; character of: 37; degradation of: 36; design for: 92; divine presence in: 28, 32; doctrine of: 144; estrangement from: 91; fulfillment of: 113; harmony of: 107; integrity of: 40; kinship with: 29; material: 36, 93; new: 35, 95, 98, 102, 106, 115, 123, 126, 130, 196, 203, 205; protection of: 97; reality of: 16; renewed: 94; right relationship with: 35; sacramentality of: 34, 38, 68; unity of: 68; work of: 35
creativity: 96–97, 128, 142; divine: 35, 38; human: 160; self-forgetful: 98; sources of: 174; springs of: 179; theology of: 35
creatures: 16; as signs of Creator: 24–25; detachment from: 32
creed, differences of: 186
crisis, cultural: 148; environmental: 40; existential: 195; migrant: 184; political: 148; social: 148
critique, cultural: vii; prophetic: xi, 87, 189
cross(es): 44, 52, 104, 129, 156, 183; mystery of: 50, 92; passage through: 48; power of: 50, 52, 54, 101, 123; presence of: 50; wisdom of: 70; word of: 20–21, 61, 77, 163
cross-purposes: 88
crows: 152
crucifixion: 60; of ego: 62
cruelty: 18, 190
Cuadra, Pablo Antonio: 165

culture(s): 22, 154; as partial: 195; as provisional: 195; category of: 195; Christian: 193, 195; crimes of: 189; commitment to: 189; differences of: 186; follies of: 189; global: 157, 187, 199; Greco-Roman: 193; non-Western: 190; religious: 187; single: 195; soulless: 157, 199; synthesis of: 195; transcendence of: 195; Western: 187–90, 192; world: 194
Cunningham, Lawrence S.: xi, 3, 88, 111, 141, 151
customs, monastic: 102

Daggy, Robert E.: xiv, 2–3, 28, 59, 104, 116, 133, 148, 187, 200
dancers, ghost: 187
Dancing in the Water of Life: 3, 28, 31, 59, 104, 116, 119, 124, 126, 133, 146–49, 152–53, 155–56, 200
Dante Alighieri: 10, 15, 98–99, 175, 188
darkness: 117, 154; of unknowing: 34; power of: 117
day: 153; resurrection of: 152
Day, Dorothy: 132
Day of a Stranger: 28, 38, 103–4, 148–56, 194
daydream, sterile: 97
Dear, John: 6
death(s): 50, 52–53, 60, 81, 86, 92, 129, 154; curse of: 53; facing: 181; forces of: 114–15, 154; Great: 62; human: 45–46; in Christ: 61; liberating: 54; mystical: 53; of Christ: 20, 43, 47–51, 53–56, 58, 60–61, 85, 112, 114, 121–22, 127, 136; pain of: 45; personal: 54; physical: 53–54; power of: 116–17, 128; series of: 48, 94; sinful: 54; sublimation of: 54; suffering of: 45; temporal: 53; to self: 204; to sin: 43; victorious: 54; victory over: 114, 117, 204
debts, forgiveness of: 80

deception: 83; forces of: 163
decision(s), last: 181; mature: 166; rational: 166; time of: 86
dedication, pseudo-: 196
deer: 147
defense of person: 85
defenselessness: 45
defensiveness: 109, 132
degradation, environmental: 5, 24; of creation: 36
Deignan, Kathleen: 5, 23, 28
delight: 76, 91
Delphi: 170
delusions: 86
denunciation, prophetic: 67, 85
dependence: 94, 163; on Creator: 91; on Lord: 80
depersonalization: 190
depth, inner: 144
dereliction: 58
desert(s): 61, 79–80, 94, 101, 103, 133–36, 141–42, 149; as wilderness of compassion: 204; demon-haunted: 106; law of: 80; layperson in: 140; temptations in: 81
design, divine: 67, 195
desire(s): 162; egocentric: 16; egotistical: 91; evil: 60; human: 89; inordinate: 92; object of: 33
despair: 113; forces of: 163
destiny, authentic: 112; true: 112
destitution: 58
destruction: 36, 86, 92, 201; atomic: 39
detachment(s): 33, 44, 79, 135, 196; from creatures: 32
development, spiritual: 34
devil: 14, 133
deviousness: 86
dharma: 192
dialogue: 104, 173, 186–87, 199; as compassion: 191; as identification: 191; as source of communion: 199; as source of insights: 199; as source of relationships: 199–200; as substitution: 191; foundation for: 173; fraternal: 172; genuine: 168–69; humble: 172; intercultural: 190–91; interreligious: vii, 6, 44, 61–62, 78, 158, 186; models of: 170–72; place of: 169; sincere: 191
diatribe: 186
Dickens, Charles: 185
Dickinson, Emily: 176
dictates, social: 158
differences, cultural: 194, 205
dignity: 129; affirmation of: 144, 198; human: 96, 127; inalienable: 85; intrinsic: 163, 190, 198; of person: 143, 190; respect for: 191; revelation of: 144
dilemma(s), shared: 153, 187
dimension, Christian: 154–55; contemplative: 192; ethical: 72; ontological: 72; religious: 154–55; sapiential: 192; spiritual: 154–55
discernment: 7, 32, 124; powers of: 165
disciple(s): 142; community of: 8; of Christ: 111–12; true: 50
discipleship, Christian: 85, 136; life of: 82; meaning of: 117; responsibility of: 126
discipline: 158; ascetic: 71; contemplative: 58; meditative: 58; spiritual: 79, 199
discrimination: 104
disguise(s): 18, 20
dishonesty, acknowledgement of: 168; moral: 190
disillusion: 132, 146
disinformation: xii
disintegration: xii; of cultural self: 196; of social self: 196
disloyalty, twofold: 190
disorder, interior: 16
disorientation, spiritual: 78
Disputed Questions: 21, 50, 55, 67, 79–80, 82, 123, 126–28, 176, 180, 197–98, 201

Index 227

dissonance, awareness of: 152
distortions: 82
distractions: 88
diversions: 88
diversity, cultural: 187, 195; respect for: 185; unity in: xii, 13
divine, openness to: 191
divinization: 47, 66, 144, 163
division(s): 79, 85, 92, 201; acceptance of: 97; artificial: 201; inner: 100; outer: 100; power of: 117; transcendence of: 97
doctrine(s): 199; and experience: 44, 56, 62; conflicting: 72; religious: 165
dogmas: 20; of incarnation: 56; of redemption: 56; of Trinity: 56
doing, busyness of: 90
Dostoevsky, Feodor: 145
Douglass, James: 132
dread: 58
dream(s), awakening from: 88, 109; of separateness: 88
dualisms: 96
duties: 142
dying with Christ: 42–43, 45–48, 54, 57–58, 61–62, 69, 92, 140, 144
dynamism, contemplative: 125; eschatological: 125; of church: 130

earth, future of: 40
Easter: 57; mystery of: 197; Vigil: 57
Ecclesiastes, wisdom of: 70–71
Eckhart, Meister: 22, 188
eclecticism, age of: 194
ecology, disturbances of: 39; mental: 153, 194
Eden: 95–96, 101, 106–7, 161; awakening in: 109; exile from: 107; freedom of: 94; garden of: 98; journey to: 94; life in: 109; monasteries as: 100; return to: 106; spiritual: 98
efficiency: 143, 157, 199
effort, ascetic: 32; human: 34

ego, contingent: 20; destructive: 20; empirical: 179; hedonistic: 20; knowing: 179; reflecting: 179; self-centered: 46, 62; self-sufficient: 46; talking: 179; transient: 54; wasteful: 20; willing: 179
egoism: 60
Egypt, monastic: 106
Eighteen Poems: 106, 108
elements, chauvinistic: 184; reactionary: 184
elevation, pseudo-mystical: 153
Elijah: 81
Eliot, T. S.: 175–76
elitism: 71; philosophic: 69
Ellul, Jacques: 165
Emblems of a Season of Fury: 59, 67, 76, 107–8, 155, 165, 173, 176–77, 190–92
empathy: 9
Empire, Holy Roman: 119; Roman: 118
empowerment: 47
emptiness: 19, 60–61, 93–94, 104, 107, 136, 180, 205; primordial: 73
enclosure, monastic: 28
encounter, existential: 197; unmediated: 32; with God: 32, 197
ends, commercial: 24; military: 24; technological: 24
enemy, ideological: 189; love of: 51
energies: 86
enigma: 72
enlightenment: 73; of Buddha: 204; personal: 158
enslavement, to idols: 95
Entering the Silence: 3, 28, 30, 101, 111, 138–39, 204
environment, exploitation of: 5, 23
epiphany: xii, 89, 205; Fourth and Walnut: 18, 88; natural world as: 34; of cosmic mystery: 75; of God: 74; of divine: 68; of wisdom: 37, 74; wilderness as: 75

equality, spirit of: 80
equity, conversion to: 80
Erdman, David: 175
eros: 76
error: 92
eschatology, realized: 116
establishment, religious: 135
estrangement: 171; from authentic self: 90–91; from creation: 91; from Creator: 90; from God: 91; others: 91; self-deceiving: 161; self-defeating: 161
ethic, environmental: 23
ethos, of exploitation: 79; of power: 79
Eucharist: 122
euphemisms: 165
Europe: 186, 189; guilt of: 97
Evagrius Ponticus: 34
evangelization, work of: 49
evasions: 82
Eve: 19, 95, 106; awakening by: 88, 109; creation of: 161
events, pseudo-: 86, 169
evil(s): 83; forces of: 115; moral: 96; pervasiveness of: 128; power of: 81, 128; victory over: 117
exchange, intercultural: 199; inter-religious: 199
exclusion, principle of: 197
exclusiveness, cultural: 185; religious: 185
exclusivity, principle of: 197; sign of: 174
existence, authentic: 113; empirical: 61; esoteric: 150; ground of: 19; kingdom: 126; lay: 151; mystery of: 20; of universe: 38, 74; redeemed: 130; secular: 60; separate: 47; state of: 19; superior: 150; wilderness: 103
expectations of society: 60
expendable: 114
experience: 10, 95, 157; actual: 112; aesthetic: 191; authentic: 158;

authority of: 136; Christocentric: 55; contemplative: 20, 72, 178; direct: 62; doctrine and: 44, 56, 62; enlightenment: 72; human: 158; immediate: 61; inner: 22; mystical: 34; of God: 11–12, 57; of reality: 55; ordinary: 174; paschal: 20, 61; religious: 62, 199; sapiential: 71; spiritual: 62, 191; theocentric: 55; transcendent: 73, 167, 178–79; trinitarian: 55
experiment, scientific: 66, 90
exploitation: 24, 32; colonial: 190; environmental: 5; ethos of: 79; of poor: 67; of things: 36; problems of: 190
exploration, inner: 144
explorer(s), Arctic: 187; solitary: 59
extenuation: 11
extinction, cultural: 184
eye(s), inner: 38, 177; of faith: 115; of heart: 177

face of God: 27, 200
failings, recognition of: 189
failure, fear of: 125
faith: xii, 66, 103, 180; act of: 54; Christian: xi, 43, 117, 121–22; Christocentric: 74; communal dimension of: 121–22; community of: 121, 128; contemplative: 124; darkness of: 122; eschatological: 124; experience of: 103; eyes of: 115; heart of: 44; incarnational: 74; life of: 11–12, 22, 49; political dimension of: 121–22; salvation by: 142
Faith and Violence: 8, 52, 70, 78–79, 82–87, 114, 117, 119, 121, 129, 164, 169, 177–78, 191, 200
faithfulness: 124; to tradition: 8
fall: 38, 77, 91, 98, 100, 104, 107, 159; of Adam: 104, 162; reversal of: 90
fallout: 189
falsity, experience of: 162

family, human: 127
fanaticisms: 83
fantasy, slave of: 20
Father(s), Church: 13, 22, 47, 93, 153; Cistercian: 9; Desert: 9, 12, 104, 134, 139, 141, 144, 146; Eastern: 139; Greek: xi, 13, 15, 32, 34, 75, 159; Latin: xi, 13; spiritual: 136, 141; Western: 153
Faulkner, William: 4, 176; sapiential outlook of: 75
fear: 162, 173; of failure: 125
feedback, parodic: 167
Ferrapont, Fr.: 145
fictions, collective: 169
fidelity: 117, 168, 189; call to: 124; of God: 83; return to: 80; to church: 87; to God: 187; to meditation: 124; to self: 171; to truth: 87
Figures for an Apocalypse: 27, 31
Finley, James: 19, 43
fire: 154
flesh: 14
flowers: 25, 74
foolishness, pathetic: 115
force, destructive: 115; of freedom: 81; of life: 81; oppressive: 115
Ford, George B.: 26
Forest, Jim: 2, 6, 108, 132
forest, silence of: 103
forgetfulness of self: 148
forgiveness of debts: 80
form, Christian: 188; detachment from: 197
formation, monastic: 137
formulas, verbal: 179
fragmentation: xiii, 66, 68, 127, 185; destructive: 187
France, southern: 188
Francis of Assisi, St.: 29, 81, 152; witness of: 6
Francis, Pope: 1, 6, 186
freedom: xii, 54, 60, 73, 76, 78, 81, 83, 95–96, 103, 128, 135, 142, 146; authentic: 138; charismatic: 59, 125, 144, 156; distorted concept of: 23; exercise of: 84; forces of: 81; from automatisms: 158; from institutional structures: 135; from routines: 158; illusions of: 84; illusory: 161; metaphysical: 99; misuse of: 92; of Christian: 142; of Eden: 94; of prophet: 84; of speech: 159, 161; perfect: 142; potential for: 112; surrender of: 166; transcendent: 199; uninhibited: 93
friction: 185
frustration, eventual: 197
fulfillment: 158; sexual: 166
fullness: 205
function, outward: 142
fury, paranoid: 201
future, utopian: 24

gadgetry, technological: 151
Gandhi, Mohandas: 78, 171–72, 192–94, 201–2
Gandhi on Non-Violence: 66–67, 78, 90, 192–94, 201–2
garden, world as: 91
Gardner, W. H.: 26
Genesis, Book of: 91, 161
genocide: 115, 164
gentleness: 109
Geography of Lograire: 186–87
Gestapo: 164
Gethsemani, Abbey of: xiv, 98–99; community of: 102; solitude of: 197
gift(s): 90, 126, 130; divine: 34, 94; eschatological: 126; God as: 76; liberation as: 83; of community: 86; of God: 76; of love: 91; of Spirit: 47, 52, 69, 114, 117, 121; pure: 191; Sophia as: 76; spiritual: 126; wisdom as: 76
glory, divine: 35; of God: 27, 33, 35, 45, 125; of kingdom: 124; to God: 25

gnosis: 33, 71
goal, divine: 163
God, art of: 25, 27; as Beginning: 172; as Center: 177; as compassionate: 203; as consolation: 102; as Creator: 15, 24, 32, 34, 36–37, 66–67, 88, 90–91, 190; as End: 172; as Father: 44, 172, 177; as gift: 76; as ground of existence: 44; as Lord of Israel: 203; as merciful: 203–4; as peace: 102; as *Principium*: 172; as source of existence: 44; as Redeemer: 34; child of: 113; children of: 156; communication with: 162; communion with: 160; dwelling place of: 93; encounter with: 32; epiphany of: 74; essence of: 25; experience of: 11–12, 57, 70; face of: 27, 200; favor of: 129; fidelity of: 83; footprints of: 29; gift of: 76; glory of: 27, 33, 35, 45, 125; glory to: 25; goodness of: 29, 70, 129; grace of: 117, 129; growth in: 113; hand of: 16; happiness of: 45; image(s) of: 18, 20, 28, 85, 91, 93, 95, 142–43, 190, 198; immortality of: 45; infinite: 177; instruments of: 127; journey to: 29; judgments of: 80; justice of: 125; kingdom of: ix, 8, 10, 12, 17, 49, 52, 59, 85, 111–30; knowledge of: 70; life of: 35, 45, 54–55, 63, 70, 100; light of: 153; likeness to: 96, 198; love for: 36, 125; love of: 19, 25, 27, 29, 39, 46, 68, 70, 97–98, 113, 129, 178, 198; mercy of: 84, 128–29, 180; message from: 181; mind of: 25; name of: 101; of Islam: 203; of justice: 85; of liberation: 85; of love: 85, 198; people of: 144; personality of: 178; praise of: 125; plan of: 85; power of: 35, 45, 168; presence of: 34, 67, 83, 95; quest for: 145; reality of: 37, 55, 160; reign of: 8, 50, 85–86, 111–14, 119, 121, 123–24, 128, 163, 196, 202–3; relationship with: 11, 162; riches of: 21; rule of: 85; secret of: 202; self of: 73; self-disclosure of: 37; sight of: 25; solitary: 197; solitude of: 21, 55, 198; sons of: 142; Spirit of: 96, 123; transcendence of: 178; triune: 56; truth of: 35, 125; union with: 35, 43, 52–53, 62, 72, 96, 124; unity in: 109; voice of: 147; will of: 4, 19, 50, 84, 113, 120–21, 123, 127–28, 202; wisdom of: 27, 33–35, 37, 39, 98; Word of: 8, 34, 69, 125, 163, 169, 172, 176; work of: 91, 96, 130, 202; world of: 17
god(s), false: 82, 163; ideologies as: 83; of Canaanites: 80
goodness, human: 129; intrinsic: 163; of God: 29, 70, 129; potential: 129
gospel: xii, 59; betrayals of: 16
grace: xii, 53–54, 58, 66, 93, 119, 126, 129, 142, 191; beauty of: 36; builds on nature: 150; inner: 147; interior: 61; liberation as: 83; life of: 57; of Christ: 105; of God: 117, 129; of sacraments: 58; reality of: 91; saving: 117
gratification, self-centered: 32
gratitude: 90, 126
grave: 154
Grayston, Donald: 155
greed: 18, 60, 85, 190, 203
Green, Julian: 188
Gregory Nazianzen, St.: 139
Griffin, John Howard: 108, 187
ground, of existence: 19; transcendent: 161
growth, in God: 113; spiritual: 32, 34
guidance: 137
guile: 154
guilt: 18; separation from: 97; spiritual life as: 155

habit, monastic: 131
haecceitas: 31
Hagia Sophia: 37, 67, 74, 76, 88, 107–9, 155
half-truths: 82
happiness, of God: 45; spiritual: 91; temporal: 127
harmony, appreciation of: 152; cosmic: 77; natural: 155; personal: 77; primordial: 90; social: 77
Hart, Patrick: 2–4, 26, 35, 46, 69–70, 91, 93, 99, 102, 112, 134–35, 139, 157, 171, 175, 196, 203, 205
hate: 154
hatred(s): 18, 51, 115, 129, 201, 203; of life: 39; power of: 128; world of: 85
He Is Risen: 50, 126
healing, instrument of: 79; of individuals: 113
heart, eye of: 177; of faith: 44; of Israel: 80; of mysticism: 44; paschal: ix, 63; Sacred: 63; simplicity of: 147
heat: 155
heaven: 15, 63, 93, 122
hedonism, intellectual: 69
hell: 53
helplessness: 11
Henry, Gray: xii, 1
Herakleitos: 170
heritage, cultural: 193; double: 190; experiential: 188; Indian: 193; intellectual: 188; of Asia: 193; of Greece: 193; of Rome: 193; spiritual: 199; Western: 189
hermit(s): 10; 137, 140, 152, 154; Egyptian: 104; movement: 137; nonmonastic: 137
hermitage: 29, 103, 126, 146–49, 194
Hidden Ground of Love: 2, 74–75, 105, 131, 137–38, 146, 149, 153, 156, 200
hiddenness: 133, 204

hierarchy: 140; Russian Orthodox: 184
Hillis, Gregory K.: 4, 6
Hinduism: 78, 177
Hindus: 65, 198
Hiroshima: 165
history: 27, 66; Christian: 16; completion of: 112; course of: 115; creatures of: 189; factual: 91; human: 196; monastic: 132, 145–46; of Israel: 86; salvation: 196; turning point of: 113; world of: 120
Hitler, Adolf: 87
holiness: 27; call to: 28; of creatures: 25–27, 74; secret: 80; transcendent: 80
hollowness: 19
Holy Spirit: 21, 46, 54–55, 62, 81, 83, 85, 94, 96, 119, 122–23, 126, 129, 135, 177; as mutual love of Father and Son: 44, 53; breath of: 65, 198; domestication of: 124; gift(s) of: 47, 52, 69, 114, 117, 121; openness to: 84; power of: 59; presence of: 124; sending of: 147; submission to: 82; undomesticated: 142–43; voice of: 87; working of: 127
honesty: 168
"Honorable Reader": 79, 197, 202–5
hope(s): 50, 52, 103, 113, 137, 203; Christian: 53; darkness of: 122; eschatological: 61, 129, 137, 202; instrument of: 79; message of: 181; sign of: 10; word of: 154
hopelessness, apparent: 61, 136
Hopkins, Gerard Manley: 25–27, 31, 34
Horan, Daniel P.: 4–5, 28, 30
Horeb, Mt.: 101
Hosea: 80
hostility, 191, 198; interreligious: 184
Hubbard, Barbara: 24
hubris, technological: 38–39; Western: 189

human being, authentic: 91
humanism, Christian: 75, 116, 144;
  new: 143; personalistic: 144
humanity, broken: 63; common: 149,
  156; communion with: 93; fulfilled: 113; goodness of: 129;
  redeemed: 36, 102; renewal of:
  113; respect for: 191; restored:
  100, 113; self-deluded: 17;
  shared: 66; sinful: 17, 63; suffering: 63; unity of: 87, 96
humanization: 144
humility: 59–60, 83, 98, 121, 126, 168, 197
humorlessness, dogmatic: 189
hunger: 146
hungry, food for: 127
Huntington, Samuel P.: 183–85, 201

iconoclasm, creative: 84; prophetic: 84
ideas: 34; sharing of: 158; worldly: 131
identification, compassionate: 143;
  cross-cultural: 200; dialogue as:
  191; self-created: 107
identity, authentic: 25, 28, 35, 89, 102,
  161, 163, 172; change of: 56;
  Christian: 144; cultural: ix; deepest: 39, 43, 91; false: 19; genuine:
  47; group: 197; in Christ: 121;
  inner: 142; inviolable: 25;
  monastic: 132, 144–45; mystery
  of: 149; new: 47; of Adam: 91;
  of church: 86–87; personal: 35,
  70, 144, 155; quest for: 103;
  recorded: 107; religious: 197;
  self-centered: 92; self-created: 92;
  shared: 198; socially constructed:
  196–97; spiritual: 53; superficial:
  19; true: 19, 83, 121
ideologies, as gods: 83; confusion of: 164
idol(s): 82–83, 143; as illusions: 85;
  as phantoms: 85; enslavement to:
  95; of mystification: 84; of power:
  84; of self: 95; of super-control:
  84; religious: 84; secular: 84
idolatry: 16, 83, 145, 163–64; abominations of: 82; denunciation of:
  82; identification of: 82; of class:
  84; of comfort: 84; of money: 84;
  of power: 84; of race: 84
ignorance: 173
illumination: 55; concrete: 72; existential: 72; intuitive: 72; of wisdom: 73
illusion(s): 32–33, 82–83, 87, 92, 162–63, 166, 197; choice of: 19;
  human: 47; idols as: 85; of
  autonomy: 45, 91, 105; of freedom: 84; of life: 80
image(s): 34, 82, 169; confusion of:
  164; divine: 13, 67, 91, 93, 112,
  127, 163; of God: 18, 20, 28, 85,
  91, 93, 95, 142–43, 190, 198;
  political: 174; uncreated: 47
imagery, advertising: 166; bridal: 42
immanence of kingdom: 120
immortality: 54; heavenly: 120;
  of God: 45
Imperato, Robert: 30
imperialist, cultural: 189
impersonality, passive: 167
improvement of life: 86
In the Dark before Dawn: 108
inattention: 88
inattentiveness: 89
incarnation: 8, 10, 74; doctrine of: 56,
  144, 172; of Christ: 30, 37, 98, 107,
  112–13; of kingdom: 125; of
  Logos: 66; of Word: 30
incoherence of contemporary discourse: 167
incomprehension, mutual: 195
independence, theocratic: 80
India: 202
Indian, American: 75
indigence: 11, 173
individual: 20, 95
individualism: 21

individuality: 25–26
inequalities: 80
inequity, temptations of: 80
inertia: 67
infidelity, to self: 171; to truth: 190
influence, spheres of: 184
information: 169; communication of: 160; jargon as: 167
inheritance, intellectual: 188; spiritual: 188
iniquity: 154
injustice: 51; power of: 128; racial: 115; victims of: 51
Inner Experience: 15, 33, 44–45, 48, 56–57, 69, 75, 95, 134, 203
innocence: 92, 105; inexpressible: 89; loss of: 107; original: 98; personal: 83; renewed: 97
innovation: 8; passion for: 7
inscape: 25–27, 31, 34; as sanctity: 37, 74
insecurity, timid: 16
inseeing: 175
insensitivity: 186
insight(s), contemplative: 199; intuitive: 173; mutual: 199; new: 47, 192; shared: 187; spiritual: 200
insignificance, human: 45
insignificant: 113
inspiration: 176
institution(s), Christian: 134; ecclesial: 118, 134; industrial: 23; military: 23; monastic: 102, 145
instrument, of justice: 85; of love: 85; of *shalom*: 85; of unity: 96
integration: xi; eschatological: 196; final: xiii, 195–96, 205; human: 125; of self and world: 148; transcultural: 125, 196; with natural world: 31
integrity, cultural: 190; personal: 143
intelligence(s), creative: 176; pure: 34
interdependence, cultural: 186
interests, selfish: 46

intimacy, covenant: 79; spontaneous: 159
intolerance: 184, 186
Introduction to Christian Mysticism: 33–36, 75, 134
intuition(s): 78; aesthetic: 178; concrete: 10; contemplative: 147, 156; inexpressible: 160; Zen: 179
invitation, sign of: 117
involvement: 79
Isaac, Abbot: 139
Isaac of Stella: 178
Islam: 78, 193; God of: 203; symbols of: 183
isolation: 53, 67, 78
isolationism: 185
Israel: 87; biblical: 184; heart of: 80; history of: 86; identity of: 79; life of: 80; nuptials of: 79; prophets of: 80; state of: 184; vocation of: 79
itinerants: 137

Jägerstätter, Franz: 87
Japanese: 203
jargon, meaningless: 167
jealousy: 60
Jeremiah: 67
Jews: 65, 198
John Chrysostom, St.: 139
John of the Cross, St.: 4, 22, 32, 46, 178
John the Baptist, St.: 204
John the Evangelist, St.: 22
John XXIII, Pope St.: 7, 169
Johnson, Thomas H.: 176
Jordan River: 204
Joseph, St.: 99–100
journey, mystical: 35; spiritual: 29, 32, 71, 180
joy: 11, 18, 61, 76, 101; eschatological: 117; infinite: 11; spiritual: 144; true: 12
Judaism: 78
judgment(s): 127, 166; avoiding: 123; good: 165; of God: 80

Julian of Norwich: 11, 22, 97, 153
justice: 52, 80, 83, 132; action for: 117; conversion to: 80; covenantal: 67; global: 201; God of: 85; instrument of: 85; racial: 39; reign of: 52; sign of: 85; social: 4, 203

kairos: 86–87, 152, 205
karuna: 180, 205
kenosis: 21, 43, 46, 62, 93, 205
Kentucky: 151
kerygma: 75, 123
Kilcourse, George: 30, 41, 43, 106
King, Martin Luther, Jr.: 202
kingdom, absence of: 115; affirmation of: 115; as gift: 126; building: 12, 117, 126–27; citizens of: 129; coming of: 8; epiphany of: 120; eschatological: 112, 118–20, 126; eternal: 127; glory of: 124; identity of: 120; immanence of: 120; instrument(s) of: 17, 121; interior: 116; language of: 111; message of: 120; messianic: 114; Muscovite: 119; of God: ix, 8, 10, 12, 17, 49, 52, 59, 85, 111–30; of heaven: 116; of life: 114; of peace: 115, 128; of promise: 103, 126; power of: 123; presence of: 120–21, 128; reality of: 115, 128; revelation of: 128; sign(s) of: 10, 17, 121; static view of: 118; true: 124; vision of: 113; witness to: 128
kinship, spiritual: 186
knowledge: 173; abstract: 77; analytical: 77; by identification: 38, 75, 176; conceptual: 158, 179; dualistic: 93; existential: 96; factual: 173; for power: 78; imaginative: 179; intellectual: 69; intersubjective: 38, 75, 176; manipulative: 78; objective: 62, 77, 178; of God: 70; practical: 173; quantitative: 77; reflexive: 179; scientific: 77; self-aggrandizing: 78

Koreans: 203
Kramer, Victor A.: 3, 38, 59, 76, 89, 118, 188

labor, painful: 77; of action: 77; of science: 77; useless: 77
Lahey, G. F.: 26
laity: 144
language: 158–73, 180; abuse of: 167; as divine gift: 162; as human accomplishment: 162; as instrument of violence: 164; as victim: 164; conceptual: 161; corruption of: 172; degradation of: 165, 174; failures of: 167; function of: 160; German: 164; impurity of: 175; integrity of: 170; limitations of: 178; love for: 180; misuse of: 163, 172; objective: 161; of Auschwitz: 165; of efficacy: 172; of *kairos*: 172; of kingdom: 111; of propaganda: 165; perversion of: 164–65; pretensions of: 179; purification of: 172; question of: 172; reappropriation of: 168–72; redemption of: 168; rejection of: 178; respect for: 180; sapiential: 73; symbolic: 174; validity of: 180; value of: 180; wisdom of: 176
Lao Tzu: 179
Laughlin, James: 30, 139, 157, 196
law: xii; canon: 132; fulfillment of: 71
Lax, Robert: 187
Learning to Love: 3, 108
Leclercq, Jean: 10–11, 22, 56
legacy, cultural: 188
legalism, religious: 164
Lent: 57
Leopold, Aldo: 23, 39
liberation: 60, 103, 197; as gift: 83; as grace: 83; contemplation as: 95; existential: 61; from conventions: 158; from limitations: 158; from mechanisms: 158; from sin: 53; from social dictates: 158; God

of: 85; search for: 204; secret of: 143; to captives: 81
liberty: 85; charism of: 142; full: 205; transcendent: 205
lie(s): 82, 161–63; acceptance of: 161; preference for: 162; world of: 171
life: 128; active: 34, 170; affirmation of: 86; as passive: 76; ascetic: 34; challenges of: 171; Christian: 44, 115, 124, 135; common: 100; contemplative: 34; cultural: 148; divine: 35, 48, 117, 122; eremitical: 126, 146; eternal: 53–54, 93; evangelical: 134; forces of: 81; free: 81; fruitful: 61; fullness of: 63; hatred of: 39; hermit: 131, 146; hostility to: 18; human: 148; illusion of: 80; imaginative: 106; improvement of: 86; in Christ: 43, 50, 61, 129–30, 140; in Eden: 109; in society: 105; in Spirit: 11; institutional: 145; intimate: 70; kingdom of: 114; lay: 131, 146; liturgical: 57, 121, 123; message of: 80; monastic: 24, 31, 58–60, 79, 100–101, 103, 117, 125, 132–33, 141, 143, 146; mystery of: 72, 114; natural: 148; new: 61, 95; of discipleship: 82; of faith: 11–12, 22, 49; of freedom: 59; of grace: 57; of God: 35, 45, 54–55, 63, 70, 100; of humility: 59; of Israel: 80; of joy: 59; of love: 59; of monk: 61; of peace: 59; of solitude: 149; of surrender: 59; of transformation: 59; of universe: 38, 74; ordinary: 147; political: 35, 153; problems of: 171; prophetic: 81; redeemed: 127; religious: 132, 141; renewed: 102; resurrected: 124; sacramental: 57, 121, 123; sapiential: 80; social: 153; spiritual: 35, 48, 71, 155; state of: 125; tree of: 93; trinitarian: 60; way of: 72; worldly: 131

Life and Holiness: 45–48, 50, 57–58, 121, 124, 126–27
Life of the Vows: 60
light: 36, 53, 96, 154; as passive: 76; blessed: 103, 126; divine: 93; of God: 153; of Logos: 37; of *theoria*: 39; of truth: 123; of wisdom: 34–35; spiritual: 115
likeness, divine: 35; existential: 199; to God: 96, 198
limitations, liberation from: 158
Literary Essays: 35, 38, 70, 75, 86, 91, 105–6, 171–72, 174, 176
liturgy: 44, 57–58, 62, 122–23; eucharistic: 57, 122
Living Bread: 50–51, 57
logo, corporate: 174
logos of creatures: 34
Logos, divine: 34; image of: 74; incarnation of: 66; light of: 37; presence of: 172; seeds of: 170; *Tao* and: 73–74; wisdom and: 69, 74–75
loneliness: 171; as mysterious: 136; as prophetic: 136; of monk: 61
Louisville, KY: 100
love(s): 10, 21, 54–55, 70, 73, 121, 128, 155–56, 191, 201; act of: 50, 54; all-encompassing: 104; as ground of being: 17; authentic: 50; authority of: 136; capacity to: 144; compassionate: 113, 117, 204; covenantal: 67; creative: 36, 68, 89; disinterested: 100; divine: 15, 35, 163; for God: 36, 125; for language: 180; free: 122; gift of: 91; God of: 85, 198; human: 174; infinite: 198; inordinate: 91; instrument of: 85; kingdom of: 123; life of: 59; maternal: 204; merciful: 46; mutual: 53, 56, 128; of Christ: 51, 55, 63, 117, 122, 128; of church: 86; of enemies: 51; of God: 19, 25, 27, 29, 39, 46, 68, 97–98, 113, 129, 178, 198; of self: 91;

one: 155–56; particular: 104, 155; power of: 52, 123, 129, 202; presence of: 78; quest for: 103; redemptive: 68, 128–29; reign of: 52; sacrificial: 129; sanctified: 122; selfless: 125; sign of: 85; sophianic: 71; sources of: 174; steadfast: 80; suffering: 49; trinitarian: 53, 124; unity of: 88, 128; unlimited: 91; unmerited: 91; victory of: 129; wisdom based on: 75
Love and Living: 46–47, 49, 52–54, 56, 58, 61, 69, 93, 102, 112–13, 118, 128, 166, 173–74, 177, 180, 203
lowly: 113
loyalty, absolute: 195
Luther, Martin: 142

"M.": 106, 108
Macarius, St.: 139
machine, institutional: 102
magic, as impurity of language: 175; as manipulation: 175; as self-fulfilling prophecy: 175; of words: 174
mahakaruna: 205
man, exterior: 48; interior: 48; mass: 174; mere: 156
mandala: 187
Manichaeanism: 15
manipulation of things: 36
marginalized: 87, 97, 137
Maritain, Jacques: 188
Maritain, Raïssa: 153
Mark, Gospel of: 81, 87, 111
market, free: 184
marketing: 84
Marxism, decline of: 184
Mary, Blessed Virgin, awakening by: 88, 109
mask: 18
mass: 57–58; celebration of: 139
master, spiritual: 136
mastery, technological: 24

materialism, crude: 189
matter: 66; cultural: 188
maturity, spiritual: 157
Maximus the Confessor, St.: 34
McBrien, Richard: xi–xii
McDonald's: 184
meaning: 7, 96; illusory: 85; quest for: 103; self-constituted: 86
mechanisms, liberation from: 158
media, mass: 169; misuse of: 171
meditation: 58
memory, communal: 7
mendacity: 166
Meng Tzu: 179
mentality, activist: 192; crusading: 158; goal-oriented: 192; pragmatic: 192
mercy: 53, 76, 109, 154; Christian: 128, 203; divine: 80, 129; great: 154; healing: 168; of God: 84, 128–29, 180
Merton, Thomas: as critic of monasticism: 132; as hermit: 32, 131, 148–56; as model: 185–86; as monk: 11; as novice master: 31–32, 149; as progressive: 7; as prophetic: 4, 6; as representative figure: 2; as sign of contradiction: 185; as sign of reconciliation: 185; as solitary: 148; as writer: 2–4, 11; audience of: 3; biography of: 2; catholicity of: 88; commitments of: 186; conversion of: 24; death of: 1; defensiveness of: 132; disillusion of: 132; last testament of: 205; literary style of: 3, 6; monastic life of: 24, 31; parents of: 188; personality of: 2, 6; poetry of: 29–30, 176–77; priesthood of: 31, 138–39; social thought of: 23; vocation of: 2, 11, 204
message, Christian: 116–17; from God: 181; of salvation: 113; prophetic: 113, 173; providential: 173

metanoia: 54, 59, 123
Middle East, conflict in: 184
millennium, new: 183, 186
mind, right: 193
mindfulness: 147, 204
mindset, conformist: 189; materialist: 189; totalitarian: 189
ministry of Jesus: 113
miracle of new life: 61
misinformation: 171
mission, of church: 87, 112; prophetic: 81
Mississippi: 154
mistrust: 198
misunderstanding, cross-cultural: 157, 191
monastery, as Eden: 100; as eschatological sign: 125; as place of dialogue: 169; as sacrament: 102
Monastic Journey: 4, 46–47, 48, 57, 59–60, 102
Monastic Observances: 27
monasticism: 44, 59, 62; as lay movement: 131–44; decay of: 102; desert: 135; early: 138; institutional: 137; primitive: 135; pure: 138; renewal of: 103; rise of: 9; wholeness of: 103
money, idolatry of: 84
monk(s), as exemplary: 59; as explorer: 59; as integral Christian: 135; as layman: 134; as man of paradise: 98; as marginal person: 143; as witness: 61; life of: 61; loneliness of: 61; mystique of: 149; role of: 158; true: 91; vocation of: 98, 135
Montaldo, Jonathan: xii, 1, 3, 28, 101, 111, 138, 204
mortality: 181
mortification: 18
Moscow: 119
Moses: 101
mosquitoes: 150–51
Mott, Michael: 2, 28, 30, 108
movement, mass: 174

Mozart, Wolfgang Amadeus: 76
Muir, Edwin: 176
multiculturalism: viii
Murdoch, Rupert: 184
music: 178; cosmic: 74, 76–77; divine: 74, 76–77
Musk, Elon: 184
Muslim(s): 65, 198, 202
mystery: 61; cosmic: 38, 75; divine: 50; Easter: 58, 197; eschatological: 125; existential: 72; of being: 174; of Christ: 60, 122–23, 170, 193; of Christianity: 20; of contemplative truth: 174; of cross: 50, 92; of human love: 174; of life: 72, 114; of mutual compassion: 45; of redemption: 56, 174, 196–97; paschal: ix, 20, 43–44, 48–49, 52–53, 56–58, 61–63, 69–70, 114–15
mysticism: 71; Christian: 43; heart of: 44; Islamic: 89
mystics, Russian: xi, 13; Spanish: xi, 13
Mystics and Zen Masters: 6, 11, 72–73, 75, 87, 96–97, 105, 169, 175–76, 186, 192–94, 204
mystification, idols of: 84
mystique, organizational: 125–26
myth(s): 66, 82, 90; confusion of: 164

nakedness: 19
name(s): 159–60; detachment from: 197; right: 106
Nash, Roderick: 23
nation, claims of: 196
nationalism, Christian: 184
Native American: 97
nature: xii, 66, 74; as sign of divine goodness and love: 29; communion in: 75; concrete: 25; divine: 93; grace building on: 150; human: 112, 176
Navajo: 187
necessity, physical: 99
needs: 203

Negro: 187
neuroses, collective: 7
New Man: 14, 35–37, 43, 45, 47–50, 53–54, 57–58, 70–71, 77, 92–93, 95–96, 114–15, 117, 121, 128, 159–62, 168, 172
New Seeds of Contemplation: ix, 14–16, 19–20, 25, 27, 30, 33, 37, 42–43, 45–47, 49–51, 55, 57, 71, 74, 91, 94–95, 166–67, 178
New Testament: 13, 38, 155, 164, 192
Newman, St. John Henry: 26, 56
Nhat Hanh, Thich: 200
night(s), dark: 48; of sense: 48; of spirit: 48
No Man Is an Island: 43, 45, 47–51, 53, 57, 168, 202
noise: 151
non-existence: 45
nonviolence: 78, 85, 172, 186, 204; and dialogue: 191; as kind of language: 172; as prophetic: 172; Christian: 129; logic of: 201
Nonviolent Alternative: 86, 165, 172
nostalgia, sterile: 7
Notes on Genesis and Exodus: 161–62
nothingness, primordial: 88; pure: 104, 156
novice: 136
nowhere, center of: 107
nuptials of Israel: 79

Oakham School: 25
obedience, inner: 72; monastic: 60; of Christ: 54, 92; strict: 136; to Truth: 92; wilderness: 103, 126
objection, conscientious: 87
objects, natural: 28; ordinary: 174
obligations: 142, 154
observance(s), monastic: 102, 145
obsessions: 7
O'Callaghan, Frank: xiv
O'Callaghan, Tommie: xiv
O'Connell, Michael J.: xiv

O'Connell, Patrick F.: vii–ix, xii, 3–6, 23–24, 27, 29–30, 32–33, 52, 60, 72, 75, 107–8, 132, 134, 139, 141, 161–62, 165, 167, 175, 177, 186
O'Connor, Flannery: 153, 176
Odorisio, David M.: 89, 94
office, divine: 107, 154
officialese: 164
Old Testament: 81
opposites, attunement of: 66
oppression(s): 51, 80–81, 83, 85, 171, 173, 204; brutality of: 85; police: 85; political: 167; power of: 128
oppressors: 113
optimism, false: 119; superficial: 39
order: 96; new world: 184, 205; of universe: 38, 74; pattern of: 74; spiritual: 92
ordinary, sacredness of: 66
ordination: 140; monastic: 137
orientation, sapiential: 72
Original Child Bomb: 165
origins, monastic: 134
Other Side of the Mountain: 3, 139, 205
Otto of Friesing: 118
outcast(s): 113, 137
outlaws: 137
Oyer, Gordon: 5–6

Pachomius, St.: 139
Padovano, Anthony T.: 2
pain of death: 45
Pakistan: 202
paradise: ix, 39, 87–88, 90–109, 133; climate of: 105; earthly: 97, 99, 102; experience of: 109; garden of: 159; gates of: 88, 92; Gethsemani as: 98–99; heavenly: 99; inner: 103; intuition of: 105; man of: 98; new: 93; recovery of: 94, 96, 101, 103–4, 106; restored: 98, 100; return to: 90–92, 94, 96, 101, 107; rivers of: 203; spiritual: 96
paradosis: 22
pardon: 168

Paris, as cultural capital: 188
parousia, imminent: 116
parrhesia: 159–61, 168
participation: 43, 54, 57, 60–61, 82, 122, 136; immediate: 62; in passion: 45; in resurrection: 45; intuitive: 62
particularism: 66
particularity: 26; concrete: 151
Pascal, Blaise: 50
passion: 60; slave of: 20
Pasternak, Boris: 123–24, 176
patriotism: 83
Paul, St.: 20, 22, 42–43, 62, 69–71, 77, 91, 93, 164
peace: 52, 59, 77, 80, 91, 101, 103, 116, 121, 127, 132, 180, 201; action for: 112; commitment to: 39; global: 201; God as: 102; kingdom of: 115, 128; of Christ: 128; on earth: 203
peacemakers: 128
peacemaking: 6, 186; Christian: 129
Pearson, Paul M.: 106, 108
penance: 123; sacrament of: 60
Pentecost, communion of: 197
people, redeemed: 122
persecuted: 51
person: 20; appreciation of: 199; defense of: 85; integrity of: 95
persona, social: 180
perspective(s), Christocentric: 62–63; cosmic: 98; dualistic: 92; holistic: 66; incarnational: 62–63; theocentric: 62–63; transcultural: 193–94; trinitarian: 62–63
perversion, crude: 164
Peter of Iberia, St.: 139
phantoms, idols as: 85
philosophers, Bantu: 186; Greek: 170
philosophy: 79, 160; civilized: 194
Pick, John: 26, 31
pilgrim, transcultural: 192
pilgrimage: 103; lifelong: xi
pine, fragrant: 155

plan, divine: 50, 85, 113
Plato: 69, 75
Platonism: 193
play: 99; wisdom at: 76; work as: 99
Plotinus: 69
pneuma: 36, 155
poem(s): 160; gnomic: 161
poet(s): 67, 87, 105–6, 174–76; business of: 174; creative intelligence of: 176; office of: 105, 176; vocation of: 67, 174
poetry: 175–76, 178; dignity of: 176; innocence of: 175; of paradise consciousness: 106–9; valid: 106
point, virginal: 156
point vierge: 89
policies, oppressive: 83; self-serving: 83
polis, Christian: 122
politician: 174
politics: 154
Polonnaruwa: 179, 205
poor: 80, 87, 113–14, 204; as Christ: 114; exploitation of: 67, 115; good news to: 81, 112
positivism: 176
possession(s): 19, 90; demonic: 113; material: 82; worship of: 82
posturing: 196
poverty: 11–12, 156
power(s): 85, 163; and elements: 164; and principalities: 132; as motive for knowledge: 78; cynical: 124; divine: 35; ethos of: 79; idolatries of: 84; idols of: 84; military: 85; nonviolent: 52; of air: 164; of Christ: 45, 50, 77; of compassion: 202; of cross: 50, 52, 54, 101, 123; of evil: 81; of God: 35, 45, 168; of kingdom: 129; of love: 52, 123, 129, 202; of sacrifice: 123; of Spirit: 59; of technology: 97; of truth: 129; of understanding: 202; of vision: 88; political: 82, 113; redemptive: 54; religious: 82;

temptations of: 80–81; transforming: 129; worldly: 81, 118, 124; worship of: 82
practice, Christian: xi, 121; religious: 87
pragmatism: 157, 199
praise of Creator: 67, 176
Prajna: 73
praktike: 32
Pramuk, Christopher: 37, 76, 108
prayer: 4, 6, 125; and protest: 132; contemplative: xi; interior: 124; monastic: 60, 125; private: 58
Prayer and the Yoke of Christ: 176
preachers, itinerant: 137
preconceptions, logical: 179
prejudice(s): 82, 196; racial: 67; religious: 67
presence, clerical: 133; divine: 93, 124, 155; of cross: 50; of God: 34, 67, 83, 95; of love: 78; of truth: 78; political: 82, 164; priestly: 133
"Present 'Crisis' in Monasticism": 4
prestige: 163
presumption, arrogant: 184
Preview of the Asian Journey: 24, 39, 138
pride: 92, 162; human: 36
priesthood: 57, 140
priests, monastic: 140
principalities, powers and: 132
principle, Socratic: 169
prisoner, visit to: 127
privilege: 163
problems, current: 189; of exploitation, 190; of mass society: 190; of racism: 190; of war: 190
production: 36; mystique of: 36
productivity: 143; as criterion: 198
profit(s): 24, 84, 157, 199
progressives: 119
promise(s), divine: 113; kingdom of: 103, 126
propaganda: 165–66, 189; political: 163, 165; violence of: 166
propagandist: 174

prophecy: 67–68, 71, 79–88, 156; authentic: 83; biblical: 4, 79; burden of: 81, 86; false: 163; leaven of: 67; mission of: 87; self-fulfilling: 119, 175; witness of: 84
prophet(s): 68; as divine instruments: 80; as solitary: 80; as voice in wilderness: 81; as witness: 80–81, 83; false: 86; freedom of: 84; Hebrew: 153; mission of: 80; of Israel: 80; Old Testament: 87; task of: 83; true: 86
prosperity: 162
protection of creation: 97
protest: 6; mission of: 87; prayer and: 132
Protestants: 65, 198
Proverbs, Book of: 36–37, 76; wisdom of: 71
Psalms: 12, 107, 154, 156
purgatory: 99
Purgatory, Mt.: 10, 88, 98
purification: 68; purgatorial: 99
purity: 92–93; of contemplation: 95; of vision: 88
Putin, Vladimir: 184
Pycior, Julie Leininger: 1
Pythagoras: 75

quest, for identity: 103; for love: 103; for meaning: 103, 187; for transcendence: 187
question, christological: 116; discipleship: 116
quietism: 67

race, claims of: 196; detachment from: 197; differences of: 186; idolatries of: 84
racism: 4–5; problems of: 190
Raids on the Unspeakable: 6, 76, 165, 173–75
rain, as gratuitous: 76; as useless: 76
ranters, English: 187
rationalism, scientific: 68

Reading Notebook #14: 138
Reading Notebook #16: 133
Reading Notebook #17: 137
Reading Notebook #24: 134
Reading Notebook #57: 140
reality: 82, 116; absolute: 104; alienation from: 91; appreciation of: 168; as sacrament: 68; awakening to: 109; contact with: 160; created: 74; desire to control: 89; fullness of: 62; goodness of: 106; insight into: 173; material: 15; of God: 37, 55, 160; of grace: 91; of kingdom: 128; ontological: 174; participation in: 174; perception of: 16; present: 128; pure: 44; relationship with: 168; religious: 174; specious: 179; structure of: 74; unity of: 106
realization, contemplative: 124, 167; human: 67
realm, future: 116; transcendent: 116
reason: xii, 66, 191
rebellion: 184
rebirth: 125, 196
reconciliation: 187; message of: 128; witness of: 201–2
redeemed, community of: 49
redemption: 14, 20, 50, 57, 66, 91, 105; doctrine of: 56, 144; effects of: 49; fullness of: 103; individual: 113; meaning of: 112; mystery of: 56, 196–97; of language: 168; process of: 168; work of: 50, 122
"Reflections on Love": 51
Regula Magistri: 140
regulations: 136
reign, earthly: 116; of death: 116; of God: 8, 50, 85–86, 111–14, 121, 123–24, 128, 163, 196, 202–3; of justice: 52; of love: 52; of sin: 113, 116; of shalom: 128; of truth: 52; power of: 112
reintegration: 79–80; inner: 93
rejection: 129

relations, web of: 201–2
relationship(s): 136; with creation: 159; with Creator: 159
relevance, passion for: 7
religion: 79; as divisive force: 183; Judeo-Christian: 193; pagan: 164; resurgence of: 183
Renaissance: 192
renewal: 8; contemplative: 78; liturgical: 121–22; monastic: vii, 102–3, 144–45; mystical: 46; of world: 103; vision of: 88
renunciation, charism of: 136
repentance: 80, 123; continued: 127
repression, violent: 118
reputation: 19
resentment: 185
resistance, contemplation and: 132; nonviolent: 128, 171; political: 201; religious: 201; social: 201; violent: 185; witness of: 201
resource(s): 86; natural: 24, 39, 97; utilitarian: 98
respect: 90; for being: 199; genuine: 198; mutual: 169, 187
response, human: 68
responsibility: 130, 154; abdication of: 166; environmental: 23; of community: 86
rest: 79, 96
restlessness: 78
restoration: 147; eschatological: 109; of inner self: 44; witness of: 202
results, measurable: 125
resurrection(s): 60, 94; eon of: 114; of Christ: 20, 35, 43–45, 47–50, 54–58, 60–61, 85, 93, 98, 112, 114, 121–22, 127–28, 136, 197
retribution: 202
return to Father: 44
reunion of Christians: xi
revelation: 75, 89, 91, 103, 147; cosmic: 37, 66, 74; creation as: 67; divine: 66, 68; messengers of: 188; moment of: 152; natural: 74;

nature as source of: 31; of incarnation: 74; of Scripture: 74; of wisdom: 39; poetic: 91; positive: 74; symbolic: 91; ubiquity of: 66
revolution, inner: 59
revolutionaries: 119
rich: 80, 85
Richardson, Jane Marie: 29, 81, 180
riches of God: 21
righteousness, personal: 103
Rilke, Rainer Maria: 175
rising with Christ: 43, 45–46, 50, 54, 57–58, 61–62, 69, 144
risk: 144; state of: 181
rite(s): 66, 90; religious: 150
rituals: 150–51
rivalries, petty: 195
Road to Joy: 2, 187
role, public: 149
Rolle, Richard: 137
Roloff, Ronald: 139
Romkema, Albert: 3
roots, cultural: 13; spiritual: 13
routine(s), freedom from: 158; monastic: 102; ordinary: 154; organized: 107; secure: 142, 144; social: 181; sterile: 58; Trappist: 101; tyranny of: 146
Rubenson, Samuel: 134
Ruether, Rosemary Radford: 131–32, 137, 149, 153, 156
rule(s): 126; of God: 85; written: 135
Run to the Mountain: 3, 26, 29, 51, 57, 99–100, 175
Russia, holy: 120
Ruysbroeck, Jan: 188

sabbath, law of: 80; true: 80
sacrament(s): 57–58, 62, 68; church as: 8; grace of: 58; monastery as: 102; reality as: 68; world as: 15, 17, 38, 66, 97
sacramentality, of creation: 34, 38, 68; of creatures: 31; of world: 24
sacredness of ordinary: 66

sacrifice, power of: 123
sage(s): 68; Eastern: 153
salvation: 8, 61, 90–91, 94, 96, 123; by faith: 142; drama of: 85; eternal: 53; fruits of: 122; meaning of: 20; message of: 113, 143; way to: 204
sanctions, judicial: 135
sanctity: 82; inscape as: 37, 74; true: 45
sanity, spiritual: 193
Sankara: 197
sapientia: 69, 69–70, 73, 77, 173
sat: 177
Satie, Erik: 188
satisfaction: 77; trivial: 166
satyagraha: 171; vow of: 171
Schillebeeckx, Edward: 138
Schlesinger, Bruno P.: 74
School of Charity: 2, 134, 139
science: 78, 160, 174
scientia: 69, 77, 173
Scotus, Bl. John Duns: 15, 29–31, 38, 107
Scripture: xii, 74, 134
Scrooge, Ebenezer: 185
Search for Solitude: xi, 3, 11, 13, 18, 88, 111, 123–24, 151
Seasons of Celebration: 33, 36, 45, 50, 57, 61, 98, 112–16, 118, 120, 122–23
secret, of God: 202; unspeakable: 103–4
secular, glorification of: 15
security: 144
Seeds of Contemplation: 15–16, 19, 24–25, 27, 32–33, 49, 51, 55, 94
Seeds of Destruction: 74–75, 78, 115, 125, 128–29, 171, 202
Seeing the World in a Grain of Sand: 175–76
Selected Essays: 5, 23, 39, 139, 186, 191, 193
Selected Letters (Laughlin/Merton): 30
self: 14, 18–22; alienated: 17, 45; as Christ: 47; as idol: 95; as image of God: 18; authentic: 19–20, 83, 90,

142; cultural; 196; deepest: 91; dying to: 121, 123; ego: 20; egotistical: 92; emptying of: 93; estrangement from: 91; everyday: 46; exterior: 44, 92; false: 17, 19, 44–45, 47, 91–92, 142, 196; familiar: 47; glorification of: 33; illusory: 20; in Christ: 20–21, 43, 55, 59–60; in God: 21; individual: 174; inner: 20, 44; liberated: 46; new: 46; of God: 73; old: 54; original: 46; private: 19; public: 149; radical: 93; real: 20–21; restoration of: 44; sinful: 53, 121; smoke: 20, 45; social: 196; spiritual: 44; superficial: 19, 196; surrender of: 104, 155; theology of; 19; transcendent: 73; true: ix, 20–21, 43–45, 47–48, 52–55, 59–60, 62, 91, 93, 197; unredeemed: 94; worldly: 20
self-abnegation: 18
self-absorption: 90
self-acceptance: 18
self-actualization: 18, 21
self-affirmation: 18–19
self-alienation: 43, 92
self-assertion: 92, 109, 197
self-betrayal: 190
self-concealment: 161
self-concern, pharisaic: 196
self-consciousness: 175
self-contradiction, sin as: 164
self-deception: 125; acknowledgement of: 168; fatal: 150
self-denial: 18, 20
self-discipline: 18
self-division, state of: 91
self-doubt: 162
self-dramatization: 102
self-emptying: 19, 21, 58, 62, 107; of Christ: 46, 205
self-examination: 150
self-expression: 159
self-fulfillment: 19, 203

self-gift: 46, 112
self-glorification: 92, 162
self-hatred: 190
selfhood: 26, 95, 159
self-interest: 125, 162
self-justification: 84, 161
self-knowledge: 180
selflessness: 94; strength of: 202
self-naughting: 19, 58
self-possession, surrender of: 166
self-realization: 20, 70, 92, 166; authentic: 61; perfect: 72
self-righteousness: 83, 119
self-sacrifice: 50
self-sufficiency: 16
self-surrender: 18, 46, 53, 203
self-transcendence: 53, 158, 203
self-transformation: 20
Selma: 154
sensibility, edenic: 105
sensitivity, moral: 119
separateness: 175; dream of: 88
separation, artificial: 155
service: 98
servitude, comfortable: 94
Seven Storey Mountain: 1, 25–26, 28–30, 98, 100–101, 175
shalom, instrument of: 85; reign of: 128; sign of: 85
Shannon, William H.: xii, 2–3, 5–7, 15, 19, 24, 33, 51–52, 69, 74, 90, 95, 98, 105, 108, 131, 134, 141, 186, 200, 203
Shaw, Jeffrey M.: 5
Shepard, Kris: 202
Short, William: 31
sick, visit to: 127, 141
sign(s): 160; eschatological: 103, 114, 125; indicative: 173; of attraction: 96; of contradiction: 10, 61, 79, 81, 84, 96, 113, 117; of invitation: 117; of justice: 85; of love: 85; of *shalom*: 85; of unity: 96; preeminence of: 174; sacramental: 61, 136; sacred: 160

Sign of Jonas: 28, 139, 204
silence: 60, 72, 80, 101, 103, 155–56, 158, 167, 180–81; abyss of: 178; black: 152; contemplative: 107; creative: 180; deepened: 180; enriched: 180; of forest: 103, 155
Silence in Heaven: 70
Silent Life: 101
Silva, Ludovico: 148
simplicity, of church: 86; paradisal: 103, 126; pure: 96; undivided: 96
simulacrum: 82–83, 162, 164
sin(s): 51, 53, 63, 71, 80, 93, 105, 120, 122, 129, 204; as self-contradiction: 164; drama of: 14; effects of: 122; evil of: 53; forces of: 114; liberation from: 53; meaning of: 90; of West: 190; original: 93; power of: 117; reign of: 113; state of: 19, 91; structural: 4; victory over: 50, 114
Sinai, Mt.: 79, 173, 191
sincerity of others: 168
sinfulness, human: 128
slave, African: 97; of convention: 20; of fantasy: 20; of passion: 20
sleep: 146
slogans: 169; meaningless: 166–67; political: 86, 169
snake, king: 150–51
society, affluent: 39; ancient: 79; Asian: 79; Christian: 118; civil: 17; compulsions of: 60; consumerist: 84, 184; expectations of: 60; life in: 105; mass: 84, 143, 164, 167, 174, 190; quantified: 190; Roman: 9; soulless: 190; technological: 77–79, 190; traditional: 79; Western: 78–79
solidarity: 127, 203; as resource: 196, 198–200; human: 84; with marginalized: 137; with victims: 85
solitaries, lay: 137
solitude: 2, 21, 49, 55, 131, 137, 140, 146, 148, 154, 169, 198, 203; as resource: 196–98; call to: 103, 155;
charismatic: 126; Christian: 134–35; divine: 197; life of: 149; monastic: 101–2; of Ascension: 197; of Calvary: 197; of Gethsemani: 197; of God: 21, 55, 198; perfect: 101; vocation to: 155; way of: 144
song, bird: 155
Song of Songs, wisdom of: 71
sonship, beauty of: 36
sophia: 37, 69, 73, 76, 155, 176
sophiology: 76
soul: 33, 66, 95, 115; purified: 98
source, divine: 163
Soviet Union: 84
spectatorship: 175
speech, free: 168; freedom of: 159, 161; meaningful: 180
sphere, supernatural: 120; timeless: 120
spirit(s), balance of: 153, 194; human: 21, 35, 93; nakedness of: 60; redeemed: 36; selfish: 92
Spirit, laws of: 21; life in: 11; of Christ: 8–9, 55, 71, 128
Spirit of Simplicity: 70
spirituality: 34; Christocentric: 41–42; contemplative: vii; creation: 15; facile: 197; Franciscan: 28–31; holistic: vii–ix, 40; incarnational: 10; inclusive: ix; Judeo-Christian: 104; lay: 132; monastic: 132, 144; paradise: 97; paschal: vii, 42–63; sacramental: 10; Sufi: 89; superficial: 197; theocentric: 41–42
spontaneity: 76
Springs of Contemplation: 29, 81, 83–86, 180
St. Bonaventure College: 29, 175
stability, monastic: xi
standards, external: 72
statement, communicative: 160; contemplative: 160
status: 143; social: 113
stewardship: 38; environmental: 39
stillness: 156; of being: 90

Stone, Naomi Burton: 46, 69, 93, 112, 119, 133, 139, 157, 196, 203
Strange Islands: 162–63
stranger(s): 5, 149, 155, 192; as friend: 192; encounter with: 97; identified with oneself: 205; shelter for: 127; voice of: 173, 191
strength, of cooperation: 202; of selflessness: 202
structure(s): 126; artificial: 146; communal: 136; ecclesial: 142; human: 119–20; individual: 27; institutional: 135, 144; monastic: 102
struggle(s): 58, 68, 94, 154, 203; prophetic: 81
submission: 18; to Holy Spirit: 82
substitution, dialogue as: 191
suffering(s): 45, 61, 129, 203–4; of death: 45; protection from: 204; victory over: 204
Sullivan, Danny: 106, 108
sunyata: 180, 205
super-control, idols of: 84
superficiality: 91
superstition(s), abominations of: 82; confusion of: 164
support, mutual: 199
surrender(s): 59; of self: 104, 155; particular: 104, 155; paschal: 53; primary: 104, 155
suspicion: 198; mutual: 184
Suzuki, D. T.: 104, 146–47, 200
Sweeney, Jon: 1
sword, flaming: 95
symbol(s), as expression of unity: 173; as vehicle of wisdom: 173; pseudo-: 174; purpose of: 174, 177; traditional: 7; true: 173; validity of: 174; value of: 174
symbolism: 167, 173–77
syncretism, age of: 194; muddled: 197; turbid: 197
synthesis: 194; cultural: 192; holistic: 6
Szabo, Lynn R.: 108

T. S. Eliot and Prayer: 176
Tao: 73–75, 105; as everyday mind: 146–47; as ultimate truth: 146; eternal: 179
Tao Te Ching: 179
Taoism: 72, 75, 105, 183
Tardiff, Mary: 131
Tauler, John: 188
tears, seed of: 12
Tears of the Blind Lions: 30–31, 106–7, 139
technics, mystique of: 36
technique: 174, 199
technology: 5, 78, 98; power of: 97
Temple of Understanding: 157
temptation(s): 94; basic: 198; in desert: 81; of comfort: 80; of complacency: 80; of inequity: 80; of power: 80–81; pervasive: 166
tendencies, bad: 60
tenderness: 76
tension: 191
Teresa of Avila, St.: 153
terms, archetypal: 167; mythic: 167
Thailand: 143, 181
theocentrism: 41–43
theologia: 32
theology, biblical-existentialist: 87; Christian: 121; Franciscan: 28–31; holistic: 34; liberation: 132; monastic: 10–11, 56; of reconciliation: 193; scholastic: 56; scientific: 34; symbolic: 177
theoria physike: 32–36, 74; light of: 39
thief, good: 92
things, essences of: 32; growing: 25; inanimate: 25; living: 25
thirsty, drink for: 127
Thirty Poems: 29
Thomas Aquinas, St.: 15, 71, 170, 193
Thomas Merton in California: 94, 100
Thompson, Ian: 106, 108
Thompson, Phillip M.: 5
Thoreau, Henry David: 192
thought: 166; discursive: 178; Oriental: 191

Thoughts in Solitude: 46, 55, 63, 163, 180–81
threats: 90, 155, 189
Thurston, Bonnie: vii–ix, xiv, 106, 108, 141
time, acceptable: 86; fullness of: 112, 114; of decision: 86; of end: 125, 196; of kingdom: 125, 196; of Spirit: 125, 196; patterns of: 151; redeemed: 125, 196; transformed: 125, 196
Tolstoy, Leo: 192
topics, literary: 131; political: 131
tourist: 191
Tower of Babel: 162–63, 167
tradition(s): vii, xii, 7, 188–89; alien: 158; ambivalence toward: 190; application of: 9, 12–13; appreciation of: 9–10, 13; appropriation of: 10–13; Catholic: 72; chain of: 22; Christian: 22, 24, 72, 186; contemplative: 22, 68; cultural: 169, 186; Dionysian: 188; distortions of: 189; European: 186; faithfulness to: 8; Franciscan: 188; importance of: 189; love for: 7; monastic: 157; of East: 68, 178; problems of: 189; religious: 157; remote: 158; respect for: 7; retrieval of: 13–14; shortcomings of: 189; sins of: 189; spiritual: 6–9, 24, 178; theological: 24; Thomistic: 188; threats of: 189; Victorine: 188; Western: 169, 187–89
transfiguration, moment of: 152
transformation: 59, 113, 128; Christian: 61; human: 144; in Christ: 58; inner: 46, 144; moment of: 152; moral: 32; of self: 171; of society: 171, 200–201; personal: 34, 53; social: 196, 200–203; spiritual: 45
travelers, Muslim: 187
tree(s): 28, 151; of life: 93; paradise: 104, 107, 156; primordial: 156

Trinity: 93; contemplation of: 32; doctrine of: 56
triumphalism: 118
triviality, mechanized: 199
trout: 27
Trump, Donald: 184
trust: 80, 95, 103, 126
truth: 72, 85, 96, 162–63, 165, 171; act of: 60; as inner law: 78; as law of being: 172; awareness of: 191, 199; commitment to: 168, 172; contemplative: 174; defense of: 172; divine: 35; fidelity to: 87; force of: 171; fullness of: 196; holiness of: 168; infidelity to: 190; kingdom of: 123; light of: 123; living: 172; manifestation of: 172; nonviolence and: 172; of God: 35, 125–26; power of: 129, 171; presence of: 78; reign of: 52; shared: 172–73; sources of: 174; speaking: 172; spiritual: 162; ultimate: 178; veneer of: 165; word of: 163
Turning Toward the World: 3, 12–13, 38–40, 59, 76, 88–89, 118–20, 126, 129, 188
tyranny, of Egyptians: 79; systematic: 164

Ukraine, invasion of: 184
unanimity, appearance of: 162
understanding, beauty of: 36; interreligious: 203; mutual: 169; power of: 202
uniformity, totalitarian: 187
union, beyond subject and object: 72; contemplative: 43, 48, 53; eternal: 124; fraternal: 80; mystical: 71; of consciousness: 70; of contemplation and eschatology: 124; of Word and soul: 42; with Christ: 20, 46, 48, 56, 93; with God: 35, 43, 52–53, 62, 72, 96, 124; with light: 93

Unisphere: 183
unity: 13, 116, 121, 127–28, 201; as divine gift: 196; as vocation: 49; celebration of: 122; desire for: 39; eschatological: 196; fostering of: 185; fragile: 162; global: 184, 196; in diversity: xii, 13, 155; in God: 109; instrument of: 96; manifest: xi, 13; of creation: 68; of humanity: 87, 96; of love: 88, 109; of reality: 106, 109; older: 182; original: 109, 182, 196, 199, 202; paradisal: 92; primordial: 90, 196; recognition of: 185; recovery of: 80, 196; restoration of: 90–92; secret: xi, 13; sign of: 96; underlying: 185; unspoken: xi, 13; visible: xi, 13; way to: 195; with creation: 80; with Lord: 80; with others: 80
universality, awareness of: 198
universe: 38; beauty of: 74; created: 32; existence of: 38, 74; life of: 38, 74; moral: 202; order of: 38, 74
university, medieval: 69
unknowing: 178; darkness of: 34
unreality, acceptance of: 162
untruth: 51

values, authentic: 143; human: 143, 164; neglected: 192; spiritual: 199; Western: 184
Van der Meer de Walcheren, Pierre: 188
vanity: 32, 60; of world: 71
Vatican Council, First: 133
Vatican Council, Second: xii, 7, 133
Venantius Fortunatus: 156
verbiage, pointless: 167
Vergil: 187
vestigia Dei: 29
via negativa: 167
via positiva: 167
victims, of injustice: 51; solidarity with: 85

victory, paschal: 122
Vietnam: 17
Vietnamese: 203
vindication of Christ: 114
Vinski, Edward J.: 5
violence: 67, 115; cycle of: 202; instrument of: 164; murderous: 129
virginity: 76
vision: 32; catholic: 187; charism of: 136; contemplative: 147; holistic: xii, 88, 92, 112; incarnational: 66; of kingdom: 113; of renewal: 88; of wholeness: 18; of wisdom: 39; power of: 88; purity of: 88; sacramental: 15, 66; spiritual: xii; transcendent: 199; unifying: 39; universal: 187
vitality: 18, 142
vocation: 8; artistic: 105; Christian: 17, 117; clerical: 140; contemplative: 170; desert: 80, 125; fidelity to: 181; modern: 39, 98; monastic: 61, 102, 131, 137, 142, 145; of Adam: 91, 95–96; of Christ: 84; of church: 9, 86–87, 149, 169; of contemplative: 174; of Israel: 79; of monk: 98; of poet: 174; pastoral: 140; prophetic: 83; unity as: 49
Vogüé, Adalbert de: 140
voice(s), feminine: 153; of God: 147
void: 61, 154; demonic: 174; false: 174
Vow of Conversation: 119, 133, 147–48
vows: 135

Waldron, Robert: 108
Walmart: 184
Walsh, Daniel C.: 29–30
war: 18, 67, 154; brutality of: 84; cold: 185; forces of: 115; Hitler's: 86; nuclear: 4; problems of: 190; Vietnam: 9, 202
Ware, Kallistos: 32
warmth: 146
Waters of Siloe: 100

way: 46; apophatic: 178; beyond concepts: 178; beyond expression: 178; beyond images: 178; beyond words: 178; illuminative: 32; of life: 72; of spiritual discipline: 79; of wise: 79
Way of Chuang Tzu: 72, 105, 179
weakness, human: 45, 91
wealth: 85, 113; worship of: 82
Weis, Monica: 5, 23
welfare, temporal: 127
West, genius of: 190
When Prophecy Still Had a Voice: 187
When the Trees Say Nothing: 28
whimsy: 196
wholeness: 80, 87; hidden: 38, 67, 109, 155; quest for: xii; vision of: 18
wilderness: 80–81, 101, 142; of compassion: 204
wilfullness: 60
will, divine: 50; dynamism of: 202; of Christ: 50, 60; of God: 4, 19, 50, 84, 113, 120–21, 123, 127–28, 202
Winandy, Jacques: 146
wind: 38; quiet: 155
wisdom: 6–7, 12, 46, 53, 66–79, 87–88, 90, 98, 109, 153, 173, 186; as communion in cosmic awareness: 176; as contemplative realization: 69; as creative agent: 69; as intersubjective knowledge: 176; as knowledge by identification: 176; as pure gift: 76; at play in creation: 76; authority of: 10, 136; banal: 163–64; based on love: 75; beauty of: 36; Christian: 71, 73; Christocentric: 71; complacent: 163–64; contemplative: 70; conventional: 164; creative: 35; dialectical: 77; divine: 15, 35, 37–38, 69, 71, 74; epiphany of: 37, 74–75; gift of: 66; human: 69; illumination of: 73; inner: 68; light of: 35; Logos and: 69, 75; manifestation of: 66; non-Christian: 73; of American Indian: 75, 176; of cross: 70; of Ecclesiastes: 71; of God: 27, 33–35, 37, 39, 98; of Proverbs: 71; of Song of Songs: 71; of speech: 77; orientation to: 199; perennial: vii; personification of: 36–37, 69; pseudo-: 77; rational: 77; rejection of: 67; respect for: 199; revelation of: 35, 39; salt of: 71; spiritual: 77; understanding of: 191; vision of: 39
Wisdom of the Desert: 9–10, 12, 135–36, 139, 144, 149
witness: 173; monk as: 61; of church: 111; of prophecy: 84, 86; of prophet: 80, 83; of reconciliation: 201–2; of resistance: 201; of restoration: 202; social: 128; to kingdom: 128
Witness to Freedom: 2, 24, 37–39, 98
woman: 161
wonder: 126
word(s): 169; empty: 167; function of: 160; magic of: 174; misuse of: 171; of cross: 163; of life: 163; of truth: 163; true: 167–68
Word, incarnation of: 169; living: 22; of cross: 20–21, 61, 77, 163; of God: 8, 34, 69, 125, 163, 169, 172, 176; preexistent: 69; proclamation of: 169
work(s): xii, 19, 79; creative: 91, 96; fruitful: 68; of Adam: 96; of charity: 58; of Christ: 35–36, 52, 66, 81, 122; of evangelization: 49; of God: 91, 96, 130, 202; redemptive: 35, 96
world(s): 14–18, 66, 85, 129, 185; affirmation of: 15; as divine epiphany: 34; as garden: 91; as mirror of human disorder: 17; as sacrament: 15, 17, 38, 66, 97; biblical: 82; child's: 107; choice of: 17; commercial: 152; concern for: 204; confusion of: 123; contemporary:

82; contempt for: 17; created: 34, 52, 66, 84, 97; darkness of: 123; disordered: 19; divided: xi, 116; fallen: 94, 161, 168; familiar: 94; fragmented: 129, 199; hostile: 129; hostility to: 16; human: 153; material: 15, 32, 34, 36; multicultural: 201; multipolar: 185; murderous: 132; natural: 24, 34, 151, 153, 174; of business: 154; of culture: 154; of division: 185; of lies: 171; of murder: 171; of peace: 171; of politics: 154; of violence: 171; of war: 154; paradisal: 106; perfect: 161; post-communist: 183; post-ideological: 183; post-lapsarian: 162; redeemed: 52, 109; rejection of: 15, 17, 132; renunciation of: 103; transformation of: 127; unfallen: 161–62; vanities of: 71; violent: 129

worldliness: 16, 133
worship: 35; of comfort: 82; of possessions: 82; of power: 82; of wealth: 82; purity of: 80
worthiness, criterion of: 198
writer, perceptive: 91
Wu, John C. H.: 75

yin/yang circle: 183

Zahn, Gordon C.: 86
Zen: 20, 62, 73, 179, 192, 194; as awareness: 75; as consciousness: 75; as metaphysical intuition: 75; as realization: 75
Zen and the Birds of Appetite: 19–21, 43, 61–62, 73, 75, 77, 92–94, 104–5, 116, 130, 146–47, 179, 195, 204
Zion, Mt.: 10
Zossima, Staretz: 145